Constitutional Reform
and
Effective Government

JAMES L. SUNDQUIST

Constitutional Reform and Effective Government

THE BROOKINGS INSTITUTION
Washington, D.C.

Library of Congress Cataloging in Publication data:

Sundquist, James L.
    Constitutional reform and effective government.
    Includes bibliographical references and index.
    1. Presidents—United States.   2. United States.
Congress.   3. Separation of powers—United States.
4. United States—Constitutional history.   I. Title.
JK585.S86   1986   342.73'04   85-26918
ISBN 0-8157-8228-4   347.3024
ISBN 0-8157-8227-6 (pbk.)

9 8 7 6 5 4 3 2

THE BROOKINGS INSTITUTION is an independent organization devoted to nonpartisan research, education, and publication in economics, government, foreign policy, and the social sciences generally. Its principal purposes are to aid in the development of sound public policies and to promote public understanding of issues of national importance.

The Institution was founded on December 8, 1927, to merge the activities of the Institute for Government Research, founded in 1916, the Institute of Economics, founded in 1922, and the Robert Brookings Graduate School of Economics and Government, founded in 1924.

The Board of Trustees is responsible for the general administration of the Institution, while the immediate direction of the policies, program, and staff is vested in the President, assisted by an advisory committee of the officers and staff. The by-laws of the Institution state: "It is the function of the Trustees to make possible the conduct of scientific research, and publication, under the most favorable conditions, and to safeguard the independence of the research staff in the pursuit of their studies and in the publication of the results of such studies. It is not a part of their function to determine, control, or influence the conduct of particular investigations or the conclusions reached."

The President bears final responsibility for the decision to publish a manuscript as a Brookings book. In reaching his judgment on the competence, accuracy, and objectivity of each study, the President is advised by the director of the appropriate research program and weighs the views of a panel of expert outside readers who report to him in confidence on the quality of the work. Publication of a work signifies that it is deemed a competent treatment worthy of public consideration but does not imply endorsement of conclusions or recommendations.

The Institution maintains its position of neutrality on issues of public policy in order to safeguard the intellectual freedom of the staff. Hence interpretations or conclusions in Brookings publications should be understood to be solely those of the authors and should not be attributed to the Institution, to its trustees, officers, or other staff members, or to the organizations that support its research.

Foreword

      As the United States prepares to celebrate the bicentennial of its Constitution, many experienced statesmen and thoughtful scholars are raising questions about the adequacy for contemporary times of the institutional structure created by that grand document. The division of policymaking authority among three centers of power—the presidency, the Senate, and the House—provides a safeguard against hasty and ill-considered action, as the framers intended. But that division can also lead to debilitating conflict that renders the government incapable of dealing with critical problems in a timely and decisive manner. Those who believe that the government is too prone to stalemate and deadlock have suggested a broad range of institutional changes designed to encourage a greater degree of harmony between the executive and legislative branches.

    In this book, James L. Sundquist reviews the framers' rationale in creating the country's unique constitutional structure and then analyzes various proposals for altering that structure or the relationships among its institutional elements. He identifies three problems as fundamental. First, the electoral system commonly leads to divided control of the executive and legislative branches between the two major parties, making policy conflict and deadlock all but inevitable. Second, the short interval of only two years between national elections tends to preoccupy presidents and legislators alike with the always-imminent next election, and to limit to only a few months every four years the "window of opportunity" for dealing with pressing matters free from electoral distraction. Third, the absence of a workable mechanism for replacing a government that has palpably failed, for any of a wide range of possible reasons, permits what may be a dangerously long wait until the next regularly scheduled election. In his analysis, the author emphasizes feasible remedial measures to alleviate or resolve these problems.

vii

In undertaking this work, Sundquist has benefited from participation in the deliberations of the Committee on the Constitutional System, which is made up of present and former government executives and legislators, scholars, and other observers who are concerned with the shortcomings in governmental performance and attribute them, in some degree, to structural causes. His views as expressed in this book are, however, his own and may not agree with positions that ultimately may be taken by that committee or its individual leaders. By the same token, those views should not be ascribed to the trustees, officers, or other staff members of the Brookings Institution, or to the foundations that contributed to the support of this study.

The author wishes to thank Paul E. Peterson, director of the Brookings Governmental Studies program, James W. Fesler, Peter P. Schauffler, Nathan Tarcov, Aaron B. Wildavsky, and an anonymous reader for their careful reviews of the entire manuscript and their penetrating criticisms and suggestions. He is grateful to Alice M. Carroll for editing the manuscript; to Pamela D. Harris, Nancy K. Kintner, and Judith H. Newman for secretarial support; to Diane Hodges for administrative assistance; and to Joel M. Ostrow for research assistance.

The Brookings Institution deeply appreciates financial assistance for this study from the American Express Foundation, the Dillon Foundation, the Ford Foundation, the William and Flora Hewlett Foundation, and the Rockefeller Foundation.

BRUCE K. MAC LAURY
President

December 1985
Washington, D.C.

Contents

CHAPTER ONE

The Constitutional Dilemma

"Nothing human can be perfect," wrote Gouverneur Morris, looking back at the work of the Constitutional Convention twenty-eight years afterward. "Surrounded by difficulties, we did the best we could; leaving it with those who should come after us to take counsel from experience, and exercise prudently the power of amendment, which we had provided."[1] Thus did the one among the founding fathers who contributed most to the style and arrangement of the Constitution agree with the one who contributed most to its substance, James Madison. "I am not one of the number if there be any such," wrote Madison after eleven of the thirteen states had approved the document, "who think the Constitution lately adopted a faultless work."[2]

The Constitution achieved two purposes. First, it created a structure of government for the new republic; it defined the unique American tripartite system of independent yet interdependent branches— executive, legislative, and judicial—prescribed how those holding national office should be chosen, and sought to draw a boundary between the powers of the national government and those of the states. Second, it provided a limited body of fundamental substantive law, relating to such subjects of controversy at the time as slavery,

1. Letter to W. H. Wells, February 24, 1815, in Max Farrand, ed., *The Records of the Federal Convention of 1787*, 1937 rev. ed., 4 vols. (Yale University Press, 1966), vol. 3, pp. 421–22.
2. Letter to G. L. Turberville, November 2, 1788, in ibid., p. 354.

civil liberties, the public debt, taxation, regulation of commerce, and titles of nobility.

When Madison was writing, public dissatisfaction centered on the second of these elements of the Constitution, its substantive provisions—specifically on the absence of a bill of rights. That omission was corrected when the First Congress proposed ten amendments that the states ratified by 1791. Since then, the Constitution has been amended only sixteen times in nearly two centuries, and most of those amendments have pertained also to substantive matters. Two of them—the Eighteenth, which prohibited alcoholic beverages, and the Twenty-first, which repealed the prohibition—left the document substantively unchanged. Of the remaining fourteen, seven further expanded the guarantees of civil rights. The Thirteenth outlawed slavery, and the Fourteenth guaranteed the rights of blacks and other citizens as well; four extended the right to vote, to blacks (the Fifteenth), to women (the Nineteenth), to young people at the age of eighteen (the Twenty-sixth), and to residents of the District of Columbia in presidential elections (the Twenty-third); and the Twenty-fourth Amendment abolished the poll tax as a requirement for voting. Two of the remaining amendments concerned the powers of the federal government: the Eleventh imposed a minor limitation on the jurisdiction of the federal courts, and the Sixteenth removed the constitutional prohibition against a graduated income tax.

Only five of the twenty-six amendments, then, dealt with the structure of the government created by the Constitution—which is the concern of this book—as distinct from the scope of its authority and the rights and liberties of U.S. citizens. And of those five, three can be considered technical or peripheral; they corrected flaws in the design of the structure or adapted it to new circumstances without altering the nature or relationships of the institutions as the framers had conceived them. The Twelfth Amendment, ratified in 1804, separated the balloting for president and vice president in the electoral college and thus accommodated to the age of parties the rather anomalous—from a modern perspective—nonpartisan presidential selection system conceived by the founders. The Twentieth Amendment, adopted in 1933, established the present January dates for the inauguration of presidents and the convening of Congresses, thus belatedly adjusting the political calendar to the development of steam transportation. The Twenty-fifth Amendment, approved in 1967, finally filled two gaps in the constitutional system that the founders had neglected to attend to. One provision established a procedure for the vice president to become acting president when the president is disabled. The second set up a process for the selection of a new vice president when that office becomes vacant—the process that was promptly used twice, when Gerald R. Ford was chosen to succeed Spiro T. Agnew and when Nelson A. Rockefeller was approved to replace Ford on the latter's advancement to the presidency.

That leaves only two amendments that have affected in any way the character of the institutions that were bequeathed to the twentieth century by the eighteenth. One was the Seventeenth Amendment, ratified in 1913, which provided that senators would be directly elected by the people rather than appointed by state legislatures. That action not only altered the constitutional balance between the federal government and the states but changed the nature of the Senate by introducing into its membership men and women of new political styles. The other was the Twenty-second Amendment, ratified in 1951, which limited presidents to two four-year terms and so decreed that each reelected president would enter his term as a "lame duck," with whatever consequences that status might have on his relations with the Congress.

Even these two amendments influenced the institutions only indirectly, by affecting the selection or retention of the occupants of offices, not by adding to or subtracting from the constellation of institutions established by the Constitution or altering the formal distribution of power among them. The country's governmental architecture has proved, then, to be amazingly durable in a world of change. While some nations have shifted from monarchies to democracies to dictatorships and back again, while some have adopted and discarded and redesigned entire constitutions, the structure that was designed for the United States government in one eighteenth century summer remains in force essentially unchanged.

Does this mean that this human document was, after all, perfect in its basic design, despite the modest disclaimer of Gouverneur Morris? Many have thought so. It was William Ewart Gladstone, the British prime minister, who described the Constitution in a moment of ecstasy as "the most wonderful work ever struck off at a given time by the brain and purpose of man."[3] Surely the durability of the constitutional structure and the growth and prosperity of the country

3. "Kin Beyond the Sea," *North American Review* (September 1878).

governed by it are a testament to the wisdom and inspiration of the framers. Had the system they designed verged at any time on outright failure, serious and sustained movements to alter its basic features would have been born. Yet in two centuries, the only two significant movements for structural change were those that produced the Seventeenth and Twenty-second amendments, and even those alterations did not reach to the fundamentals of the institutional system. In all that time, no failed movement of any consequence can be added to the short list of reform efforts.

The Current Constitutional Debate

If the constitutional structure has served the country so well for so long, the question is appropriate: Why discuss reform at all? The cliché "If it ain't broke, don't fix it" makes a valid point. Trying to improve something that is working reasonably well can sometimes make things worse.

Yet that counsel is too negative. Its message is that breakdown must be awaited, not averted. Moreover, breakdown is not usually an absolute but a matter of degree. Weaknesses in a governmental system can debilitate and devitalize a government, short of outright collapse. Should a partial breakdown, reflected in simple inefficiency and ineffectiveness, be tolerated on the supposition that the cure will be worse than the ailment? After all, most of the world's great inventions, in technology and social affairs alike, have sprung from somebody's urge to make better what, at the time, most of the people undoubtedly considered good.

Few would deny that the American governmental system, in its two centuries, has shown weaknesses and inefficiencies. Defenders of the status quo respond simply that this is as it was meant to be, and should be. Writing just before his retirement in 1984, Barber Conable, the veteran Republican representative from New York, acknowledged "the well-known mess which at any given time clutters up the Washington landscape" and the "laggard" character of the American government but argued that the system was intended to work that way and "we are better for it." "The Founding Fathers," wrote Conable, "didn't want efficient, adventurous governments, fearing they would intrude on our individual liberties. I think they were right, and I offer our freedom, stability, and prosperity as evidence."[4]

The danger lies in the fact that a government has objectives that all will agree are good and necessary—national security and economic prosperity, to name but two—in addition to whatever objectives some may deem unworthy. And the good and bad cannot be separated. A government too inefficient to embark on adventurous efforts to change society will also be, by necessity, too inefficient to meet its inescapable, imperative responsibilities. United States history abounds with illustrations of governmental failures that, if they did not destroy "freedom, stability, and prosperity," at least threatened and sometimes impaired them. What constitutes failure may, of course, be disputed, but contemporary popular opinion as well as the retrospective judgment of history may be called on to help in the identification of some of them.

The most indisputable of all the instances of failure—secession and Civil War—perhaps could not have been averted by any American government however structured. Maybe the same can be said of the crash of 1929 that precipitated the Great Depression. But the paralysis of the government for more than three years after that crash, in the face of increasing and intolerable suffering, is harder to explain away as reflecting virtue in the system. The constitutional structure provided no mechanism by which the people, when it was clear they had lost confidence in their leaders, could place in office new ones, with a fresh mandate to use the powers of government vigorously to alleviate suffering and restore prosperity. They could replace only a part of the government, in 1930, and that only intensified the policy deadlock that prevailed until the presidential election two years later.

The country's foreign affairs, in this century, offer innumerable examples of ineffective policy, brought about by the inability of leaders to harmonize all of the institutional elements that, under the Constitution, must act in concert before any decisive policy can be carried out. The country could participate in the sacrifices of World War I, by the will of the majority, but it could not join in the League of Nations that its president helped to design to construct and maintain the peace—not because the majority did not similarly will it, but because the constitutional system empowered the minority to

4. *Roll Call* (April 19, 1984); reprinted in *This Constitution: A Bicentennial Chronicle* (Winter 1984), pp. 42–43.

rule. In Vietnam, the United States lost its first war—surely a failure by any objective standard—because it could not muster sufficient unity either to do whatever was necessary for victory or to disengage and withdraw cleanly at an early stage. Since then, conflict between the president and the Congress has repeatedly rendered American policy ineffective—most conspicuously, in the 1980s, in the case of Nicaragua, where neither the president's policy, which conceivably might have succeeded in overthrowing the Sandinista government, nor the policy of his opposition, which conceivably might have co-opted the Sandinistas and ultimately weaned them away from the Soviet-Cuban bloc, could be pursued with firmness and decision.

In retrospect, the country clearly approves of social security, unemployment compensation, medicare, civil rights, and federal efforts to raise standards of education, housing, and nutrition and to alleviate poverty. During the Reagan administration, the national commitment to some programs in these areas has been scaled back but few have been eliminated; the structure of the welfare state that remains in place reflects a genuine national consensus. But the welfare state came late to the United States; most of its major elements were adopted here decades later than in the industrial democracies of Europe. Civil rights legislation was stalled for years, even decades, until the logjam was broken by the televised images of law enforcement officers using police dogs and fire hoses on peaceful demonstrators. If these legislative measures are deemed necessary and useful now, they would have been equally useful earlier, and the delays—the laggardness—that are the consequence of America's constitutional structure have been the nation's loss.

In 1973 and 1974, the country witnessed the collapse of an administration mired in crime but lacked the means to place a new leader in the White House—until by lucky accident an Oval Office tape recording was finally discovered that implicated the president in criminal activity beyond a reasonable doubt. President Nixon's resignation restored the government, but only partially. The deadlock between the Republican president and the Democratic Congress that had rendered the government immobile in the Nixon period continued under Gerald Ford, with incessant quarreling between the branches over the whole range of foreign and domestic policy.

In the mid-1980s, the country's gravest domestic problem was universally adjudged to be its unprecedented peacetime budgetary deficit, running in the $200-billion-a-year range as far ahead as anyone could see. In 1985, the Senate and the House finally reached agreement on a modest program that made a start in reducing that deficit, but only a start, and given the arduous process required to enforce any agreement on fiscal policy, there was no assurance that even a significant beginning would be made. Meantime, with the approach of the 1986 midterm election, every participant would be increasingly reluctant to take difficult decisions that would alienate significant voting blocs—from old-age pensioners to defense contractors to Amtrak riders and employees, and above all the taxpayers whose benefits conferred in 1981 brought on the problem. Yet, in that 1986 election, or even in the presidential election in 1988, the voters would be unable to fix responsibility on either the Republicans or the Democrats, for neither had controlled the government—only part of it. The parties were joined in a kind of coalition government, unsought and involuntary, formed by political adversaries whose natural mission was not to cooperate, but to discredit and defeat each other. Such a coalition, as experience all over the world has shown, is bound to be fractious, torn by dual leadership and philosophical dissension, and consequently weak. And irresponsible as well, for each party can sidestep the initiative for taking unpopular actions and shift the blame for whatever adverse consequences may result from failure to act decisively. And unaccountable; the electorate cannot render a clear verdict on the conduct of either party and deliver its mandate through the only means at its disposal—its ballots.

Whenever the people sense that their government is failing, their tendency is to blame the individuals who hold elective office, usually the one who occupies the White House. It was not the system that failed, in the public view, but Herbert Hoover, or Lyndon Johnson, or Richard Nixon, or whoever. The process by which leaders are selected is a crucial part of any governmental system, of course, and some selection methods may produce better results than others. But granting that none of them can assure that ideal leaders will be chosen, the American constitutional system places extraordinary obstacles in the path of any leader. A president is expected to lead the Congress, but its two houses are independent institutions and, most of the time of late, one or both are controlled by his political opposition. And when a president fails as leader—whether because the Congress chooses not to follow or because of any of the many possible forms of personal inadequacy—the system has no safeguard. The government cannot be reconstituted until the calendar announces that the day of the next presidential election has arrived. Unless one contends that all of the historical episodes cited here as examples of governmental failure were in fact successes, one is impelled to ask whether the constitutional system inherited from the eighteenth century is indeed adequate for the twentieth. Specifically, five questions recur.

Would an electoral system that encouraged unified party control of the three centers of decisionmaking—presidency, Senate, and House— make for more effective, responsible, and accountable government?

Would longer terms for the president or for legislators, and a longer span between elections, enable leaders to rise to a higher level of statesmanship in confronting crucial issues, permit the resolution of issues that now go unresolved because of the short two-year life of each successive Congress, and permit greater deliberation and care in the legislative process?

Can a better solution be devised to deal with the immobility of government brought about by leadership failure, or deadlock and quarreling between the president and the Congress, than simply waiting helplessly until the next presidential election comes around?

Can harmonious collaboration between the executive and legislative branches be induced through formal interlocking of the branches or through strengthening the political parties that are the web that binds administrators and legislators to a common purpose?

Should any of the constitutional checks and balances, by which the executive and legislative branches are enabled to thwart each other, be modified to permit one or the other branch to prevail more readily and thus facilitate decisions?

Questions such as these (which are the subjects of chapters 4 through 8 of this book) are being asked more insistently now, by more national leaders of experience and stature, than probably at any time in history. This is evidenced by the incorporation, late in 1983, of the Committee on the Constitutional System (CCS), with a former cabinet member (Douglas Dillon, secretary of the treasury in the Kennedy administration), a former White House counsel (Lloyd N. Cutler, counsel to President Carter), and an incumbent senator (Nancy Landon Kassebaum, Republican of Kansas) as cochairmen, and enrolling in its membership a significant number of present and former members of the Congress and high officials of the executive branch, as well as constitutional scholars, journalist observers of the Washington scene, and others.

"Our governmental problems do not lie with the quality or character of our elected representatives," contends Dillon. "Rather they lie with a system which promotes divisiveness and makes it difficult, if not impossible, to develop truly national policies." The division of power between the president and the Congress makes "stalemate" inevitable, and "no one can place the blame," continues Dillon. "The President blames the Congress, the Congress blames the President, and the public remains confused and disgusted with government in Washington." The country cannot speak with "one, clear voice" in foreign affairs, and it lacks ability "to act promptly and energetically in the face of a crisis."[5] Cutler puts it in similar language. "In parliamentary terms," Cutler wrote in the last year of Carter's administration, "one might say that under the U.S. Constitution it is not now feasible to 'form a Government,'" one formed of an elected majority that is "able to carry out an overall program, and is held accountable for its success or failure."[6]

The words *stalemate* and *deadlock*—or, in their latest variation, *gridlock*—recur as a constant theme in the critiques of the reformers. The historian James MacGregor Burns, a founder of CCS, described in 1963 what he called *The Deadlock of Democracy*: a "somber and inexorable cycle" that leads this country's public affairs from "deadlock" to "drift" to the enactment of "bits and pieces" of an election mandate during a "short honeymoon" between the president and the Congress, then back once more to "the old cycle of deadlock and drift."[7] Burns was writing then of the failure of the Congress to enact the liberal program of John F. Kennedy, just as supporters of Franklin Roosevelt's New Deal had complained of the legislators' "obstruction" of their hero's legislative proposals a quarter century before. One source of constitutional reform sentiment, then, has been the frustration of activists with a government that, because of the division

5. Douglas Dillon, address at Tufts University, May 30, 1982; reprinted in Donald L. Robinson, ed., *Reforming American Government: The Bicentennial Papers of the Committee on the Constitutional System* (Westview Press, 1985), pp. 24–29.

6. Lloyd N. Cutler, "To Form a Government," *Foreign Affairs*, vol. 59 (Fall 1980), pp. 127, 132; reprinted in Robinson, *Reforming American Government*.

7. *The Deadlock of Democracy* (Prentice-Hall, 1963), p. 2.

of policymaking authority, has so often proven incapable of moving boldly and decisively in dealing with domestic problems. To the conservatives, of course, the relative sluggishness of the U.S. government in intervening in domestic matters is a merit of the Constitution rather than a fault. They agree that the American system has an endemic tendency to deadlock, stalemate, delay, and indecision. But, they contend, with Barber Conable, that the founding fathers were right to contrive just such a system, to check impulsive, demagogic, and egalitarian legislation. And if the system requires an extraordinarily high degree of consensus for action to be taken, they argue, that is a necessary foundation for enforceable legislation anyway. Deadlock forces compromise, and minority views must be accommodated, and that confers legitimacy on the policies ultimately adopted.

To a degree, then, constitutional reform has been a debate between liberals and conservatives, the former seeing the separation of powers as a barrier to, and the latter as a protection against, governmental activism. That debate is essentially unresolvable, for the two sides are influenced heavily by value judgments relating to the ends and role of government. Would a government capable of translating an election "mandate" into quick, decisive action do more good than harm? The activists say it would, but that is because they have been traditionally optimistic about the beneficial effects of governmental intervention. The conservatives have tended to be less sanguine about the wisdom of politicians and the competence of administrative agencies. Beyond that, the two sides can never agree on what is truly beneficial. All of the constituent programs of the welfare state—social security, education, health, housing, and all the rest—redistribute resources from taxpayers to the recipients of the governmental benefits, which means usually from the upper to the lower ranges of the income scale. Whether one regards the redistribution as "beneficial" depends largely on whether one views the transaction from the top or from the bottom, on where one's sympathies lie.

Yet there are other themes in the constitutional debate beyond the liberal-conservative argument over domestic policy, and these provide the basis for a broader, less partisan and ideological, discussion. A second impulse toward constitutional reform has come from those who have helped to conduct the nation's foreign affairs, and here the liberal-conservative split is less apparent. The liberal Woodrow

Wilson was defeated when the Senate rejected the Versailles treaty, and the liberal-backed Strategic Arms Limitation Treaty (SALT II) negotiated by Jimmy Carter had to be withdrawn, but the conservatives Richard Nixon, Gerald Ford, and Ronald Reagan found their foreign policies undercut by congressional liberals, leaving the country often with no clear foreign policy at all.

In the Reagan years, the country witnessed an unprecedented political configuration—a determined, activist conservative president encountering increasing resistance from a moderate Congress more disposed to defend the status quo. It was the conservatives' turn to experience the frustration of the separate powers. Nevertheless, not many Reaganites identified the constitutional structure as a problem to be concerned about; perhaps the phenomenal success of their president in 1981 in mobilizing the Congress—including even the Democratic-controlled House—to enact the essential features of his program was still too fresh a memory. Yet his inability, after the 1981 success, to lead the government significantly further in the direction he had set did arouse some alarm on the conservative side of the ideological divide. "We're learning that our worst fears about the inability of our institutions to function are turning out to be right," warned Alan Greenspan, chairman of President Ford's Council of Economic Advisers, commenting on the government's failure to come to grips with "the real long-term budget problem."[8] Earlier, David A. Stockman, about to retire as President Reagan's budget director, had deplored the "political division and policy conflict within our governmental institutions" that had "reached such an extreme and intense state that it is nearly impossible to see where the political will and consensus will come from that is necessary to enact any plan big enough to balance the books—or even substantially close the gap."[9]

8. "Waiting for the Crisis: An Interview with Alan Greenspan," *Washington Post*, August 4, 1985.
9. Speech, June 5, 1985, *New York Times*, June 29, 1985. While not questioning the basic constitutional structure, conservatives, including President Reagan, were rallying behind the item veto as one reform they considered necessary, but their main effort was directed at accomplishing the change by statute rather than through constitutional amendment. They also supported the proposal for an amendment to require a balanced federal budget except in certain circumstances and to limit the growth of spending. That would be a substantive rather than structural change (as would an antiabortion or school prayer amendment) and therefore is not considered in this book.

If the conservatives continue to elect presidents, and then find themselves confronting the same deadlocks that liberal presidents experienced most of the time in their years in power during the past half century, conservatives and liberals may some day find constitutional reform, for the first time, a common cause. But perhaps not. If conservatives begin to decry the obstacles in the constitutional structure that blocked Franklin Roosevelt or John Kennedy from achieving their policy objectives, liberals may find new merit in the obstacles that similarly blocked the path of Ronald Reagan.

That is the constitutional dilemma. An institutional structure that enables the government to move decisively to do good things will also enable it to move with dispatch to do bad things, whatever one's definition of those terms. To support constitutional reform, one must be prepared to gamble. In the old dispute between liberals and conservatives, each side must be ready to gamble that it can win elections, most of the time, and make its policy views prevail. On less partisan issues—foreign policy in particular, but perhaps also the general outlines of fiscal policy—a national consensus must arise that a government able to concert its powers and act decisively will, most of the time, take the right action, that its positive achievements will outnumber its mistakes, that when it speaks with the one clear voice it will speak mostly wisdom and not folly. And that, when it does err, a government capable of decisive action is best able to correct mistakes.

The Barriers to Constitutional Reform

If the founders wanted those who came after them to "exercise prudently the power of amendment," as Morris suggested, they still erected enormous barriers to that exercise—obstacles that proved to be greater, undoubtedly, than they anticipated. Approval of each amendment by two-thirds of both houses of the Congress, followed by its ratification by three-fourths of the states, can on occasion be attained, as the twenty-six successful efforts attest. But this is more easily accomplished on a substantive matter, such as prohibition of alcoholic beverages or the repeal thereof, when waves of popular enthusiasm can be aroused. Issues pertaining to the structure of government do not stir mass excitement, in the absence of outright governmental collapse. Such questions are examined closely by few except officeholders and politicians, and they are apt to appraise each proposal from the standpoint of its direct and immediate consequences to themselves, the offices they hold, and the parties they belong to.[10]

Within the political elite, for an amendment to clear the barriers to passage, its acceptance must come close to unanimity. For one-third plus one of those voting in either the Senate or the House can kill it. Or, if it survives that hurdle, one-fourth plus one of the states—today, thirteen of fifty. Yet the approval level in the states must be, usually, even higher than that, for with one exception the states have two-house legislatures. Thus as few as thirteen of ninety-nine state legislative bodies can defeat the ratification of a congressionally approved amendment; stated in reverse, as many as eighty-six of the ninety-nine—or 87 percent—may still be insufficient, which amounts to a requirement for virtual national unanimity. The Constitution does provide a unicameral alternative to ratification by bicameral state legislatures; the Congress may specify that the states shall act through conventions, as they did in ratifying the Constitution itself. But only one of the twenty-six amendments—repeal of prohibition—was adopted through that procedure.

The requirement for such extraordinary majorities means that, in the case of structural amendments, any significant political bloc possesses an effective veto. To succeed, then, a proposed amendment either must have no adverse effect on anybody—as, say, the amendment that rescheduled inauguration days and congressional sessions—or must distribute its adverse effects so nearly neutrally that no substantial interest is offended. It must be neutral in its impact on the president and the Congress, for either one can probably block it (while the president is not part of the approval process, his influence and that of past presidents and former executive branch officials who defend presidential prerogatives would usually be sufficient to give supporters of the presidency an effective veto). It must be neutral in its impact on Republicans and Democrats, on incumbent officeholders and challengers, on liberals and conservatives, on professional politicians and amateurs, or on any other of the dichotomous groups

10. The Constitution provides an alternative to the Congress as the initiator of amendments—a constitutional convention called on petition of two-thirds of the state legislatures—but this method (which is discussed further in chapter 9) has never been employed.

between which the political world can be divided. And structural amendments, by their very nature, are rarely neutral. Altering an institutional structure inevitably redistributes power, taking from some and giving to others. In the long run, the country as a whole, and both parties, may be better off by a redistribution. But it is in the short run that politicians plan their careers. In the absence of a manifest collapse of government, the power losers can be counted on to exercise their veto. Those who worry about the shortcomings of their government, then, have traditionally sought remedies that do not involve the obstacle-strewn route of constitutional reform. Laws can be changed more readily, with simple majorities in both houses; political party rules and institutions can be altered, and politicians can be exhorted to change their ways.

But if these remedies are exhausted and the deficiencies of government remain, then there is no recourse but to reexamine the constitutional structure itself.

The Parliamentary Model—and Incrementalism

Those who have been frustrated with the stalemates of the American system, over the years, have looked longingly across the Atlantic and northward toward Canada and admired the streamlined unity of other democratic governments. In the parliamentary democracies, the legislative majority is sovereign, and a committee of that majority—the cabinet—both leads the legislature and directs the executive branch. Power is unified. Responsibility is clearly fixed. Strong party discipline assures prime ministers and their cabinets that they can act quickly and decisively without fear, normally, of being repudiated by their legislatures. Yet the leaders are held accountable by the requirement that, to remain in power, they must maintain the confidence of the parliamentary majority that chose them. In two-party parliamentary systems, of which Great Britain is the model, votes of nonconfidence are rare, but on occasion the majority has forced a prime minister in which it has in fact lost confidence to resign—as when Neville Chamberlain was compelled to give way to Winston Churchill early in World War II. In the multiparty parliamentary systems of the European continent, governments are usually formed by coalitions, and they collapse when the parties making up a government fall into conflict. As long as they can resolve disagreements—or postpone or evade issues—within their cabinets, however, they are as certain of legislative support as are the governments of Britain. Under any of these parliamentary systems, governments can be formed, in Lloyd Cutler's phrase. They can act. They can speak, on the world scene, with a single, clear voice.

Douglas Dillon, for one, has suggested that the answer to this country's governmental stalemate "could well be some form of parliamentary democracy."[11] Former Senator J. William Fulbright of Arkansas, long chairman of the Senate Foreign Relations Committee, also advocates "a different system, one incorporating the principle that the executive and legislature shouldn't be separated."[12] Cutler, on the other hand, suggests that "the most one can hope for is a set of modest changes that would make our structure work somewhat more in the manner of a parliamentary system, with somewhat less separation between the executive and the legislature than now exists."[13] Many of the specific changes that have been under consideration by the CCS are adapted from parliamentary systems, but for most constitutional reformers the parliamentary system represents only a source of ideas for incremental steps that might bring more unity to the American government, each such step to be considered on its own merits in terms of its adaptability to American tradition and institutions. Parliamentary democracy is not a model to be adopted in its entirety, supplanting the entire U.S. constitutional structure with something new and alien.

What Changes Might Work?

The purpose of this book is to examine what some of the incremental steps might be, if it turns out at some point that the Dillon-Cutler diagnosis is the correct one and something must indeed be done. It does not attempt to make the general case for constitutional reform, beyond what has been said already. It is directed primarily toward those who are already persuaded that the tripartite constitutional

11. Tufts University address, May 30, 1982.
12. *Washington Post*, July 18, 1982.
13. "To Form a Government," p. 139.

design has evident and serious weaknesses and the question is not so much *whether* constitutional change is needed as *what* changes might work best. My object is to contribute to practical thinking about what might best be attempted, if one day a national consensus emerges that the United States government is indeed too congenitally divided, too prone to stalemate, too conflict-ridden to meet its immense responsibilities.

The next chapter presents the rationale for the structure of government designed two hundred years ago, as expressed by the more articulate among the fifty-five men who met in Philadelphia to create it. That is followed by an account of the few serious attempts made in two centuries to alter that structure. The next five chapters analyze each of the principal proposals that have been advanced for incremental change in the constitutional system (including not only constitutional amendments but statutes and changes in political party rules and processes), as a guide to those who, during the bicentennial season, will wish not only to celebrate the grand document of 1787 but to consider whether and how the structure of government created by and under it might be improved. A final chapter summarizes what appear to be the more constructive and feasible of the array of possible changes and then reviews the difficulties that must be overcome to accomplish any change at all.

CHAPTER TWO

Origins of the Constitutional Structure

The men who made up the Federal Convention of 1787 wavered during the course of their deliberations on most of the specific features of the constitutional structure they evolved, but they never vacillated on its central principle. That was the doctrine that the powers of government must be separated into independent branches—legislative, executive, and judicial. Nearly all the delegates arrived in Philadelphia clearly committed to that objective.

And so, clearly, were the constituents of the delegates. In the *Federalist* papers that explained the new Constitution to the country, James Madison of Virginia referred to the separation of powers as "the sacred maxim of free government,"[1] and during the intense debates over ratification nobody disputed that precept. The opponents of the Constitution did not take their stand on the ground that the new charter separated the powers of government too cleanly, that a more unified government would serve the country better. They attacked, rather, from the other side, charging that the new charter did not separate the powers of government cleanly enough, that the branches were not sufficiently protected against encroachment of one on another. The British government was cited as the model, but not today's British government. It was the government that existed—or was understood to exist—at that time, which was a government of

1. *The Federalist*, no. 47 (New American Library, 1961), p. 308.

17

separated powers. Nobody advocated the kind of unified government
that has since evolved in Britain, the one that current critics of the
U.S. Constitution often put forward as a model. Insofar as the framers
of the Constitution foresaw the coming rise to supremacy by the
House of Commons, they were mostly alarmed by the prospect. The
overwhelming majority of them wanted no single group, legislative
or executive, to be supreme in the new republic on this side of the
Atlantic.

For the men of 1787 lived in the fear of despotism. Their generation
in Europe and America was emerging from a long era of rule by
monarchs, sometimes benevolent but too often tyrannical. And the
philosophers who spoke for that generation were those who heralded
the rights of man. When the framers turned to designing a new
government, then, they sought "vigor" and "dispatch" and "strength"
and "efficacy"—characteristics that the Continental Congress had so
conspicuously lacked—but they also were determined to erect safeguards to protect the citizenry from abuse of power by the invigorated
organs of the state. To that end, power would have to be dispersed
among branches of government capable of checking and controlling
one another. Madison cites "the celebrated Montesquieu" as the
"oracle who is always consulted and cited" on the principle of
separation of powers, and that philosopher had said, "There can be
no liberty where the legislative and executive powers are united in
the same person, or body of magistrates" or "if the power of judging
be not separated" also.[2] Under the Articles of Confederation, the
powers had been united in the Continental Congress with no loss of
liberty, but that body was devoid of any final power, being wholly
dependent on the consent of the states to all its actions. And, in any
case, it was no model to be copied; its failure was the reason that
the convention had been assembled in the first place to propose
amendments to the Articles that would give the new nation a better
and a stronger central government.

The delegates had had experience, however, with other and more
potent governments that verged on unity—those of the new states
during the interval between 1776 and 1787. And they were the
proximate cause of the framers' fear of despotism. King George III

2. Ibid., pp. 301–02.

and the concentrated executive power that he represented were more than a decade in the past; the new state legislatures were very much in the present. "Our chief danger arises from the democratic parts of our constitutions," Governor Edmund Randolph of Virginia said in introducing the Virginia plan that became the basis of the convention's deliberations. "It is a maxim which I hold incontrovertible, that the powers of government exercised by the people swallows up the other branches. None of the constitutions have provided sufficient checks against the democracy."[3] Expanding on this theme in the next few days, Randolph attributed "the evils under which the U.S. laboured" to "the turbulence and follies of democracy."[4] Elbridge Gerry of Massachusetts agreed: "The evils we experience flow from the excess of democracy," he declared, citing the "most baneful measures" enacted in his state in response to "popular clamour"; he was still a republican, but "had been taught by experience the danger of the levilling spirit."[5] In *The Federalist*, Madison specified the nature of the leveling: "A rage for paper money, for an abolition of debts, for an equal division of property, or for any other improper or wicked project."[6] In the processes by which the states chose their delegations to the convention, the dread levelers had somehow been effectively excluded, so there was none to take issue with Madison and defend such acts, and the Randolph-Gerry-Madison view as to the prime source of danger to the public liberty prevailed. James Wilson of Pennsylvania even observed that the colonists had revolted not against the king but against parliament, "not against an unity but a corrupt multitude."[7]

If the legislative branch was "omnipotent" in the states, if it was "everywhere extending the sphere of its activity and drawing all power into its impetuous vortex," as Madison claimed, then the

3. Max Farrand, ed., *The Records of the Federal Convention of 1787*, 1937 rev. ed., 4 vols. (Yale University Press, 1966), vol. 1, pp. 26–27, proceedings of May 29, notes of James McHenry.

4. Ibid., p. 51, May 31, notes of James Madison. Unless otherwise indicated, quotations from the convention records are from Madison's notes.

5. Ibid., p. 48, May 31.

6. *Federalist*, no. 10, p. 84.

7. Farrand, *Records*, vol. 1, p. 71, June 1, notes of Rufus King. The same observation is attributed to King himself in ibid., vol. 3, p. 466, T. H. Benton on King's retiring from the Senate.

other branches of the new government had to be protected against legislative usurpations. As Madison put it, "it is against the enterprising ambition of this department that the people ought to indulge all their jealousy and exhaust all their precautions."[8] Much of the intellectual energy of the convention was accordingly devoted to considering how best to check the ambition of the legislature.

Yet, not everyone at Philadelphia would go so far as Madison in asserting that *all* the jealousy of the people ought to be directed toward the ambition of the legislative branch. While fear of democratic demagogues was a dominant theme in the convention, dread of tyrannous executives was a secondary one. The venerable Benjamin Franklin of Pennsylvania expressed from time to time his foreboding that the new republic would inevitably drift to monarchy, seeing a "natural inclination in mankind to Kingly Government." George Mason of Virginia rose repeatedly to warn against establishing in the new presidency "a more dangerous monarchy, an elective one," and at the close he declined to sign the Constitution because, among other reasons, "it would end either in monarchy, or a tyrannical aristocracy; which, he was in doubt, but one or the other, he was sure." And men like Randolph, even as they denounced the excesses of popular legislatures, could wax equally eloquent against the "foetus of monarchy," as Randolph termed it, whenever they sensed that the structure of government was overbalanced in favor of the executive. "He will be an elective King, and will feel the spirit of one," warned Hugh Williamson of North Carolina. During debate on the executive's veto power, Pierce Butler of South Carolina observed that "Gentlemen seemed to think that we had nothing to fear from an abuse of the Executive power. But why might not a Cataline or a Cromwell arise in this country as in others."[9]

The concerns of both groups—or the concerns of individual delegates about both dangers—merged naturally into a general theory of "checks and balances," by which all three branches would be protected against encroachments by one another. The system to be evolved would be one in which "ambition must be made to counteract ambition."[10]

8. Ibid., vol. 2, p. 36, July 17; *Federalist*, no. 48, p. 309.

9. Farrand, *Records*, vol. 1, p. 83, June 2, and p. 101, June 4; vol. 2, p. 632, September 15; vol. 1, p. 66, June 1; vol. 2, p. 101, July 24; vol. 1, p. 100, June 4.

10. Madison, *Federalist*, no. 51, p. 322.

Checks on the Congress

In the founders' plan, the all-powerful legislative branch would be checked in two ways. First, it would be weakened by dividing its own powers between two branches. Second, the executive and judicial branches would be provided means of self-protection. For the judiciary, that means would be its power to declare unconstitutional any laws that it found invaded the judicial powers.[11] For the executive the most important safeguards would be the independent election of the president and his right to veto legislation that encroached on his powers.

Bicameralism

Dividing the legislature into two branches, wrote Madison in the *Federalist*, "doubles the security to the people by requiring the concurrence of two distinct bodies in schemes of usurpation or perfidy, where the ambition or corruption of one would otherwise be sufficient." And, to decrease the likelihood of "sinister combinations," the two houses should be rendered, "by different modes of election and different principles of action, as little connected with

11. While the power of the judicial branch to invalidate laws on grounds of unconstitutionality was not stated explicitly in the Constitution and was not established until the Supreme Court's 1803 decision in *Marbury* v. *Madison*, it was clearly envisioned by at least some of the framers. When the convention was considering whether the power to veto legislation should be vested in a "council of revision" that would include representation from the judiciary, Elbridge Gerry observed that the judges "will have a sufficient check against encroachments on their own department by their exposition of the laws, which involved a power of deciding on their Constitutionality." Similarly, Rufus King of Massachusetts noted that "the Judges will have the expounding of those Laws when they come before them; and they will no doubt stop the operation of such as shall appear repugnant to the constitution." When the convention returned to the subject, James Wilson, Luther Martin of Maryland, George Mason, and Gouverneur Morris of Pennsylvania all acknowledged that the judiciary would have that power. John Francis Mercer of Maryland and John Dickinson of Delaware protested that the judiciary ought not to possess the authority, but Dickinson "was at the same time at a loss what expedient to substitute." Farrand, *Records*, vol. 1, p. 97, June 4; p. 109, June 4, notes of William Pierce; pp. 73, 76, 78, July 21; pp. 298–99, August 15. That the veto was ultimately placed solely in the president suggests that the majority of the delegates agreed with the Gerry-King view of the judicial role.

each other as the nature of their common functions and their common dependence on the society will admit."[12]

If the principle of separation of powers was universally taken for granted by the delegates when they arrived in Philadelphia, the concept of a bicameral legislature had almost as wide an acceptance. George Mason said the concept was "well settled" in "the mind of the people of America." All the states except Pennsylvania had created two-house legislatures, he pointed out, and the unicameralism of the Continental Congress was one of the factors that made the people averse to conferring greater powers on it. Pierce Butler, acknowledging that he had been among those opposing a stronger Congress, said on seeing that the Virginia plan proposed a two-house legislature he would approach the subject with an open mind. Explaining the Constitution to the North Carolina ratification convention the next year, William R. Davie reported that approval of a strengthened national government by the convention had depended on dividing the legislature into two branches, so that a longer-tenured group of men who were "more experienced, more temperate, and more competent to decide rightly" could check a popular branch "which might be influenced by local views, or the violence of party." George Washington put it more simply in his famed interchange with Thomas Jefferson. When Jefferson asked over the breakfast table why a second legislative chamber had been created, Washington asked, "Why did you pour your coffee into your saucer?" "To cool it," Jefferson answered. "Even so," said Washington, "we pour legislation into the senatorial saucer to cool it."[13]

Delegates were explicit that the new Senate would be designed "to secure the rights of property," as George Mason put it. Gouverneur Morris reasoned that if the Senate was to check the excesses of the House of Representatives, its members should have a "personal interest" in doing so, and they should therefore be persons of "great personal property," as well as an "aristocratic spirit," and they should be unpaid, to assure that only the rich would serve. The House of Lords was the ready model. John Dickinson of Delaware lamented the difficulty of nurturing on American soil the "House of Nobles"

12. *Federalist*, no. 62, pp. 378–79; no. 51, p. 322.
13. Farrand, *Records*, vol. 1, p. 339, June 20, and p. 34, May 30; vol. 3, p. 340, debate in North Carolina convention, July 24, 1788, and p. 359, anecdote of Washington and Jefferson.

that was essential in any perfect government, but he urged the delegates to create a Senate whose members would be distinguished "for their rank in life and their weight of property, and bearing as strong a likeness to the British House of Lords as possible." Elbridge Gerry yearned for a "house of peers."[14]

This concept of the role of the Senate determined both the length of senators' terms and the method of selection. Morris held that to protect the independence of the Senate from the more democratic House of Representatives, its members should be chosen for life,[15] but that was too blatant a departure from republican principles to win acceptance. Stability would be guaranteed by giving the senators a longer term than that accorded members of the House; the delegates initially approved a term of seven years, but later shortened it to six to facilitate the staggering of terms.

As for the method of selection, the Virginia plan proposed that senators be chosen by the members of the House from lists of persons nominated by the state legislatures, but this scheme ran at once into the criticism that it violated the principle of bicameralism by making the senators' election dependent on the very House whose excesses the Senate was being created to check. Charles Pinckney of South Carolina suggested at the outset that the Senate be the body in which the states showed their "sovereignty,"[16] and this idea quickly gained wide acceptance. Popular election of senators was discarded, then, on three grounds—first, that one popularly elected branch of the legislature would not be well designed to check another branch similarly chosen; second, that popular election could not be relied on to place men of experience, stature, and wealth in the republican counterpart of the House of Lords; and third, that if the states were to control the senate, the members of that body had to be appointed by the states themselves rather than elected by the people. So selection of senators by the state legislators was approved by unanimous vote of the state delegations. To George Mason, this mode of election added another to the checks and balances in the Constitution; the states would have the power through the Senate to defend themselves against encroachment by the federal government, just as the presi-

14. Ibid., vol. 1, p. 428, June 26; pp. 512–13, July 2; p. 87, June 2; p. 150, June 7; p. 221, June 12, notes of Robert Yates.
15. Ibid., p. 512, July 2.
16. Ibid., p. 59, May 31, notes of Pierce.

dential veto enabled the executive branch to defend itself against the legislature.[17]

There being no "levelers" in the convention, scarcely any argument for the unicameral alternative was advanced at any time. Franklin reportedly considered two houses unnecessary, but he did not speak out, and bicameralism was initially adopted without discussion or, apparently, dissent. Roger Sherman of Connecticut subsequently remarked that, on principle, he saw no need for a two-house legislature, but concluded by saying that if bicameralism was necessary to solve the quarrel between the large states and the small states over the formula for representation in the legislature, he would agree to the creation of two houses.[18] Bicameralism did turn out to be the magic solvent for that great dispute that had threatened to destroy the convention. The large states would get in one house the representation on the basis of population they had demanded, while the small states would gain in the other the equal representation of states on which they had been adamant. The large states would control the House, the small states would have their disproportionate weight in the Senate. When that great compromise saved the convention, it riveted the principle of bicameralism into the Constitution.

As an element of the compromise, the House was given the exclusive power to originate revenue bills. As originally proposed by the committee that drafted the compromise, the provision denied the Senate the right to amend such bills—a feature copied from the similar restriction on the British House of Lords—but this yielded to the argument that in this as in other matters the more deliberate Senate should serve to check the impulsive House. The original version covered appropriations as well as revenue bills, but the narrower wording that came from a later committee—the famed Committee on Postponed Matters—was not challenged.

Independent Election of the President

The Virginia plan that was the basis for the convention's deliberations provided that the chief executive should be selected by the legislature. This obvious breach of the separation of powers principle was at once recognized as such, and inventive members turned their

17. Ibid., pp. 155–56, June 7; p. 407, June 25.
18. Ibid., p. 48, May 31; vol. 3, p. 297, Franklin letter of April 22, 1788; vol. 1, pp. 341–43, June 20.

minds to devising a suitable—and salable—alternative. But it took all summer, and recurrent intense debate, before they could agree on one. "This subject has greatly divided the House," said James Wilson in September, as the convention neared adjournment with the issue still unsettled. "It is in truth the most difficult of all on which we have had to decide."[19]

Wilson had been the first to oppose this element of the Virginia plan, and it was he who first suggested the electoral college scheme that finally found its tortuous way into the Constitution. But the initial reaction was that the general electorate would be too poorly informed to make a wise choice of electors, and the "great trouble and expense," as Hugh Williamson put it, made the plan unaccept-able. In the first test of Wilson's idea, on June 2, he could not even carry his own state, and election by the legislature was affirmed by a vote of eight states to two. After that, however, the convention formally changed its mind three times. On July 19, it voted for an electoral college, six states to three. Five days later, it reverted to selection by the legislature, seven states to four. On a reconsideration, on August 24, the electoral college plan lost by a five-to-six vote and again on a four-to-four tie vote, with two states divided and the eleventh absent. It was this deadlock, more than any other, that occasioned the appointment of the Committee on Postponed Matters, consisting of one member from each of the eleven participating states, and that body after four days of intensive deliberation came down on the side of taking the election of the president out of the hands of the Congress. That settled the matter, and the novel idea of the electoral college was decisively approved.

Had this close decision gone the other way, the United States would have had a form of government much more closely akin to those of the parliamentary democracies of the world, where the chief executive—the prime minister—is chosen by, and from, the legislature and remains in office only so long as he or she holds the confidence of the majority of that body.[20] But throughout the summer, the opponents of the original Virginia proposal hammered away at the

19. Ibid., vol. 2, p. 501, September 4.
20. In bicameral legislatures, practices vary, but typically the more popular, or "lower" chamber has the dominant or exclusive role in the selection and removal of prime ministers. In Britain, the model for many parliamentary systems, the House of Commons has the exclusive role, the House of Lords having long since been reduced to a minor and essentially advisory legislative capacity.

argument that for the legislature to choose the chief executive would destroy the independence of that office and make its occupant "subservient" to the will of the legislators. The Virginians had recognized this problem and had tried to resolve it by making the executive ineligible for a second term; this provision, argued George Mason, would remove "a temptation on the side of the Executive to intrigue with the Legislature for a re-appointment." To most of those who favored limiting the executive to a single term, it seemed logical that that term should be a long one, and a length of seven years was initially approved, by a one-vote margin, over the objection of those who, like Gunning Bedford, Jr., of Delaware, worried about what would happen to the country "in case the first magistrate should be saddled on it for such period and it should be found on trial that he did not possess the qualifications ascribed to him, or should lose them after his appointment." Impeachment, he pointed out, "would reach misfeasance only, not incapacity."[21]

But the seven-year, single-term solution still fell short of satisfying those who were most concerned about assuring the independence of the executive. Even if he were barred from reappointment, the initial appointment would make him "the mere creature of the Legislature," particularly since he would also be impeachable by that body, argued Gouverneur Morris. "If the Legislature elect, it will be the work of intrigue, of cabal, and of faction . . . real merit will rarely be the title to the appointment." And, in the absence of an independent executive to serve as "the great protector of the Mass of the people," "usurpation and tyranny on the part of the Legislature will be the consequence." James Wilson agreed that the executive would still be "too dependent to stand the mediator between the intrigues and sinister views of the Representatives and the general liberties and interests of the people."[22]

Their position was immensely strengthened when, in mid-July, the convention reversed itself on the question of the single term. Ineligibility for a second term, Morris had contended, would tend "to destroy the great motive to good behavior, the hope of being rewarded by re-appointment." Roger Sherman and Rufus King added the argument that "he who has proved himself to be most fit for an

---

21. Farrand, *Records*, vol. 1, pp. 68, 69, June 1.
22. Ibid., vol. 2, pp. 29, 31, July 17; p. 52, July 19; p. 30, July 17.

Office, ought not to be excluded by the constitution from holding it."[23] On the strength of these arguments, the one-term limit was removed on July 19, six states to four. That permitted a shortening of the executive's term, but it was reduced only from seven to six years. And it precipitated the July 19 swing over to the electoral college method of choosing the executive, even Virginia joining the majority.

The electoral college was still, however, too novel an institution. Delegates wondered whether first-rate men would choose to serve as electors, and whether introducing a new group of officials into the structure would not make the new government too complex. With New Jersey and Delaware changing sides, the convention on July 24 rescinded its decision of five days earlier and restored the power of presidential selection to the legislature. The related decisions on the presidential term were reversed as well, and the delegates were back where they began, with a single seven-year term for their new executive.

But the matter remained far from settled, for the advocates of an independent executive were more adamant than ever. Morris was still insisting that an executive chosen by the legislature would be its "mere creature." He, along with Wilson, King, and others, still contended that the country should be enabled to retain an able president in office for another term, even if the first were as long as seven years. And their ranks attracted an influential recruit: the principal author of the Virginia plan, Madison himself, who had finally thought the matter through and concluded that in this particular feature his plan did indeed violate his own exalted principle of independent branches and separated powers. For the legislature to choose the chief executive encountered now, in his mind, "insuperable objections." He summed up the opposition case. It would "agitate and divide the legislature so much that the public interest would materially suffer by it." The candidate would intrigue with the legislature, and foreign powers would join in the intrigue. Above all, the appointee would be "subservient" to the majority faction that selected him; and that must not be, for legislatures "betrayed a strong propensity to a variety of pernicious measures" and one object of creating an executive with the power of veto was "to control the

23. Ibid., p. 33, July 17; p. 55, July 19.

National Legislature, so far as it might be infected with a similar propensity."[24]

All these arguments were reiterated by Gouverneur Morris when the matter was again considered, on August 24, but in another test vote the electoral college was defeated, six states to five. The proponents had won back New Jersey and Delaware but lost Maryland. A week later, the convention did what such bodies have always to do (and this convention had already done on the great controversy between the large and small states over representation in the legislature); it appointed a committee. Among the eleven members chosen by ballot, one from each state, happened to appear the two most eloquent and insistent enemies of selection of the executive by the legislature, Morris and Madison. Perhaps that ordained the ultimate victory of the electoral college.

Once the committee had agreed that the president would be chosen by electors, two related decisions came easily. The president could be made eligible for reelection, as most delegates had desired all along. And, that being the case, his term could be shortened, and four years was agreed on. As for how the electors would be chosen, that was left to the state legislatures. And their distribution reflected a compromise between the large and small states, with the number of electors assigned to each state equal to its representation in the Senate and House of Representatives combined. The electors would meet in their respective states, and each would cast two votes, only one of which could be for a resident of his own state—an idea advanced earlier in the summer as an answer to the contention that electors would invariably vote for candidates from their own states (at least after George Washington had completed his expected service), making it impossible for anyone to receive a majority. If, despite that precaution, no candidate received a majority, the Senate would choose from among the top five; or, in cases when two candidates received majorities but tied, from the top two. In each of these selection processes, the runner-up would become the vice president.

When the plan was presented, on September 4, defenders of the original Virginia plan for presidential selection by the legislature grumbled but on a test vote could muster the support of only two states. Debate then focused not on the central question of independent

24. Ibid., p. 103, July 24; pp. 109–10, July 25.

electors but on the role of the Senate when the electors failed to produce a clear majority. To many delegates, indeed, this became the overriding issue, for they envisioned the electoral college as little more than a nominating body, consisting of men who would meet in scattered state capitals and, out of touch with one another, disperse their votes among many candidates. Some delegates argued that more and more leaders with national reputations would emerge, but none of the men of Philadelphia—with all their experience and sagacity—were able to look even two decades into the future and foresee the emergence of national political parties with central nominating processes and national campaigns. Nineteen times in twenty, predicted George Mason, the president would be chosen by the Senate.[25] Many were less gloomy than that, but no delegate, probably, would have dared predict that the electoral college would work as well as it has done, failing only twice in the first forty-nine presidential elections under the Constitution to give one candidate a clear majority.[26]

This, then, raised the specter of too much power in the Senate. Charles Pinckney foresaw the president as a "mere creature" of the Senate, who would ally with that body against the House of Representatives and thus fix himself in office for life. When the president became its "minion," argued Wilson, the Senate would control all appointments, including those to the judiciary, and since it also was being given the power of trying impeachments and making treaties, all three branches of government would be "blended" into the Senate.[27] After a couple of days of floundering, two members of the committee that had designed the proposal, Williamson of North Carolina and Sherman of Connecticut, hit on a scheme that would allay delegates' fears of an overweening Senate yet preserve for the small states the voting parity with the large states that they enjoyed in that body. The House of Representatives would be given the

25. Ibid., p. 500, September 4.
26. Those were the elections of 1800 and 1824, and the first failure was the result of the peculiar provision in the electoral college plan that gave each elector two votes. When the Republican party nominated Thomas Jefferson and Aaron Burr, with the intent that Jefferson serve as president and Burr as vice president, the party's electors cast ballots for both, with the result that both received a majority but tied. This flaw in the Constitution was corrected by the Twelfth Amendment, which was ratified before the next presidential election.
27. Farrand, *Records*, vol. 2, p. 511, September 5; pp. 522–23, September 6.

disputed responsibility, but there the members would vote by states, with each state having a single vote. Thus was resolved the "most difficult" of the convention's problems of governmental architecture.

The Presidential Veto

In a government of separated powers, the legislative branch could not hold an absolute power to make laws. If so, it could encroach on the powers of the other branches and so, in the phrase Madison liked to repeat, "draw all power into its impetuous vortex." The questions before the convention, then, were not whether a veto should exist but who should exercise it, whether the legislature should have the power to override the veto and, if so, by a majority of what size.

The Virginia plan had called for a "council of revision," consisting of the executive and an unspecified number of judges, with power to veto laws but subject to being overriden by an extraordinary majority of both houses (the size of the majority left blank).

Granting the veto power to both the executive and judicial branches, acting jointly, was proposed on the logical ground that both were in equal need of a mechanism of defense against an ambitious legislature. The weakness of this argument was that the veto power was more than a defense mechanism; it was needed also, said George Mason, to "discourage demagogues" in the legislatures from attempting to pass "unjust and pernicious laws," and Gouverneur Morris was explicit as to the types of laws: "emissions of paper money, largesses to the people—a remission of debts and similar measures." If the judges were to participate in vetoing laws on policy grounds, they would be "meddling in politics and parties," as Sherman put it, and they would be biased in interpreting laws they had played a part in writing. "The judges ought never to give their opinion on a law till it comes before them," contended John Rutledge of South Carolina, the presiding judge of his state's supreme court.[28] As for defending the judiciary against legislative encroachment on its powers, some delegates observed that the judges had their power to declare any such laws unconstitutional. These arguments prevailed each time in repeated tests of the issue, leaving the veto power in the executive branch alone.

28. Ibid., pp. 78, 76, July 21; p. 300, August 15; p. 80, July 21.

A few delegates, notably Wilson and Alexander Hamilton of New York, thought the logic of separation of powers required that the executive have an absolute veto. "Without such a Self-defense," said Wilson, "the Legislature can at any moment sink it into non-existence."[29] But an all-powerful executive was only somewhat less fearsome than an unchecked legislature, and not a single state supported it. Debate then centered on the size of the legislative majority required to override the veto. Two-thirds of each house was the proportion chosen in June. In August, when the plan still called for the executive to be chosen by the legislature and delegates worried about his becoming the legislators' captive, the figure of three-fourths was substituted. But in September, when the executive had been strengthened by the plan for independent election, delegates feared that the three-fourths requirement gave him excessive power. With the support of only a small minority of legislators, protested Sherman, he could prevail over the "general voice" and "mistake or betray" the "sense of the people."[30] In one of its last decisions before adjourning, the convention restored the two-thirds figure.

Checks on the President

As the convention went about creating a strong executive to check what most delegates perceived to be the more dangerous branch of the new government—the legislature—the safeguard advanced originally by Randolph and others who feared monarchy was a plural rather than a unitary executive, to be composed of three men representing different regions. But this proposal was never able to attract the support of more than three states. A plural executive, argued Wilson, would lack "energy, dispatch, and responsibility." Instead, it would produce "nothing but uncontrolled, continued, and violent animosities." All of the states, he observed, had unitary executives.[31]

True, replied his opponents, but they all had a council of some sort to advise and restrain their executives. This became the line of retreat for those who feared an elective king. Gerry, Madison, Mason,

29. Ibid., vol. 1, p. 98, June 4.
30. Ibid., vol. 2, p. 585, September 12.
31. Ibid., vol. 1, p. 65, June 1; p. 96, June 4.

Sherman, and Franklin were among influential members who insisted on some form of council—although they disagreed on whether it should be strictly advisory to the executive or should possess a veto power over executive actions—and in August, Oliver Ellsworth of Connecticut suggested one consisting of the president of the Senate, the chief justice, and the heads of the executive departments, to be limited to advisory functions. The Committee of Detail added the Speaker of the House to this body and named it the privy council, after the group who advised the British king. Mason proposed an alternative, a council elected by the House of Representatives. But the Committee on Postponed Matters resolved the question by giving to the Senate the right to "advise and consent" on the two elements of executive power that most concerned the delegates—the power to make appointments and the power to make treaties—and a separate council then became superfluous.[32] The Senate, Luther Martin of Maryland advised his state's ratifying convention, was to serve as a "privy council" for the president, residing permanently in Washington. Rufus King of Massachusetts, a member of the Committee on Postponed Matters, summarized for his state's convention the reasons that the council was abandoned. Since every state would insist on having at least one member, any council would be similar to the Senate. Under the Constitution as drafted, the Senate would advise the president on some matters and he could obtain the opinions of other officers on others. Finally, "secrecy, despatch, and fidelity were more to be expected than where there is a multitudinous executive." None of these arguments satisfied George Mason, who gave among his reasons for not signing the Constitution the absence of the constitutional council that "any safe and regular government" must have. Without such a council, the president would rely for advice on "minions and favorites" or become "a tool to the Senate," Mason gloomily predicted.[33]

The principal checks on the executive, then, in addition to the oft-cited power of the purse, were to lie in the Senate's control of

32. Alexander Hamilton identifies the power to make treaties and the power of appointment as "the only instances in which the abuse of the executive authority was materially to be feared." *Federalist*, no. 77, p. 464.

33. Farrand, *Records*, vol. 3, p. 194, Luther Martin to the Maryland legislature, December 28, 1787; p. 269, Rufus King in the Massachusetts convention, January 28, 1788; and vol. 2, p. 638, September 15.

appointments and of treaties, the legislature's retention of the power to declare war, and the power of the legislature, in extremity, to remove the president from office through impeachment. In addition, legislators would be protected from executive influence by denying the president the right to offer them positions in the executive branch as long as they remained in the legislature.

Senate Confirmation of Appointments

The original Virginia plan assigned the power to appoint judges to the legislature (a practice followed to this day in Virginia), but in its early consideration of the subject the convention restricted the power to the Senate. The "more numerous" House of Representatives, Madison had argued, would be inclined to "intrigue and partiality" and would be too disposed to appoint from its own membership or from lawyers who had served its members. The Senate, as "a less numerous and more select body," would do a better job. But to many delegates, even the Senate would be too numerous, "too little personally responsible," and too much given to "intrigue and cabal," as Nathaniel Gorham of Massachusetts put it.[34] He suggested appointment by the executive with the "advice and consent" of the Senate, a method used in his state for one hundred and forty years. But others thought that the executive, too, would be subject to intrigue, and the small states rallied as usual around the Senate, the one institution in which they enjoyed an equal status. The proposal lost on a tie vote, four states to four, and here the matter stood until the final days of the convention.

The argument was finally resolved as part of the grand reconciliation of interbranch relationships worked out by the Committee on Postponed Matters. It adopted the Gorham proposal and applied it not only to appointment of judges but also to selection of ambassadors (which the Committee of Detail had earlier assigned to the Senate also) and to the appointment of "all other officers of the United States." Almost as an afterthought, among last-minute amendments, Gouverneur Morris pointed out that "all" was too many, and a clause was added permitting the Congress to vest the appointment of

34. Ibid., vol. 1, p. 120, June 5, and pp. 232–33, June 13; vol. 2, pp. 41–42, 44, July 18.

"inferior officers" in the president alone, in the courts of law, or in the heads of departments. Morris, one of the architects of the compromise, summed it up: "As the President was to nominate, there would be responsibility, and as the Senate was to concur, there would be security."[35]

Senate Approval of Treaties

The question of who should exercise the treaty-making power had been left to the Committee of Detail, and that body placed the authority in the Senate. When that proposition was considered, in late August, some members protested that the House of Representatives should have a right of approval of the Senate's handiwork, while others contended that the president should be involved. With that much disagreement, the treaty-making power took its place among the other interbranch issues on the agenda of the Committee on Postponed Matters. That body reduced the Senate role to one of "advise and consent" and gave the treaty-making power to the president, but with the proviso—adapted from the Articles of Confederation—that two-thirds of the Senators present must concur.[36] A motion to add the House to the approval process won the support of only a single state. A motion to reduce the Senate approval requirement to a simple majority likewise was backed by but one state, but a proposal to reduce the requirement to a majority of the entire Senate membership was defeated by only a single vote, six states to five.

The War Power

From the beginning, it was understood that the executive would be the commander in chief of the army and navy, but that he would be restrained by the ultimate power of the legislative branch to determine when, and against whom, the country would be at war. Thus, in the report of the Committee of Detail, the authority "to make war" was listed among the powers of the Congress.

35. Ibid., vol. 2, p. 539, September 7.
36. In *Federalist*, no. 38, p. 238, Madison still held to the original concept, writing that the Constitution "empowers the Senate, with the concurrence of the executive, to make treaties." But Hamilton, in ibid., no. 69, p. 419, places the power "to make treaties" in the president, subject to senatorial concurrence.

In the only discussion of this issue, Charles Pinckney of South Carolina objected to assigning the responsibility to both houses of Congress, because the House of Representatives would meet only once a year, its proceedings would be "too slow," and it would be "too numerous" for such deliberations. He suggested, accordingly, that the power to make war should be vested in the Senate alone. But his colleague Pierce Butler observed that the same objections would lie, to a great degree, against the Senate also, and proposed that the power be assigned to the president, "who will have all the requisite qualities, and will not make war but when the Nation will support it." That aroused Elbridge Gerry, who expressed shock at the thought that in a republic the executive would be empowered alone to declare war, and George Mason agreed that the president could not safely be entrusted with such power. Madison and Gerry hit on the compromise that satisfied nearly everyone. The president would be empowered "to repel sudden attacks" but not to thrust the nation into war. To this end, the congressional power was narrowed from "to make war" to "to declare war," and that wording was accepted.[37]

Impeachment

When the convention met, impeachment was a well-established—though infrequently used—process in Britain for the removal of errant officers of the crown, and like other elements of the British constitution the concept had found its way into constitutional doctrine in America as well. Accordingly, when the Virginia delegates put their plan before the convention, they listed among the functions of the judiciary the power to try impeachments that that branch of government exercised under the Virginia constitution. The plan was silent, however, on what body would be empowered to initiate the impeachment and bring it before the judges.

Since the president would be by far the most important of the "National officers" subject to removal, the question entered into the complex calculus of interbranch relationships in three aspects. Who would have the power to impeach the president? What would be the permissible grounds? And who would try the impeachment and render the verdict?

37. Farrand, *Records*, vol 2, pp. 318–19, August 17.

Few were prepared to go as far as Roger Sherman of Connecticut, the convention's leading advocate of legislative supremacy, who considered an independent executive "the very essence of tyranny" and wanted him "absolutely dependent" on the legislature, because it was that branch's will "which was to be executed." To this end, he contended that the legislature should not only appoint the executive—as the convention initially agreed to propose—but have the power to remove him "at pleasure."[38] In a test vote when the convention was only a week old, only three states were prepared to transfer the removal power from the judicial to the legislative branch.

Nor were many prepared to go to the other extreme and protect the executive from impeachment altogether. The idea of impeachment was "dangerous," protested Gouverneur Morris; if the executive "is to be a check on the Legislature, let him not be impeachable." But Morris announced after another day's debate that he had been converted by arguments such as those of George Mason: "Shall any man be above Justice? Above all shall that man be above it, who can commit the most extensive injustice?" And Franklin: "What was the practice before this in cases where the chief Magistrate rendered himself obnoxious? Why recourse was had to assassination."[39] Morris then retreated to the position that the grounds for impeachment should be limited and defined. Only two states voted to make the executive unimpeachable.

The Committee of Detail, offering the definition Morris had suggested, limited impeachment of the president to cases of "treason, bribery, or corruption." It also made its choice of the impeaching body: the House of Representatives—which, in a phrase deleted from its final language, the committee had initially held "shall be the grand Inquest of this Nation."[40] These proposals were approved without a roll call vote.

It was Morris, again, who objected to making the Supreme Court the trial body and got the matter referred to the Committee on Postponed Matters. In that committee, Morris must have won a debate with Madison, for the group decided to make the Senate the adjudicator of impeachments brought by the House, but with a two-thirds vote required for conviction and removal. It also limited the

38. Ibid., vol. 1, p. 68, June 1; p. 85, June 2.
39. Ibid., vol. 2, p. 53, July 19; p. 65, July 20.
40. Ibid., p. 154, Committee of Detail records.

grounds to treason and bribery, but on this matter Mason had the last word. This, he objected, "will not reach many great and dangerous offences. . . . Attempts to subvert the Constitution may not be Treason as above defined." With Gerry seconding him, he proposed to add "maladministration," but when Madison protested that this would amount to the president's serving "during pleasure of the Senate," Mason substituted "other high crimes and misdemeanors," and in this form the language was approved, eight states to three. At this point, Madison renewed his argument in favor of trial by the Supreme Court or by some special tribunal outside the legislative branch, for if the House were empowered to impeach—"and for any act which might be called a misdemeanor"—and the Senate to convict, the president would be "improperly dependent." But Morris responded that the Supreme Court "were too few in number and might be warped or corrupted" and Sherman reminded the delegates that the Court would be made up of presidential appointees.[41] Madison could win the support of only two states, and the Senate was confirmed as the trial body.

Prohibition of Dual Officeholding

As a safeguard against corruption of the legislature, the authors of the Virginia plan proposed that members of that branch be ineligible for appointment to offices in the executive and judicial branches during the terms to which they were elected, and for an unspecified length of time (later set as one year) thereafter. Without such a prohibition, its advocates predicted, legislators would create unnecessary offices that they would then seek to fill. "If not checked," contended Mason, "we shall have ambassadors to every petty state in Europe—the little republic of St. Marino not excepted." Elbridge Gerry saw a legislature mired in "intrigues of ambitious men for displacing proper officers, in order to create vacancies for themselves."[42] Others, led by Madison, argued against an absolute disqualification, on the ground that it would discourage able men from seeking legislative service.

But delegates saw that the issue was not simply one of preventing

41. Ibid., pp. 550–51, September 8.
42. Ibid., vol. 1, p. 380, June 22, Yates notes; p. 388, June 23.

venality in the legislature but one of power also. For the distribution of appointments would be a prime source of influence for the new national executive that was to be created, and the proponents of a strong executive were loath to exempt the members of the legislature from the range of that influence. Thus Alexander Hamilton argued, quoting a British politician, that what "went under the name of corruption" was in fact "an essential part of the weight which maintained the equilibrium of the Constitution." If the executive is deprived of influence by rendering the members of the legislature ineligible for executive offices, agreed John Francis Mercer of Maryland, "he becomes a mere phantom of authority."[43] Those who, like Mason and Sherman, preferred, if not a phantom, at most a weak and controlled executive, supported the prohibition.

Eventually, the convention found what Madison called "a medium between the two extremes."[44] First, the delegates removed the restriction, in the case of House members, on appointments to positions in the executive branch after their terms expired, and the Committee on Postponed Matters removed that prohibition for senators as well. That committee also turned the clause into a two-way restriction; not only could legislators not be appointed to offices in the executive or judicial branches during their terms but any civil officeholder must resign his post if elected to the Congress. The delegates then, by the narrow vote of five states to four, limited the disqualification to only those offices that were created, or whose salaries had been increased, during a legislator's term, thus making him eligible for appointment to any other office provided he resigned his seat.

The Process of Amendment

The Virginia plan proposed that the articles of union the delegates were to draft should include a process for amendment, but it did not define that process except to specify that "the assent of the National Legislature ought not to be required thereto." The proviso, explained George Mason, was necessary because the legislature "may abuse

43. Ibid., p. 376, June 22; vol. 2, p. 284, August 14.
44. Ibid., vol. 3, p. 316, debate in the Virginia ratifying convention, June 14, 1788.

their power, and refuse their consent on that very account."[45] Responding to this concern, the Committee of Detail placed the responsibility for initiating amendments in the state legislatures, proposing that on application of two-thirds of the legislatures the Congress would call a convention for the purpose, and that procedure was approved.

The matter was not reopened until the final days of the convention, when Alexander Hamilton urged that a second means of amendment be added—initiation by the Congress. "The National Legislature," he argued, "will be the first to perceive and will be most sensible to the necessity of amendments" and should, therefore, be empowered to call a convention on its own motion, by a two-thirds vote of each house. Madison remarked that the language was still vague, asking "How was a Convention to be formed? by what rule decide? what the force of its acts?" His questions were only partly answered as the delegates pondered the procedure. First, they modified Hamilton's idea by providing that when the two houses of Congress by two-thirds votes agreed on the need for amendments, they submit them directly to the states rather than call a convention. After voting down, by a six-to-five margin, a proposal that amendments take effect on ratification by two-thirds of the states, the delegates agreed to require approval by three-fourths. Madison then succeeded in adding language authorizing the Congress to decide, in the case of each amendment, whether ratification should be by state legislatures or state conventions called for the purpose. Finally, in the last act of the convention before the Constitution was engrossed, the delegates responded to "circulating murmurs of the small States" by agreeing, without debate, that no state without its consent could be deprived of its equal representation in the Senate.[46]

45. Ibid., vol. 1, p. 22, May 29; p. 203, June 11.
46. Ibid., vol. 2, pp. 558–59, September 10; p. 631, September 15.

CHAPTER THREE

Two Centuries of Constitutional Debate

At no time in the two centuries of national life under the 1787 Constitution have its fundamental principles been subjected to any serious challenge. As noted in chapter 1, only a half dozen of the twenty-six amendments adopted since the Constitution was ratified have affected the governmental structure at all, and none has altered its essential architecture. Even more significant, no amendment that would contravene the separation of powers principle has ever been debated on the floor of either house of Congress, and few have even been proposed. One can search the more than one million pages of the *Congressional Record* and its predecessor publications without finding anything more than the rarest of muted and tentative suggestions that the founding fathers might have erred in designing the unique American system of independent executive and legislative branches replete with checks and balances, that the republic might have fared better with a more unified governmental structure like those that have evolved in Europe, in Canada, and in other nations of the British Commonwealth. Such criticism of the fundamentals of the constitutional system as has been spoken by scholars and observers outside the government has aroused no echo in the public utterances of presidents, senators, and representatives—the men and women who have borne the responsibility for making the system work. The great debate of 1787–88 has never been reopened, despite the expectations of the framers themselves that their decisions made in a single summer—and some by narrow and shifting votes—would be subject to review by every succeeding generation.

When structural amendments have been debated in the halls of Congress, proponents have been at pains to insist—if the question were raised at all—that their proposed changes would certainly not weaken, or would even reinforce, the constitutional structure of checks and balances. In this context, however, important changes in various elements of the constitutional system have been on occasion debated, as historical experience appeared to cast doubt on some of the details—if not the basic principles—of the framers' design.

Presidential Tenure

The most persistent, recurring topic of debate bearing on the constitutional structure has been the question of presidential tenure. The argument has revolved around two questions. First, did the right of a president to run for reelection for an unlimited number of terms threaten the United States with "an elective monarchy"? Second, if the president were restricted to a single term, should that term be lengthened from four to six years?

George Washington had set the precedent of an eight-year limit on presidential tenure by declining to run for a third term in 1796, and Jefferson and Madison had followed his example. By James Monroe's day, the two-term limit was seen as an element of the country's "unwritten constitution," yet as Monroe was nearing the end of his seventh year in office, supporters of the various candidates to succeed him considered it prudent to fix the principle in writing. Historians have reported no evidence that Monroe ever considered violating the precedent set by his three illustrious predecessors, but the Senate in January 1824, by a 30-to-3 vote, approved a constitutional amendment placing a two-term limit on presidential tenure. The House saw no need for any such precaution, and the effort ended there.[1]

Monroe's successor, however, was chosen in a process that ended in charges of scandal and corruption, and the subject was reopened in a new context. When the electoral college cast its votes following the election of 1824, none of the four candidates—John Quincy

1. Two years later, the Senate reaffirmed its position by a 25-to-4 vote, but again the House did not act.

Adams, Henry Clay, William H. Crawford, and Andrew Jackson—
had a majority, and the choice was thrown into the House of
Representatives for the second—and, as of now, last—time. Andrew
Jackson had a plurality of electoral votes, and a plurality of the
popular vote in those states that chose their electors by direct election,
but Clay threw his support to Adams in what Jackson's supporters
condemned as a "corrupt bargain" by which Clay would be named
secretary of state. When Adams, thus elected, appeared to confirm
the charge by appointing Clay to that office, the Jackson followers
had a campaign issue for the whole four years leading up to the
election of 1828. Successful in that election, Jackson set out to reform
the Constitution to prevent the recurrence of the kind of episode that
he felt had denied him his rightful reward four years before.

In his first annual message to the Congress, Jackson proposed that
the electoral college be abolished and the president be chosen by
popular vote, with a runoff election between the two high candidates
if none achieved a majority in the initial ballot. Incidental to his
principal recommendation, the president included a single sentence
suggesting that "it would seem advisable to limit the service of the
Chief Magistrate to a single term of either four or six years."[2]

A year later, in his second annual message, Jackson presented the
rationale for the one-term limit that was missing from his original
recommendation. Such a limit, he said, would "strengthen those
checks by which the Constitution designed to secure the independence of each department of the Government." A president ineligible
for reelection would "as far as possible be placed beyond the reach
of any improper influences." He would be able to approach the
"solemn responsibilities" of his office "uncommitted to any course
other than the strict line of constitutional duty."[3] Jackson reiterated
his proposals in every one of his six succeeding annual messages,
but his recommendations were not considered on the floor of either
house.[4]

2. Jackson suggested, however, that the popular preference could be registered by
states, each state to cast the same number of votes as it would cast in the electoral
college. "Message of December 8, 1829," in James D. Richardson, ed., *A Compilation
of the Messages and Papers of the Presidents (1789–1897)*, vol. 3 (Bureau of National
Literature, 1897), p. 1011.
3. "Message of December 6, 1830," in ibid., p. 1082.
4. Jackson did not pause to explain why he had not imposed a one-term limit on

After Jackson, no president won reelection until Abraham Lincoln in 1864, so the question remained quiescent. But Lincoln was shot early in his second term and the office passed to the hapless Andrew Johnson, who fell at once into the conflict with the Radical Republicans over Reconstruction policy that led to his impeachment. In the lame-duck session that followed the midterm election of 1866, the Senate Judiciary Committee reported a resolution introduced by the Radical Ben Wade of Ohio that would bar from a second term any president, including one succeeding to that office on the death of his predecessor. While the measure was aimed obviously at Johnson, the brief debate that was accorded it rose to the level of principle. Even the "greatest and best" of presidents, argued Wade, had been tempted to adopt measures "looking quite as much to the continuance of the incumbent in office as to the public good"; the desire for reelection "will sway the judgment of any man, whether he knows it or not." Those who supported Wade divided on whether the single term should run for four years or six. Advocates of the six-year term contended that every four years was too often to suffer the "great agitation and excitement" of the presidential campaign and, if a president chosen for so long a term proved incompetent or otherwise unsatisfactory, the Congress could render him "impotent"—as it had already done in the case of Johnson. But opponents waxed passionate on the danger of so long a tenure for a chief executive who proved unsuitable. Wade denied that a president who disagreed with the Congress could be rendered harmless. "His word is law," insisted the Ohioan; "and suppose the people make a mistake, as they are always liable to make a mistake . . . and get a man who is false to all they wanted of him, who thwarts all their ideas, who overthrows all their principles; and there he sits, clothed with a power that you cannot get rid of." Asked Jacob M. Howard, a Michigan radical: "Was it not a most fortunate thing for this country and the cause of human liberty" that the term of Lincoln's predecessor, Democrat James Buchanan, expired in four years instead of six? "The government would have been destroyed," cried Howard. "It is in the nature of our institutions that the people may from time to time be imposed upon by an incompetent, faithless, or traitorous Chief Magistrate." Against the one-term limit was presented the same argument used in 1787: the people's freedom to

himself, beyond a remark in his second inaugural address that his reelection was "unsolicited." Ibid., p. 1222.

choose their chief executive should not be limited. After a single session of inconclusive discussion, the Senate did not return to the measure before adjournment.[5]

The next serious discussion of term limitation came nearly half a century later, in the aftermath of the clash between President William Howard Taft and Theodore Roosevelt for the Republican nomination in 1912 and the subsequent third-party candidacy of Roosevelt that brought about the election of the Democrat Woodrow Wilson. Senator John D. Works of California, a Republican, introduced a single-six-year-term amendment with a vivid condemnation of the manner in which both Roosevelt in 1904 and Taft in 1912 had, in his view, misused the resources of the federal government to obtain renomination and, in Roosevelt's case, reelection. Thousands of federal officeholders, he charged, had been mobilized into a "political army," working for the candidate rather than the country. And, after Roosevelt's reelection, pending suits against trusts that had supported him were dismissed. Senator Works continued:

> The effort to elect a President to a second term is a prolific source of political corruption, neglect of official duty, and betrayal of trust on the part of public servants. It is degrading to the President himself, and brings his great office into disrespect, often contempt. . . . A large part of his time that should be devoted to public service is given over to politics and the effort to secure his reelection. . . . He expects every man he appoints to support his political aspirations. . . . The White House is turned into the headquarters of a political party.[6]

Taft himself agreed with at least a part of the indictment. Even if a president does not divert his energies, his appointees do, the president conceded after his defeat. "It is difficult," said Taft, "to prevent the whole administration from losing part of its effectiveness for the public good by this diversion to political effort for at least a year of the four of each administration." If reelection were to be prohibited, Taft preferred a six-year term, because four years were "too short a time in which to work out great governmental policies."[7]

Senator Elihu Root, New York Republican, argued that the government of a president seeking reelection is immobilized not just for a single year but for two, as was demonstrated in the last half of

5. *Congressional Globe* (February 11, 1867), pp. 1140–45.
6. *Congressional Record* (December 9, 1912), pp. 295–97.
7. Speech at Lotus Club, New York City, quoted by Senator Works, ibid. (December 10, 1912), p. 361.

President Taft's term. Just when a president "gets to the point of highest efficiency," argued Root, "people in the Senate and in the House begin to figure to try to beat him. You cannot separate the attempt to beat an individual from the attempt to make ineffective the operation of the Government which that individual is carrying on in accordance with his duty."[8]

But, countered Henry Cabot Lodge, Republican of Massachusetts, a president barred from reelection would still use the powers of his office to elect a successor of his own party, one in sympathy with his views, who would carry out the uncompleted policies of the incumbent. And William E. Borah, Republican of Idaho, agreed. Having attended the last two GOP conventions, he "could not discover any perceptible difference between the effect of the influence which was exerted upon the convention in 1908 by the gentleman [Roosevelt] who was nominating his successor [Taft] and that exerted in 1912 by the gentleman [Taft] who was nominating himself." If a president is fit to be in the White House, "he will be a political leader and will direct the political fortunes of his party. . . . He . . . will seek to lead his party, if not for his cause, then to the advantage of his successor." Besides Roosevelt, Borah cited Jefferson and Jackson as presidents who had run "aggressive" campaigns for their chosen successors.[9]

John Sharp Williams, Democrat of Mississippi, drew from the executive-legislative deadlock of 1911–12 a conclusion opposite to that of Senator Root. The 1910 election, which gave the Democrats control of the House of Representatives while the Republican Taft remained in the White House, ushered in two years of divided government—what Williams called "lame and impotent and unsatisfactory government." But a six-year presidential term would extend any such period of divided government for two additional years, thus "emphasizing rather than diminishing the defect of our system as it is." Joseph L. Bristow, Republican of Kansas, concurred that the six-year term would result in suspension of governmental action for four years instead of two and make the government "less flexible and more irresponsive to the public will." It would entrench the president in office beyond the reach of the people, "regardless of the character of his administration," said Bristow, suggesting a provision

8. *Congressional Record* (January 30, 1913), p. 2265.
9. Ibid., pp. 2259, 2269.

for recall of the president at any biennial election. And Miles Poindexter, Republican of Washington, put it simply: Six years "is entirely too long for a bad man, and it is too short for a good man." Trust the people to decide at the end of the fourth year was his theme.[10]

An amendment by Senator Bristow to reduce the proposed six-year term to four years was beaten, 25 to 42, and the resolution cleared the Senate, 47 to 23. But it went to a House controlled by the Democratic party, and now that party was looking forward to the inauguration of President Wilson and to complete control of the government for the first time in nearly two decades. In the summer, the Democratic platform had endorsed a single-term constitutional amendment and pledged the party's nominee to "this principle," but Wilson had also promised to "say what I really think on every public question." The president-elect said what he thought in a letter that killed the resolution:

> Four years is too long a term for a President who is not the true spokesman of the people, who is imposed upon and does not lead. It is too short a term for a President who is doing, or attempting, a great work of reform, and who has not had time to finish it. To change the term to six years would be to increase the likelihood of its being too long, without any assurance that it would in happy cases be long enough. . . . As things stand now the people might more likely be cheated than served by further limitations of the President's eligibility. His fighting power in their behalf would be immensely weakened. No one will fear a President except those whom he can make fear the elections.[11]

The next president to win election twice was Franklin Roosevelt, and he steered the reform movement in a different direction. When, in the 1946 election, the Republicans won control of the Congress for the first time since before the age of FDR, they came to Washington intent on inflicting posthumously on their long-time adversary the defeat they could never visit on him in four presidential election campaigns. Barely a month after the Eightieth Congress assembled, the Republicans pushed through a resolution to fix in the Constitution the two-term limit on presidential tenure that Washington, Jefferson,

10. Ibid., pp. 2265–66, 2271.
11. Letter to Representative Alexander Mitchell Palmer, Democrat of Pennsylvania, February 5, 1913, in Arthur S. Link, ed., *The Papers of Woodrow Wilson* (Princeton University Press, 1978), vol. 27, pp. 98–101.

and all their successors had voluntarily adopted—until Roosevelt breached that precedent not once but twice.

Quoting George Washington on the dangers of monarchy, Republicans contended that the destruction of Washington's precedent made a constitutional amendment necessary to protect the country against "totalitarianism" and "dictatorship." Representative John M. Robsion of Kentucky, one of the amendment's authors, contended that the growth of the powers of the executive enabled a president who enjoyed indefinite tenure not only to gain a "very large control of the legislative branch" but also to appoint most members of the judicial branch, posing a "real threat to our republican form of government." "The simple issue," said Representative Edward J. Devitt of Minnesota, "is whether or not we shall add one more check to our present system of checks and balances" as a safeguard "against the possible—even the probable—rise of an executive dictatorship." In the Senate, Alexander Wiley, Wisconsin Republican, likened the "long-time continuance in office by so-called indispensable leaders" to the *"fuehrer prinzip."* And for the anti-New Deal Democrats, Senator John H. Overton of Louisiana warned that a strong president could "make a life termer of himself," from which the country could "drift into an undemocratic form of government . . . a dynasty."[12]

Democrats countered that the people should not be denied the freedom to reelect their president if they wished. "To have had a constitutional limitation on the Presidential tenure of office in 1940 and again in 1944 would have been disastrous," urged Representative Joseph R. Bryson, Democrat of South Carolina; "in the face of a grave national crisis in 1940 the people . . . believed it inadvisable to change their Chief Executive; and . . . in 1944 . . . the people believed that such a change would have thrown our Nation into chaos and jeopardized our security in the face of the gravest military crisis in our Nation's history." "For the people to have the privilege of choosing whom they please to be their leader is democracy, real democracy," argued Sam Rayburn of Texas, the minority leader. Do not put future generations "in a strait-jacket" that might result "in the destruction of our country," pleaded John W. McCormack of Massachusetts, the minority whip. But to this line of argument, the sponsors had a ready reply: The people were not being shackled; on

12. Ibid. (February 6, 1947), pp. 850, 859–60; (March 5, 1947), pp. 1681, 1775.

the contrary, they were being given the right to decide for themselves through the ratification process whether they wanted the two-term limit in their Constitution.[13] The resolution was adopted by the House by 285 votes to 121 and in the Senate by 59 to 23. Not a single Republican in either chamber voted in the negative. A substitute proposal offered in the House for a single six-year presidential term was defeated by a voice vote, without serious discussion.

A "tainted amendment," political scientist Clinton Rossiter called it a few years after its ratification, one "based on the sharp anger of a moment rather than the studied wisdom of a generation." The Constitution, said Rossiter, is "not the place to engage in a display of rancor." He predicted that the amendment would prove to have permanently weakened the presidency. "Everything in our history tells us," he wrote, "that a President who does not or cannot seek reelection loses much of his grip in his last couple of years, and we no longer can afford Presidents who lose their grip."[14] President Eisenhower, asked during his 1956 reelection campaign whether as a lame-duck president his influence would be lessened during his second term, conceded that "in some directions, it may be" but the power of the presidency would still be great. He considered the amendment "not wholly wise."[15] Resolutions to repeal the amendment have been introduced on occasion, but none has made headway in the Congress—even Congresses fully under the control of Democrats fiercely loyal to the memory of Franklin Roosevelt.

The single six-year term has continued to have advocates as well. In 1971, two veteran senators, Democratic Leader Mike Mansfield of Montana and Republican George D. Aiken of Vermont, proposed this reform in order "to allow a President to devote himself entirely to the problems of the Nation and . . . free him from the millstone of partisan politics" and from constant "harassment and embarrassment" by political opponents.[16] Senator Strom Thurmond, Republican of South Carolina, added another argument in introducing a six-year-

13. Ibid. (February 6, 1947), pp. 844–48.
14. Letter of March 18, 1957, to Representative Stewart L. Udall of Arizona, ibid. (March 25, 1957), p. 4323.
15. "News Conference of October 5, 1956," *Public Papers of the Presidents: Dwight D. Eisenhower, 1956* (Government Printing Office, 1958), p. 860.
16. *Congressional Record* (April 1, 1971), p. 9182.

term amendment four years later: it would "enhance the relationship between the President and Congress" because the legislators, "knowing that the President could not be reelected for a second term, would be more likely to work through consultation rather than confrontation."[17] In 1982, backers of the measure organized the Committee for a Single Six-Year Presidential Term to press for its adoption. The committee cited statements in support of the idea by Presidents Eisenhower, Johnson, Nixon, Ford, and Carter and included representatives of all those administrations, as well as of the Reagan administration, in its leadership. Cochairmen of the committee were William E. Simon, President Ford's secretary of the treasury; Griffin B. Bell and Cyrus R. Vance, members of President Carter's cabinet; and Milton S. Eisenhower, President Eisenhower's brother and close adviser.

Linking Cabinet and Congress

One of the earliest authoritative suggestions for altering the constitutional relationship between the Congress and the executive branch came from Justice Joseph Story of the Supreme Court, in his *Commentaries on the Constitution of the United States*, published in 1833. His clause-by-clause critique of the Constitution is, for the most part, a long paean to the wisdom of the framers, but one provision troubled him. That was the paragraph barring officials of the executive branch from membership in the Congress. Citing the principle of executive accountability, Story argued that the prohibition compelled the executive "to resort to secret and unseen influences, to private interviews, and private arrangements," to "all the blandishments of office, and all the deadening weight of silent patronage" to get its measures introduced and passed, instead of taking "open and public responsibility" and making "a bold and manly appeal to the nation in the face of its representatives." He also contended that if members of the cabinet had to advocate and defend their measures in the Congress, presidents would be forced to appoint as heads of departments "statesmen of high public character, talents, experience, and elevated services . . . who . . . could command public confi-

17. Ibid. (August 1, 1975), p. 26809.

dence," instead of "personal or party favourites" of "gross incapacity" and "ignorance."[18]

A generation later, this issue did reach the stage of debate on the House floor, but in the form of a statute rather than a constitutional amendment. A bill offered by Representative George H. Pendleton, Democrat of Ohio, during the Civil War proposed to authorize cabinet officials to participate in debate on matters affecting their departments and require them to be present for questioning twice weekly, at specified times. In approving the bill, in 1864, a select committee chaired by Pendleton repeated Story's argument that if cabinet officers had seats in the House their influence on the legislature would be "open, declared, and authorized, rather than secret, concealed, and unauthorized," but the proponents appeared to be concerned less with the jurist's concept of executive accountability than with their own notion of congressional responsibility. Protesting executive branch secrecy in the conduct of the war, they complained of a "table . . . groaning with the weight of resolutions asking information from the several Departments that have not been answered" and sought face-to-face confrontation with department heads as a means of obtaining information and thus enhancing their own ability to influence and control administrative action.[19] But, by agreement, the debate was deferred until the final day of the Thirty-eighth Congress, and the bill died without a vote when the Congress adjourned. A similar bill by Pendleton—by then a senator—was endorsed by a select Senate committee in 1881 but was shelved without debate. In both cases, opponents challenged the constitutionality of the proposed statutes, but supporters argued that the constitutional prohibition applied only to full membership with voting rights, leaving the Congress free to admit anyone it might choose to mere participation in debate.

18. Joseph Story, *Commentaries on the Constitution of the United States*, 2d ed. (Charles C. Little and James Brown, 1851), pp. 605–06. The *Commentaries* appeared at a time when congressional followers of President Jackson were attacking the Second Bank of the United States but Jackson was distancing himself from the conflict.

19. Stephen Horn, *The Cabinet and Congress* (Columbia University Press, 1960), pp. 53–71; quotation from Representative James A. Garfield, Republican of Ohio, during floor debate January 26, 1865. By coincidence, the Confederate States of America were engaged in the same debate during the same period. The Confederate constitution specifically authorized the Congress to grant department heads nonvoting seats in the legislature, but measures to admit the cabinet officers were defeated by the House in 1862 and the Senate the following year. Ibid., pp. 38–45.

In the post–Civil War decades, when parties fought their battles over the spoils of office and offered little in the way of program, reformers saw still another merit in giving cabinet members seats in the Congress: they would provide a nationally minded leadership for a locally oriented and fragmented legislature. In 1873, Gamaliel Bradford, who advocated the reform consistently and constantly for more than forty years, was deploring the "absence of progress" by the Congress on a broad range of pressing problems and attributing it to a lack of clear responsibility in any institution for formulating proposals and initiating action. Presidents in those days left legislating to the legislative branch—and congressmen insisted that they do so—but within the Congress, responsibility was parceled out to committees that were more aware of local than of national interests. If cabinet members sat in the Congress, contended Bradford, when they presented proposals they would arrest the attention of the country and stir a national response.[20]

The Pendleton idea was kept alive by Bradford, the historian Henry Jones Ford, and others, and in the next century gained the important support of Henry L. Stimson. As secretary of war in the administration of President William Howard Taft, Stimson enlisted the president as a protagonist. If Taft were successful in his effort to establish an executive budget system, Stimson persuaded him, it would be of little avail to any president unless department heads could present and defend the president's budget in congressional debate. Just before leaving office, Taft sent a special message to the Congress proposing that cabinet officers be granted nonvoting seats in the legislature, but his successor—the same Woodrow Wilson who had advocated even broader reforms as a young scholar—was satisfied that strong presidential leadership, informal collaboration between cabinet members and the Democratic congressional leaders, and the use of party caucuses by the latter to develop unity and discipline would make the existing system effective. In Wilson's first two years, that proved to be the case, for Wilson's New Freedom program was written into law by cohesive Democratic majorities.[21] Wilson's own

20. "Should the Cabinet Have Seats in Congress?" *Nation* (April 3, 1873), p. 234. This editorial quotes Bradford's argument, presented in a lecture, and goes on to question whether cabinet members would in fact have that much influence.

21. Horn, *Cabinet and Congress*, pp. 104, 114–18; James L. Sundquist, *The Decline and Resurgence of Congress* (Brookings Institution, 1981), pp. 130–32.

successor, Warren G. Harding, favored the Pendleton scheme, describing it as "one of the most constructive steps that can be taken," and most of his cabinet were advocates as well, but congressional supporters could muster no corresponding enthusiasm on Capitol Hill.[22] The idea was revived in the 1940s by Representative Estes Kefauver, Democrat of Tennessee, in the more limited form of a question period, when cabinet members would be admitted to the floor to answer inquiries, but neither President Franklin Roosevelt nor the House leadership responded favorably and the effort died.[23]

Direct Election of Senators

The Seventeenth Amendment, which provided for the direct election of United States senators, did little more than confirm the transformation of the Senate that had been proceeding for more than a century.

By 1913, when the amendment was ratified, the Senate had departed in two major respects from the body the framers had designed. First, it had ceased to be—more accurately, it had never become—a kind of privy council for the president. Second, it had ceased to be the instrument by which the states participated, as states, in federal policymaking.

In its council role, the Senate was to share in two categories of executive decisions—appointment of officials and making of treaties. As soon as President Washington took office and the First Congress convened, questions arose as to how and where the Senate would give its advice to the president and consent to his actions. A Senate committee, appointed to discuss these questions with the president, evidently preferred that the executive come to the Senate chamber with his proposed nominations or treaties, justify them orally and answer questions, and at the conclusion of the discussion receive the Senate's consent or nonconsent. To Washington, such meetings would be liable both to embarrass the president and restrain the senators, and he insisted that the decision in each case whether to submit a proposal orally or in writing should be left to the president.

22. Horn, *Cabinet and Congress*, pp. 128–30.
23. Ibid., pp. 136–67.

Experience would determine the most satisfactory and effective methods of communicating.[24]

Experience was not long in coming. Having encountered delays in response to two written messages dealing with diplomatic affairs, President Washington took the oral discussion route on a proposed treaty with the southern Indians. Accompanied by the secretary of war, he appeared at the Senate chamber and asked for advice and consent to a series of propositions. But the Senate asked for time and referred the matter to a committee. The president "started up in a violent fret," protesting that his purpose in coming to the Senate chamber was defeated, and after getting a commitment for a report within two days, sullenly withdrew, declaring "that he would be damned if he ever went there again."[25] Washington did return for the second meeting, which concluded amicably, but thereafter no president repeated the experience. Communication of treaties and nominations has been in writing, and no president has entered into oral discussion with the whole Senate. Particularly since rejection of the Versailles treaty by the Senate after World War I, presidents have been careful to seek advice informally from senators before embarking on major diplomatic initiatives and have even admitted senators to the negotiating process—as when President Franklin Roosevelt appointed senators (and House members as well) to the United States delegation to the conference that adopted the United Nations Charter—but such consultation and collaboration have been with influential individual leaders and members, not with the entire Senate as a collective council. In the case of nominations, through the practice of "senatorial courtesy," advice of individual senators on local appointments has often become in fact dictation.

Clearly, the Senate never could have developed as a body of presidential councillors. Its growth in size would alone have precluded any such possibility. So would the constitutional independence of the Senate. When the king of England met with his privy council, he was consulting with advisers of his own choice; no presidential council, no matter how small, made up of persons in whose selection

24. George Henry Haynes, *The Senate of the United States* (Russell and Russell, 1960; orig. copyright 1938), vol. 1, pp. 55–56.

25. The account of the meeting comes from the journal of Senator William Maclay of Pennsylvania, and the departing comment was repeated by William H. Crawford and reported in the memoirs of John Quincy Adams. Ibid., pp. 63–67.

he had no direct voice, and perhaps dominated by political opponents eager to discredit him, could possibly serve his purpose.

The concept of the Senate as a body representing the states (like the Bundesrat of today's West Germany) disappeared more gradually. In discussing the Senate, the framers saw it as an organ of the states; when that body acted, it was the states themselves taking collective action. And that conception carried over into the early decades of government under the Constitution. State legislatures commonly took stands on national issues, and communicated those positions to their senators as instructions, much as governments have always instructed the ambassadors who represent them in faraway capitals. And a senator could ignore or contravene his instructions only at risk of being denied reelection by his state's legislature at the expiration of his term. In the post–Civil War decades, however, as the states developed a broader range of activities of their own, their lawmakers ceased trying to share in the direction of national affairs as well. And senators, as powerful and influential state politicians in their own right—the majority party's preeminent leader, or "boss," normally held one of his state's two seats and often chose his colleague—were more likely to be able to control the legislators than the other way around. So as ambassadors they became plenipotentiaries, disciplined not by those who sent them but by the powerful party organizations within the Senate that they joined on arrival. And to complete the transformation of senators from state representatives to autonomous federal officials, beginning late in the nineteenth century some states found ways to circumvent the Constitution and arrange for senators to be chosen—though still nominally by the legislatures—in fact by the people through direct election.

With the Senate thus altered, when early in this century agitation grew for adoption of direct elections in all the states, no one even called attention to the fact that the states would be giving up what the framers had conceived as the ultimate guarantee of their place in the federal system. Either the states no longer saw the Senate as the guardian of the states against federal intrusion, or they had ceased to feel the need for such protection. And, if the Senate was to represent not the states as such but the people of those states, the contention that the people themselves should make the choice became irrefutable.

Direct election of senators therefore took its place in the long series of election reform measures that were central to the Progressive creed, all aimed at taking governmental institutions out of the hands of corrupt party machines and making them responsive to the people directly—a series that included also the initiative, referendum, and recall; the secret ballot; nonpartisan local elections; and nomination of party candidates, and even presidential electors, through direct primaries. Senators delayed as long as they could; all of them beneficiaries of the existing process, they were bound to see little to gain and much to risk through change. Five times the House passed the proposed amendment, over a span of twenty years, before the Senate finally allowed the proposition to come to a vote. But by 1912, public sentiment could no longer be resisted. Muckrakers condemned the "millionaires' club" and decried the influence of corporate wealth as state legislators filled the Senate seats; the same year that it finally approved the amendment, the Senate had to expel one of its members, William Lorimer, Republican of Illinois, when it learned that a corporate "slop fund" had been used to bribe legislators on his behalf. Nineteen state legislatures, as of 1911, had petitioned the Congress to call a constitutional convention to relieve them of their onerous responsibility.[26] The proposal had been a staple in Democratic platforms since 1900, and of the Populists and other minor parties since as early as 1876. When Secretary of State William Jennings Bryan proclaimed the amendment ratified, in 1913, he exulted that the Senate would no longer be "filled up with the representatives of predatory wealth."[27]

The amendment affected the makeup and character of the Senate only gradually, for if party organizations could control legislatures they could also control nominating conventions. But many factors, including the whole body of Progressive reforms, were contributing to the weakening of party organizations, and the direct election of senators was both the product of the antiparty movement and contributed to it. As the direct primary spread, the way was opened for insurgent politicians to challenge entrenched party organizations

26. Statement of Senator Weldon B. Heyburn, Republican of Idaho, in Senate debate, *Congressional Record* (May 24, 1911), pp. 1539–40. Heyburn was an opponent of the measure; a supporter, Senator Joseph L. Bristow, Republican of Kansas, had a year earlier claimed the backing of thirty-three state legislatures, but some of these presumably had not formally petitioned for a constitutional convention. Heyburn's figure was not disputed in the 1911 debate.

27. Quoted by Haynes, *The Senate*, vol. 2, p. 1042.

and defeat them, and when the rebels arrived in the Senate they brought their independent attitudes with them. The tightly disciplined party organizations that characterized the Senate in the last decades of the nineteenth century were already beginning to disintegrate when the Seventeenth Amendment was adopted, but that action speeded their dissolution. Steadily, the Senate—and the House as well—moved from party cohesion and discipline to individualism, and the direction of change has not been reversed.

The Amendment Process

In that heyday of reform, the Progressive Era, when advocates of social change were pressing for a whole series of constitutional amendments—to bring about, among other things, the direct election of senators, woman suffrage, the income tax, prohibition of alcoholic beverages, banning of child labor—it was natural that they should direct their reforming zeal also to the amendment process which made the achievement of any of their goals exasperatingly difficult. Theodore Roosevelt's Progressive party of 1912, in the same platform that endorsed four of the above proposals, pledged itself "to provide a more easy and expeditious method of amending the Federal Constitution." The platform did not say how, but individual Progressives had been pushing for a federal version of the process that they had succeeded in inserting into various state constitutions, whereby amendments could be adopted through popular initiative and referendum, bypassing the state legislatures altogether. One resolution, introduced by Senator Robert M. La Follette, Sr., of Wisconsin, would amend the Constitution to provide that on application of ten states or a majority of both houses of Congress, a constitutional amendment could be submitted to referendum and would be adopted if a majority of all voters, and a majority in each of a majority of states, approved it.

For the immediate purposes of the reformers, however, that proved unnecessary. Even as the Progressives met in 1912, the income tax and direct election of senators were on their way to ratification by three-fourths of the states—each achieving that goal in 1913. Prohibition entered the Constitution in 1919 and woman suffrage the following year. The proposed child labor amendment was submitted by the Congress to the state legislatures in 1924.[28]   Then it was the turn of the conservatives to be upset with the amendment process. Spurred by reports that some legislatures had ratified Prohibition and woman suffrage through irregular and questionable procedures, Republican Senator James J. Wadsworth of New York, an opponent of both of those constitutional innovations, proposed an amendment to require that each state legislature's action be subjected to a popular referendum within the state. As reported by the Senate Judiciary Committee, however, the amendment simply substituted the popular vote for the legislative vote as the ratifying action, reducing the legislature to an advisory role if it chose to act at all. Wadsworth contended that he sought only a "more deliberative" process, but answered affirmatively when asked whether his "underlying motive" was to "make it more difficult to amend the Constitution in any way." In the case of the Prohibition amendment, he pointed out, the voters of five states had rejected the amendment in advisory referenda but the legislatures had approved it anyway, and when the woman suffrage amendment was submitted to the states, the same sequence occurred in four instances.[29] Wadsworth and his allies charged that these amendments—to which some southern senators added the Fifteenth Amendment (Negro suffrage) as well—had been "railroaded" or "stampeded" through the legislatures by "fanatics," "agitators," "organized minorities," and "professional reformers." "I would rather trust the conservatism of all the people," said Frank B. Brandegee, Republican of Connecticut.[30]

The remnants of the Progressive movement took the occasion to demand that the amendment process be made easier, not harder. Smith Brookhart, the insurgent Iowa Republican, argued that the right of amendment should rest squarely on the people in a democracy, and that the Congress should therefore be able to submit amendments by a simple, rather than a two-thirds, majority. "We

28. Only twenty-eight states ratified this amendment—four short of the necessary two-thirds—but the Supreme Court in 1941, reversing an earlier decision, held that Congress had the power to regulate child labor and so made the amendment unnecessary.

29. *Congressional Record* (March 10, 1924), pp. 4495, 4497, 4489. In the case of the Eighteenth Amendment, the five states were California, Iowa, Maryland, Massachusetts, and Ohio; in the Nineteenth, the four were Massachusetts, Missouri, Texas, and West Virginia.

30. Ibid. (March 20, 1924), p. 4566.

have fenced around the amendment of our Constitution by so many barriers," pleaded Brookhart, "that it is only after a generation of campaigning and of education that we are able to get an amendment at all."[31] But several test votes made clear that none of the proposed changes in the amending clause could muster two-thirds of the Senate and after several days of debate the effort was abandoned.

Approval of Treaties

As World War II approached its end and statesmen began conceiving of a world organization to prevent any third cataclysmic conflict, some remembered the struggle over an earlier body designed to preserve the peace—the League of Nations. After the First World War, President Woodrow Wilson had been an architect of the League of Nations, but after an arduous campaign that sapped his energies and ultimately left him incapacitated, the Senate rejected the Treaty of Versailles and, with it, United States membership in the League. A majority of senators approved the treaty—49 votes to 35—but that fell 7 votes short of the necessary two-thirds. Similarly, American adherence to the World Court had been blocked—the last time, in 1935, by 36 opponents overriding 52 proponents.

Even as representatives of the victors of the Second World War were gathered in San Francisco in 1945 to create the United Nations as successor to the League of Nations, the House Judiciary Committee reported a constitutional amendment that would make it impossible for as few as thirty-three of the ninety-six senators to block U.S. membership in the new world organization. The amendment, sponsored by Hatton W. Sumners, Democrat of Texas and chairman of the committee, would alter the treaty clause to rest congressional approval on a majority vote of both houses, as in the case of ordinary legislation or even a declaration of war. It was anomalous, suggested Sumners and his committee, that the Constitution rendered it more difficult to make peace than to make war, and the committee report quoted James Wilson's remark during the 1787 convention: "If two-thirds are necessary to make peace, the minority may perpetuate war, against the sense of the majority."[32]

31. Ibid., p. 4564.
32. Ibid. (May 1, 1945), p. 4011.

The original reasons for the two-thirds requirement, argued the committee in its report, had disappeared, as the conflicts between the northern and southern states that caused the framers to fear rule by simple majorities—disputes over old issues such as fishery rights and new questions arising from the westward expansion of the nation—had been resolved. The Senate had never become the intimate advisory and consultative body to the president that had warranted its special role in treaty-making to the exclusion of participation by the House. Members of the House served as long as senators, and acquired as much expertise. And because treaties normally had to be implemented through legislation and appropriations, in which the House held a parity of power with the Senate, it should play an equal part in treaty-making also. In the day when the nation was protected by its ocean barriers, "the emasculation and rejection of our treaties by a minority of the upper House of Congress could be tolerated," said the committee, but now "the very life and death of the Nation depends on smooth-working machinery for regulating our international relations." And the two-thirds requirement "ties the hands of our negotiators."[33]

The opposition based its case on the special nature of treaties under the Constitution. Unlike the legislative power, which is restricted to the purposes enumerated in the Constitution, the treaty-making power is unlimited. It overrides all state laws and constitutions. And it is not subject to judicial review.[34]

A proposal to require House approval, but by a two-thirds vote as in the Senate, was defeated, 61 to 103. Then a modification to require that the approval in each house be by a majority of the total membership was adopted, and the proposed amendment was approved overwhelmingly, 288 to 88. But the Senate never considered the measure. Each house may be viewed, perhaps, as asserting its self-interest. But in the case of the Senate, ironically, its inaction served not to protect the interest of the majority of its members but to preserve, rather, the power of a minority, in any instance, to defeat the majority will.

The United Nations was accepted by the Senate with virtually no objection, and the other treaties that embodied much of the postwar

33. Ibid., pp. 4011–12.
34. Summation by Representative John W. Gwynne, Republican of Iowa, ibid., p. 4019.

U.S. foreign policy—including the North Atlantic Treaty and the Southeast Asia Treaty—were approved with relatively little struggle. In a spirit of bipartisan and legislative-executive cooperation, the country rejected the isolationism that had marked the previous postwar period and entered wholeheartedly into a role of world leadership, and the question of the extraordinary majority required for treaty ratification lost its urgency.

But a cry of alarm soon came from the opposite direction. Organs of the United Nations were preparing to carry out their duty under the charter of promoting human rights and economic and social reforms; and the United States, in signing the charter, had pledged itself to support such programs. Conservatives suspicious of socialist and communist influence in the United Nations protested that the United States might join in approving, through treaties or executive agreements entered into under those treaties, measures having the force of law in the United States without the direct approval of the Congress. In so doing, moreover, the federal government could act in fields that under the Constitution had been reserved to the states.

A constitutional amendment to limit the executive's treaty-making power, introduced by Senator John W. Bricker, Republican of Ohio, plunged the Senate into acrimonious debate for an entire month in early 1954. As redrafted by an American Bar Association committee and reported by the Senate Judiciary Committee, the amendment would provide that no treaty or executive agreement could become effective as internal law except through legislation "which would be valid in the absence of treaty." Thus the amendment would both restore a degree of congressional control over executive agreements and restrain the federal government from usurping the powers of the states.

President Eisenhower objected that the amendment as written would put the country back to the days of the Articles of Confederation, when any state had the right to repudiate a treaty, and said he could not accept any amendment that would "change or alter the traditional and constitutional balances among the three departments of Government."[35] Both Republican and Democratic leaders in the Senate then sought the basis for a compromise. One proposed by Senator Walter F. George, Democrat of Georgia, that eliminated most

35. "News Conference, January 13, 1954," and "News Conference, February 3, 1954," *Public Papers: Eisenhower, 1954*, pp. 51–53, 225.

of the objectionable language was accepted by a 61-to-30 vote, but lost on final passage by 60 to 31, a single vote short of a two-thirds majority. Senator Bricker vowed to continue his fight, but in that year's election the Democrats recaptured their congressional majorities and interest waned.

Congressional Tenure

The two-year term for members of the House of Representatives is "too brief for the public good," President Lyndon B. Johnson said in a special message to the Congress in 1966 recommending that the term be extended to four years. In his plan, all 435 members of the House would be elected in the presidential election year.

The longer term, argued the president, would free the representatives from the "inexorable pressures" of biennial campaigning. A congressman "is scarcely permitted to take his seat in the historic Hall of the House, when he must begin once more to make his case to his constituency." That reduces his effectiveness as a legislator, deprives his constituents of full representation in the Congress, and increases the cost of holding office. All this discourages some of the country's best men from aspiring to serve in the House, concluded the president, himself a former representative.[36]

These arguments repeated those of one earlier debate. The House considered a four-year term for its members in 1906, when the proposal was attached by committee to an amendment providing for direct election of senators. The four-year term was not voted on separately, and the resolution containing both proposals was approved that year by only an 89-to-86 vote, substantially short of the two-thirds required for constitutional amendments.[37]

By 1966, the volume of legislation had increased as the scope of government expanded, and a Congress that in 1906 could adjourn in June to permit its members to go home to campaign now stayed

36. "Special Message to the Congress Proposing Constitutional Amendments Relating to Terms for House Members and the Electoral College System, January 20, 1966," *Public Papers of the Presidents: Lyndon B. Johnson, 1966* (GPO, 1967), bk. 1, pp. 36–39. Oddly, as late as 1966 a president could still refer to potential congressional candidates as "men."

37. Charles O. Jones, *Every Second Year: Congressional Behavior and the Two-Year Term* (Brookings Institution, 1967), pp. 16–17.

in session in even-numbered years until September or October. Burdened by a constantly increasing work load, longer sessions, and higher campaigning costs—for primary as well as general elections— members of the House might have been expected to embrace the proposal for a longer term as heaven-sent relief. Informal polls had suggested that they would. One survey of House opinion on a four-year term, conducted by Representative Abraham J. Multer, Democrat of New York, in 1949, obtained 319 favorable responses to 110 opposed, and a similar inquiry in 1965 by Representative Frank Chelf, Democrat of Kentucky, found 254 members favorable against 41 opposed and 67 doubtful.[38] In eight days of hearings in 1965–66— four before Johnson's message and four after—66 members supported a longer term (65 for four years and 1 for three) as against a lone opponent. Yet, after the hearings, the proposal died in the Judiciary Committee without ever being considered on the floor.

One reason was that the committee's chairman, Emanuel Celler, Democrat of New York, was among those hostile to the measure. But, clearly, many of the resolution's less committed supporters simply changed their minds after close examination of the probable consequences of a four-year term.

The central issue was the timing of the congressional election, but that question became significant because of a more profound consideration, the balance of power between the Congress and the president. Whereas Johnson proposed the congressional election coincide with the presidential, sixty of the sixty-five proponents who testified before Celler's committee had advocated electing half the members each two years. Johnson justified his position on the ground that the voter turnout is higher in presidential years. A system of staggered terms, he contended, would render the House less representative than the Senate and the presidency, by "perpetually condemning half its membership to a shrunken electorate."[39] Members were bound to suspect a less altruistic motive in a president renowned for political realism and toughness, and Attorney General Nicholas deB. Katzenbach supplied it. "In presidential years," Katzenbach testified before the committee, "the public in general elects a Congress that is running

38. *Congressional Tenure of Office*, Hearings before the House Judiciary Committee and Subcommittee No. 5, 89 Cong. 1 and 2 sess. (GPO, 1966), pp. 29, 19.

39. "Special Message of January 20, 1966," p. 39; see also Jones, *Every Second Year*, pp. 30–31.

on the platform of the President. . . . Those elected candidates of the same political complexion as the President are basically in sympathy with the views of their party. In this climate, the President and the Congress are more likely to be able to carry out a program without unreasonable deadlocks. . . . And I would think we had in this country, by and large, better government in times when a majority of the Houses were in basic philosophical sympathy with the President than when they are not. When they are not, it makes it much more difficult to do anything."[40]

The apparent unspoken Johnson objective, then, was to produce a Congress more to the president's liking and enhance his power over it. The Republican minority, of course, was quickest to sense the implication. Democrats, from the first Franklin Roosevelt victory in 1932 through Johnson's, had won seven of the last nine presidential elections. And, whether because of the "coattail" effect, the larger voter turnout in presidential years, or other reasons, Republican congressmen had been swept out of office, the GOP accruing a net loss of 210 seats in the seven elections. But in every midterm election after losing the presidency, except 1934, the Republicans had snapped back; in the eight midterm polls between 1932 and 1964 the GOP had recorded a net gain of 132 seats, and it was headed for another midterm victory (which turned out to be a smashing 47 seats) in 1966.[41] "Small wonder," observed Charles O. Jones, "that the overwhelming majority of minority party members oppose the concurrent-term proposal."[42] Of 92 Republicans who expressed a view on the four-year concurrent term in responding to a questionnaire Jones distributed in 1966 to all House members, 90 were opposed, with 2 neutral and not a single one favorable. Staggered four-year terms, with half the members elected each two years, were approved by 33 percent of Republicans responding, but the overwhelming majority preferred no change at all. Responding to the "no change" option, 73 percent approved, only 15 percent disapproved, and 12 percent were neutral.

But neither did Democrats rally behind the Johnson concurrent-term proposal. Only 25 percent of 142 majority party members who

40. *Congressional Tenure*, Hearings, pp. 183, 204.
41. Jones, *Every Second Year*, p. 43; Norman J. Ornstein and others, *Vital Statistics on Congress, 1982* (Washington: American Enterprise Institute, 1982), pp. 29–30.
42. *Every Second Year*, p. 43.

expressed a view on the questionnaire approved the plan, with 65 percent opposed and 10 percent neutral. Staggered terms won majority support, 55 to 37 percent with 8 percent neutral, but the "no change" option was approved by a slightly larger margin, 52 to 33 percent, with 15 percent neutral. When the returns for Republicans and Democrats were combined, even the most popular form of the four-year-term idea—staggered elections—could not win majority approval. Only 47 percent of the respondents expressed favor, with an equal number disapproving and 6 percent neutral. No change was approved by 61 percent and disapproved by only 25 percent.[43] "Certainly . . . as of 1966," Jones concluded, "there was very little enthusiasm for a change. . . . The number opposed to any change is impressive and those who favor some change cannot agree on the form it should take."[44]

Removing a Failed President

Eight decades after President Garfield lay incapacitated for eighty days before dying from an assassin's bullet, four decades after President Wilson spent sixteen months in seclusion after a stroke, but less than one decade after Eisenhower suffered three serious illnesses, the Congress finally came to grips with the question of how to maintain the country's leadership "in a nuclear age . . . fraught with danger" when the president became disabled. The outcome was the Twenty-fifth Amendment, which established a procedure for removing an incapacitated chief executive (as well as a method of filling a vacancy in the vice presidency). The objective was not contested—sixty-nine senators had cosponsored a constitutional amendment offering a solution—and George A. Smathers, Democrat of Florida, presented it to the Senate in 1965 as "not an effort to revise" the Constitution but simply one "to remedy an obvious defect."[45] But the committee had been forced to wrestle with

43. Ibid., pp. 110, 106. Of the 433 House members at the time, 318 returned their questionnaires (73 percent) but some members did not express a view on every alternative. Respondents were not asked to choose among the options, and some approved one or more of the proposed changes and "no change" as well.

44. Ibid., pp. 107, 112.

45. *Congressional Record* (February 18, 1965), pp. 3168–69.

a difficult question. Who should have the authority to declare the president incapacitated? One suggestion was to let the Congress decide, but the committee rejected that as violating the principle of separation of powers. The responsibility was therefore assigned to the executive branch itself. The president could declare himself disabled and devolve his powers upon the vice president or, if he was unable to do so or chose not to, the vice president "and a majority of either the principal officers of the executive departments, or of such other body as Congress may by law provide," could take the initiative. If the president protested the action and the vice president and the cabinet majority insisted on it, the Congress by a two-thirds vote of both houses could overrule the president and continue to repose the presidential powers in the vice president.

The amendment provides a useful safeguard under circumstances where the president recognizes his inability and has full confidence in his vice president—as was the case when President Reagan delegated his powers to Vice President George Bush during his cancer surgery in 1985. If a seriously impaired president were to insist on retaining his responsibilities, however, the amendment could be invoked only by a kind of palace coup engineered by the president's own appointees. The vice president, as the prospective inheritor of the presidential duties, would be in a particularly awkward position to take the initiative. So the original question of whether it is sufficient to locate the power to initiate removal of a disabled president solely in the executive branch did not wholly lose its pertinence when the Twenty-fifth Amendment was adopted.

A few years later, the question of presidential removal arose in a different form: what to do about a president who was disabled not physically but morally, who had lost the capacity to lead the country but was not removable under the new amendment and was not guilty of the "high crimes and misdemeanors" that under the Constitution must be the basis for impeachment. In May 1973, as the Watergate scandals were destroying President Nixon's standing and respect, Representative Jonathan B. Bingham, Democrat of New York, proposed an amendment to authorize the Congress to call a new presidential election by law (which would require two-thirds majorities, since the president could be expected to veto any such bill) whenever it found that, in Bingham's words, "the President has lost the confidence of the people to so great an extent that he can no longer effectively perform his responsibilities." The president would be eligible to run in the special election. This procedure would circumvent the impeachment process, which Bingham argued was a dangerous expedient because it would bring the government "to a halt" while the president was on trial.[46] Representative Edith Green, Democrat of Oregon, introduced a few weeks later a slightly different version; her amendment would empower the Congress to call an election by a two-thirds vote of both houses without referring the action to the president if it found that the chief executive had exceeded his powers, failed to execute the laws, or executed them illegally. "We presently have no option between the extreme option of impeachment or the other extreme of maintaining in office for as long as three years an administration whose stature and ability to govern has been greatly impaired," she argued. As in the Bingham resolution, the president would be eligible to run in the special election.[47]

Still a third approach was developed by Representative Henry S. Reuss, Democrat of Wisconsin. His proposal would permit the Congress to remove the president by a "no confidence" vote of 60 percent of each house, but as a deterrent to opportunistic, partisan action provided that all seats in the Congress as well as the presidency and vice presidency would be filled in a new election. The question provoked enough academic interest that one law journal devoted an entire issue to a symposium on the Reuss resolution,[48] but when Nixon resigned in August 1974 the issue died. A new president was sworn in, the country enjoyed the fresh start under new leadership that the Bingham, Green, and Reuss proposals were designed to make possible, and the previously anxious public relaxed in the confidence that once again "the system worked."

The War Power

At the height of the national turmoil over the Vietnam War and the extension of that conflict into Cambodia and Laos, the Congress set out to clarify the ambiguity in the Constitution that had once

46. Ibid. (May 8, 1973), p. 14579.
47. Ibid. (July 17, 1973), p. 24232.
48. *George Washington Law Review*, vol. 43 (January 1975).

again touched off a quarrel between the branches. Just how far could the president go unilaterally, under his authority as commander in chief, to plunge the country into hostilities without asking for the formal declaration of war that only the Congress could provide?

Senator Jacob K. Javits, Republican of New York, the principal initiator of what became the War Powers Resolution of 1973, announced an ambitious goal: to define precisely, or "codify," the president's authority as commander in chief. He proposed to restrict the president's use of the armed forces, in the absence of a declaration of war, to repelling attack, to protecting the lives and property of Americans abroad, and to complying with national commitments to which both the executive and legislative branches were a party. His measure passed the Senate by a lopsided margin in 1972, and again in 1973, but the House Foreign Affairs Committee, and particularly its ranking Democratic member, Clement J. Zablocki of Wisconsin, contended that the Congress could not anticipate all contingencies a president might face and therefore should not attempt to codify his power. The committee's bill, therefore, omitted any such restrictive language, and after the House approved it, the House-Senate conference committee constructed an ingenious compromise. It moved the Javits definition of presidential power from the substantive body of the bill to a preamble, which the conferees then in a signed statement interpreted as nonbinding. The operative provisions left it to the president to decide when he should introduce the armed forces "into hostilities or into situations where imminent involvement in hostilities is clearly indicated by the circumstances." But the resolution required him to consult with the Congress whenever possible before doing so, to report within forty-eight hours afterward, and to cease the action if the Congress did not approve within sixty days. At any time during the sixty-day period, the legislature could terminate the action by concurrent resolution.[49]

But the Congress had chosen as its instrument for clearing up the constitutional ambiguity—insofar as it had succeeded in doing so— not a constitutional amendment but a statute. President Nixon vetoed

49. This provision has presumably been invalidated by the Supreme Court's 1983 decision in *Immigration and Naturalization Service* v. *Chadha*, which outlawed the use of the concurrent resolution by the Congress to veto executive branch actions. For a fuller account of the origin and evolution of the War Powers Resolution, see Sundquist, *Decline and Resurgence*, chap. 9.

the statute on the ground that it was not only unwise but unconstitutional. The Congress enacted it over his veto, so it took its place on the statute books. But while Presidents Ford, Carter, and Reagan each adhered more or less faithfully to its terms, each also either reiterated the Nixon rejection of its constitutionality or expressed doubt. The executive branch therefore, in effect, reserved the right for any future president to flout the resolution at any time he might elect to do so, and the constitutional issue is no nearer to being settled than it was before the Congress acted.

Efficiency, Leadership, and Accountability

While reformers were failing to achieve even the modest link between the executive and legislative branches envisaged in the Pendleton and Kefauver proposals to give cabinet members a congressional role and in Lyndon Johnson's measure for four-year House terms, an occasional scholar, publicist, or retired statesman has risen to challenge the central principle of separation of powers that is embedded in the Constitution. Recognizing the constitutional dilemma confronted by the framers, they have chosen the opposite solution. In 1787, they have argued, protection of the infant republic against the danger of tyranny may have properly been an overriding concern, and governmental power may have had to be dispersed to assure freedom, whatever the costs in efficiency and decisiveness. But times have changed, and the prospect that the presidency might grow into an elective monarchy or the Congress might ride roughshod over the rights of the people no longer seems so large a menace. The danger now, in the reasoning of these critics, lies in the very dispersal of power that was at the heart of the founders' design. They ask questions that were not heard in 1787, that have been brought to the fore by the growth over two centuries in the responsibilities of government, in the complexity of the national economy, and in the interdependence of the nations of the world. How can institutions set in competition with one another be brought into a sufficient degree of harmony for timely decisions to be made and governmental action organized effectively? How can strong and decisive leadership be assured in a government of divided powers? How can the people fix responsibility when power is scattered and so, through the electoral process, hold their elective officers accountable?

The earliest systematic criticism of the constitutional system, and still among the most trenchant and pertinent, came from the pen of Woodrow Wilson, the only political scientist to attain the presidency. While still a senior at Princeton University, in 1879, Wilson picked up the Story-Pendleton-Bradford idea and carried it several steps further, proposing not merely that cabinet members have seats in the Congress but that they be chosen from among the legislators and resign when their proposals were rejected, as in Great Britain. That, as Wilson saw it, would clearly fix responsibility and accountability in a government where both were now hopelessly dispersed.[50] In his classic *Congressional Government*, completed in 1884, he developed his critique of the American system as it had evolved, terming it "a government by the chairmen of the Standing Committees of Congress" and condemning it in eloquent language:

> *Power and strict accountability for its use* are the essential constituents of good government. . . . It is, therefore, manifestly a radical defect in our federal system that it parcels out power and confuses responsibility as it does. The main purpose of the Convention of 1787 seems to have been to accomplish this grievous mistake. . . . Were it possible to call together again the members of that wonderful Convention . . . they would be the first to admit that the only fruit of dividing power had been to make it irresponsible.
>
> As at present constituted, the federal government lacks strength because its powers are divided, lacks promptness because its authorities are multiplied, lacks wieldiness because its processes are roundabout, lacks efficiency because its responsibility is indistinct and its action without competent direction.[51]

But Wilson did not reiterate his support for a constitutional amendment to provide for a cabinet drawn from and responsible to the legislature or propose other changes in the tripartite governmental structure, although his preference for the British parliamentary system is clear.

Since Wilson, others who have pondered the American system have reached much the same conclusion about the weaknesses of the constitutional structure and put their minds to redesigning it.

50. Thomas W. Wilson, "Cabinet Government in the United States," *International Review*, vol. 7 (August 1879), pp. 146–63.

51. Woodrow Wilson, *Congressional Government: A Study in American Politics*, 15th ed. (Houghton Mifflin, 1913; originally published 1885), pp. 102, 284–85, 318.

Half a dozen of these efforts produced book-length products, but singly and collectively the books aroused little interest even in the academic community—and none at all in the world of practical politics.

William MacDonald in 1921, terming the American system "rigid and irresponsible," thoughtfully set forth the advantages of the British parliamentary system. To convert the United States government into a parliamentary form, he proposed that the president select a "premier" from among members of the Congress, that the premier head a cabinet made up of legislators, and that the cabinet resign whenever it lost the confidence of both houses. The cabinet would administer the executive branch, and the president would become a ceremonial head of state whose only consequential duty would be the designation of the premier in the event this was not predetermined by the parties in the legislative branch—much as in the parliamentary republics of Germany and Italy today.[52]

William Yandell Elliott's rethinking of the constitutional design, published in 1935, was clearly a product of the times—the crises of the Great Depression and Franklin Roosevelt's New Deal. Seeing the need for national planning and the "control" of industry by government, Professor Elliott found the system of constitutional checks and balances "unworkable" and outlined a scheme for much stronger executive power—ratifying, in effect, the shift in real authority from the legislative to the executive branch that, in the emergency, had already taken place. To strengthen the president, Elliott proposed that members of the House of Representatives be given four-year terms concurrent with the president's, and that the executive be granted the right to dissolve the House and order a new election once during the four years. After the election, the president would lose his veto power for the rest of his term, permitting the Congress to set policy. The right of dissolution might extend to the Senate as well, but to reduce the power of that body, its right to act on money bills would be reduced to one of delay, and approval of treaties would be by a simple majority rather than a two-thirds vote. Elliott would also authorize the president to veto items in appropriation bills and riders (that is, nongermane provisions) in any bills.[53]

52. William MacDonald, *A New Constitution for America* (B.W. Huebsch, 1921), p. 37; see chap. 8.

53. William Yandell Elliott, *The Need for Constitutional Reform: A Program for National Security* (Whittlesey House, 1935), pp. 86, 207; see pp. 31–34, 200–02.

Seven years later, journalist Henry Hazlitt saw the exigencies of war as demanding a flexible, parliamentary form of government for the United States. "The grave defects in our Constitution," he contended, "are in large part responsible for our failure to organize efficiently for the conduct of the war. . . . We cannot permit ourselves to lose this war, or even to prolong this war, merely because we have become too hidebound to reexamine and to change that document." His reasoning, and his constitutional design, owe more to MacDonald (and to the nineteenth century English critic Walter Bagehot) than to Elliott, but he did concur in the latter's proposal to reduce the powers of the Senate. Having done that, Hazlitt would center power in a cabinet drawn only from the House and responsible to it, headed—like MacDonald's cabinet—by a premier designated by the president. Since the president's role would be so largely ceremonial, Hazlitt would dispense with direct election and permit the Congress, with the two houses sitting jointly, to choose the chief of state. If the premier lost a vote of confidence, he would have the choice of resigning or dissolving the Congress. In the latter case, a new election would fill all the legislative seats and the new Congress would either support the outgoing premier or choose a new one. Hazlitt also argued for a simplified amendment process.[54]

As the war approached its end, Thomas K. Finletter, a wartime assistant to the secretary of state, feared that the postwar need for "creative and affirmative" foreign and domestic policies would outstrip the capacity of a government "designed to achieve political negatives and the *laissez-faire* state." "You cannot," he wrote, "have a government capable of handling the most difficult problems that peacetime democracy has ever faced with the two main parts of it at each other's throats." His solution was to have simultaneous election of the president and all members of the Senate and House for six-year terms, which he assumed would result in unified party control of both branches and both houses. A joint executive-legislative cabinet would set policy. If a deadlock arose between the Congress and the joint cabinet, the president could call a new election for the presidency and the entire legislature, which would produce "a unified government, armed with a fresh authority from the people."[55]

54. Henry Hazlitt, *A New Constitution Now* (Whittlesey House, 1942), pp. 15, 8; see pp. 9–14, 102–05, 180.

55. Thomas K. Finletter, *Can Representative Government Do the Job?* (Reynal and Hitchcock, 1945), pp. 5, 6, 9, 111; see pp. 106–12.

Nearly three decades passed before another full-scale study of constitutional reform appeared—probably a testimony to the effective working of the government in the postwar decades, when the United States enjoyed prosperity and economic growth at home and successfully led and organized the free world's resistance to communist advance. But in the 1960s, this record of success gave way to inflation, an unpopular war in Southeast Asia, and riots in the ghettoes and on the campuses, and by 1973 Charles M. Hardin could write that "America was gripped by its gravest political crisis since the Civil War," with the presidency "all too often . . . out of control," the incumbent president threatened with impeachment, and bureaucracies "unbridled" and arrogant. Professor Hardin conceded the need for "strong executive leadership" but proposed to bring the presidency under control through "party government." But unlike other political scientists who had been advocating strengthened and disciplined political parties as the key to attaining a workable degree of cohesion between the executive and legislative branches, Hardin contended that "constitutional surgery" was a precondition for successful party government. He proposed to reduce the Senate's legislative power to one of delay, strip it of its right to approve treaties, extend House terms to four years concurrent with the presidential term, give the party winning the presidency one hundred at-large representatives in order to assure that party's control of the House, grant a smaller number of at-large seats to the minority party to provide it with a rostrum for its leader, permit the House to override a presidential veto by a simple majority, and provide that elections would be set by law rather than by the calendar, thus shortening the length of campaigns.[56]

In the same year that Hardin's book appeared, Rexford G. Tugwell, an original member of Franklin Roosevelt's "brain trust," published his model of a new constitution, based on discussions at the Center for the Study of Democratic Institutions. Without relating his new language closely to supporting argument, Tugwell rewrote the Con-

56. Charles M. Hardin, *Presidential Power and Accountability: Toward a New Constitution* (University of Chicago Press, 1974), pp. 1, 2; for his proposals, see especially chaps. 1, 10. Notable among other works proposing measures to strengthen party organizations were American Political Science Association Committee on Political Parties (chaired by E.E. Schattschneider), *Toward a More Responsible Two-Party System* (Rinehart, 1950), and James MacGregor Burns, *Uncommon Sense* (Harper and Row, 1972).

stitution in its entirety, renaming some governmental offices and institutions and introducing new ones. He proposed a nine-year term for the president, subject to removal by a 60 percent vote of the electorate after three years; three-year terms for House members, with one hundred elected at large; a Senate with life membership, made up of former officials and candidates and of presidential appointees, some of them selected from private groups and associations recognized by the president as "nationally representative."[57]

These voices raised outside the halls of Congress have at no time aroused response within. In their unconcern, the legislators have reflected faithfully the voters whom they represent, for the critics have inspired no mass movement. Structural amendments, in the absence of a governmental breakdown that is indisputably traceable to institutional rather than individual failure, are inherently technical and abstract, not likely to arouse emotion. But the very fact that government has not broken down attests, in the popular mind, to the wisdom of the constitutional design. The absence of criticism surely reflects a faith that the structure that has survived so long without formal alteration must have served the country well since the beginning and can be counted on to serve it no less well in times to come.

This does not mean that the balance of power between the branches, and the relationships between them, have remained constant for two centuries. As Don K. Price has emphasized, the written Constitution was flexible enough to permit "the evolution of a richly varied unwritten constitution that can be adapted by political bargaining to new needs and circumstances."[58] It has permitted the Congress to delegate extraordinary power to the president, as in wartime and during the economic catastrophe of the Great Depression, but to curtail that power when circumstances change. The Congress may submit to presidential leadership, but it does so voluntarily and for only as long as it may choose. The president may act unilaterally, particularly in foreign relations, but he does so at the peril of having his policy undermined, or repudiated, by the Congress later. Throughout this century, until the 1970s, the Congress accepted—and to

57. Rexford G. Tugwell, *The Emerging Constitution* (Harper's Magazine Press, 1974), chap. 14.

58. *America's Unwritten Constitution: Science, Religion, and Political Responsibility* (Louisiana State University Press, 1983), pp. 149–50.

some extent initiated—the strengthening of the presidency as the essential point of national leadership. But when the "imperial presidency" overreached itself in the 1960s and 1970s, the Congress was aroused to rein it in, through such measures as the War Powers Resolution of 1973, the Congressional Budget and Impoundment Control Act of 1974, and the intensification of congressional oversight of administrative actions.[59]

In a very real sense, the public acts as an invisible referee as the bargaining among the branches takes place. The American people have never waivered in their support of the essential concept underlying the tripartite structure of the government, that power shall not be concentrated, that none of the branches shall be unduly aggrandized at the expense of the others. And, while the appropriate balance of power is neither stable nor precisely definable, the people— aroused by vocal public officials, elder statesmen, and other opinion leaders—sense when it is upset and support those who seek to restore the balance. Through democratic processes, the judgment of the people prevails.

The reform proposals that are considered in the next five chapters have all been advanced, however, on the assumption that the effectiveness of government can be impaired when the bargaining and rivalry between the executive and legislative branches degenerate, as they often do, into conflict and stalemate. The object must be to bring the branches to collaborate in greater harmony without subordinating either. Specific measures are thus analyzed from the point of view of whether, and how, they will contribute to the unity of the government—while preserving the balance of its elements—and hence to its efficiency, the strength of its collective leadership, and its accountability to the people.

59. The phrase is from Arthur Schlesinger, Jr., *The Imperial Presidency* (Houghton Mifflin, 1973). Sundquist, *Decline and Resurgence,* reviews the evolution of the legislative-executive balance through the 1970s.

CHAPTER FOUR

Forestalling Divided Government

Those who believe that a basic weakness of the United States government is the recurrent conflict and deadlock between the executive and legislative branches must turn, at the outset, to the problem of divided government.

When one party controls the executive branch and the opposing party has the majority in one or both houses of the Congress, all of the normal difficulties of attaining harmonious and effective working relationships between the branches are multiplied manifold. For, by the nature of party competition in a democracy, the business of political parties is to oppose each other. Competition between the two major parties in the United States is a constant of political life—and it must be, as a safeguard against abuse of power and as the means of assuring the citizenry a genuine choice of leaders and of programs. In an overriding emergency, partisan competition may be set aside, but only temporarily. As soon as the crisis is surmounted, the competition must resume.

When government is divided, then, the normal and healthy partisan confrontation that occurs during debates in every democratic legislature spills over into confrontation between the branches of the government, which may render it immobile. The president and the Congress always promise as their terms begin to collaborate unselfishly across the party boundary, but the dynamics of party competition inevitably thrust them into conflict, with each party mobilizing resources of the branch that it controls to advance its partisan program and defeat the proposals of its adversary. When the president sends

a recommendation to the opposition-controlled Congress, the legislators are virtually compelled to reject or profoundly alter it; otherwise,
they are endorsing the president's leadership as wise and sound—
and, in so doing, strengthening him or his party for the next election.
Conversely, if the congressional majorities initiate a measure, the
president must either condemn it and use his veto or else acknowledge
to the nation the prudence and creativity of his political opponents.

There have been, of course, times when political adversaries have
collaborated across the chasm that separates the branches. Much of
the fabric of the Western alliance that sustains the postwar world
was woven at a time of divided government, in 1947–48, when
President Truman and leaders of Republican congressional majorities—notably Senator Arthur H. Vandenberg of Michigan—together
committed the nation to the Marshall Plan, the North Atlantic Treaty,
the Truman Doctrine, and major programs of military and economic
aid to allies overseas. But this was the exception, explained by the
clear menace of a hostile and aggressive Soviet Union and an
extraordinary degree of consensus in the country at large that the
spread of communism had to be stemmed. Much more typical was
the country's experience during the short presidency of Gerald Ford,
when the Democratic Congress took foreign policy into its own
hands, refusing to support commitments the Nixon administration
had made to South Vietnam, wrecking negotiations with the Soviet
Union over a trade agreement, and thwarting the president's foreign
policy in Cyprus, Angola, and elsewhere.[1] Observers may debate
whether the president or the Congress had the superior policy, in
each instance, but what is not contestable is that when the two
branches pursue divergent policies, the country can have no foreign
policy at all. The deadlock was equally pronounced on domestic
matters. President Ford exercised his veto no fewer than sixty-three
times in his twenty-nine-month tenure, sparing hardly any important
measure, as recriminations flowed back and forth between the White
House and the Capitol.

Periods of divided government have recurred throughout American
history, but until the midtwentieth century they were relatively rare.
During the first hundred years after the Republican party was formed
in 1854 and Democratic-Republican competition became the structure

---

1. James L. Sundquist, *The Decline and Resurgence of Congress* (Brookings Institution,
1981), pp. 106–07, 273–93.

of American politics, only twice did an incoming president have to confront an opposition majority in either house of the Congress. President Rutherford B. Hayes faced a Democratic House after the 1876 election, and Grover Cleveland had to contend with a Republican Senate at the outset of his first term. On a dozen occasions, the midterm election gave the opposition control of one or both houses, but a president could normally count on at least two years of undivided party government.[2] Since 1954, however, the concept of what is normal has had to be reversed. Between that date and 1986, Republican presidents have occupied the White House most of the time— for twenty of the thirty-two years—but the Democrats have organized the House during the entire period and the Senate during all of the twenty-six-year span from 1955 through 1980. President Eisenhower had to deal with Democratic majorities in both houses during all of his last six years in office. So did Presidents Nixon and Ford for all of their eight years. And President Reagan confronted a Democratic House during his first six years.[3]

In the Eisenhower years, the president's foreign policy received bipartisan support, but on the domestic side the period was unproductive. The president and his Democratic opponents quarreled over what to do about education, health insurance, housing, jobs, water pollution, and many other questions. Each side had the capacity to block initiatives by the other; neither a Republican nor a Democratic program could be enacted, and action on pressing domestic issues had to await the establishment of unified Democratic control after the election of 1960. The Nixon-Ford years, likewise, saw the emasculation of such presidential initiatives as the family assistance plan and the New Federalism, and by the end of Nixon's first term relations between the branches had degenerated into open warfare. In his second term, Nixon wrote in his memoirs, "I had thrown down a

2. Norman J. Ornstein and others, *Vital Statistics on Congress, 1984–1985* (Washington: American Enterprise Institute, 1984), pp. 32–35.

3. The post-1954 phenomenon is the product of what has been called "split-level realignment," as many conservatives in the South, and to a lesser degree elsewhere, have become reliable Republican voters at the presidential level but remain Democrats in congressional voting. But the Republican gains have been slowly extending to offices below the presidential level, as results of the 1980 senatorial races in the South show most clearly, and eventually the split-level Republicans can be expected to vote Republican for the House as well. As this realignment continues, the probability that the government will be divided after any given presidential election will gradually lessen. This trend is discussed in chapter 6.

gauntlet to Congress, the bureaucracy, the media, and the Washington establishment and challenged them to epic battle."[4] The Congress took up the challenge and, even after forcing Nixon out of office, continued the battle with his successor. President Reagan, confronting a Democratic House, did succeed in driving through his radical economic program, but his victories were confined, for the most part, to his first year in office. After that, relations steadily deteriorated, and by the third year the government was once again reduced to ineffectiveness. The House—and to some extent the Republican-controlled Senate as well—was resisting further domestic budget cuts, and it was frustrating the president's foreign policy, particularly in Central America. But the government's impotence was reflected most dramatically in its incapacity to cope with gigantic and unprecedented budget deficits. As the revenue shortfall reached $200 billion annually, the president and spokesmen for both parties in both houses of the Congress separately warned the nation of impending disaster, but together they could not muster the will to act.

Nor, in a divided government, could anyone be held accountable. In the 1984 election, the Democrats could—and did—charge the president with responsibility for the record deficits, but he in turn could—and did—blame the Democratic House. Yet both parties were entirely right in denying responsibility, because neither *was* responsible. And the voters, having declined in 1980 and 1982 to vest an undivided authority in either party, could not in 1984 register a clear-cut approval or disapproval of what had happened, and so set the future course of government, by either returning a responsible party to office or turning it out of office. An electoral verdict on the conduct of a divided government is perforce a muddy and a muddled mandate.

Designing a Solution

As recently as forty years ago, unified party control of government was still the rule, divided government the exception. But even then, powerful forces at work within the American political system had for several decades been eroding the foundations on which the unity of government rested. The straight-ticket voting that characterized the nineteenth century had been giving way to the ticket-splitting that

4. *RN: The Memoirs of Richard Nixon* (Grosset and Dunlap, 1978), p. 850.

typifies the twentieth, and that has by now made divided government the norm.[5] To resolve the problem of divided government, then, will require checking and reversing one of the central trends of modern political history.

Ticket-splitting is the electoral expression of the antiparty, or at least nonparty, ideology that has attracted a growing proportion of the voting public since the beginning of this century. Revolting against the corruption of the patronage-oriented political machines that dominated political life in the latter half of the nineteenth century, the reformers of the Progressive Era struck at the parties as institutions, seeking to supplant the venal and self-seeking party bosses with a new leadership free of party ties and hence of party taint. In the newer states of the West, nonpartisan municipal elections were introduced to eliminate the influence of political parties altogether in city politics. In the older states, partisan local elections were too well established to be supplanted, in most cases, but the reformers often organized independent reform parties or backed independent candidates in mayoralty and city council races. At the state level, direct primaries were instituted to enable reformers to challenge the machines and their bosses for party nominations.

For the reformers to succeed, aroused citizens had to be willing to shed their established party allegiances and cross the party line, if necessary, to vote for the antimachine progressives on whatever ticket they might be running. In short, the good citizen had to become nonpartisan in thought and action. Political independence and ticket-splitting became civic virtues. By being free to support the best-qualified candidates regardless of party label, it was argued, the independent voter could weed out the "party hacks" on each party's slate and compel the organizations to nominate honest and competent individuals for every elective office. The new independent newspapers that arose in the Progressive Era to replace the party-affiliated journals of the nineteenth century had to demonstrate their independence by endorsing a split ticket in every election, as a matter of principle. Interest groups and civic organizations that laid claim to political independence had to do likewise.

A precondition to independent political action, of course, was

5. The proportion of congressional districts carried by the presidential candidate of one party and the House candidate of the other still averaged only 3.8 percent in the three elections of 1900–08 but rose to 13.5 percent in the four Roosevelt elections, 1932–44. Ornstein and others, *Vital Statistics, 1984–1985*, p. 56.

fundamental reform of the ballot itself. Presidential elections in the nineteenth century were bound to lead, normally, to united party control of the presidency and the House because ballot procedures made it difficult, if not impossible, for voters to split their tickets.[6] Ballots were customarily printed by party organizations rather than by governmental agencies, and the individual voter on arriving at the polling place simply obtained his party's ballot, marked it, and dropped it in the box. The single publicly printed ballot, marked in secret, that nowadays seems so central to the democratic process that one assumes it must always have existed, was in fact one of the many electoral innovations of the Progressive Era—imported from Australia.

Even after the universal adoption of the Australian ballot early in this century, however, both tradition and the form of the ballot encouraged straight-ticket voting. In most states, the election officials listed each party's nominees in separate columns, with a square or circle at the head of the column that could be checked by those who wished to vote for a party's entire slate. A straight ticket could be voted quickly; to split one's vote required time and care, and party workers could identify the ticket-splitters simply by observing the length of time the individual voter spent in the polling place. To protect voters against pressure from party organizations, reformers in many states—backed up, of course, by the minority party in each state—gradually brought about alterations in the form of the ballot to eliminate the straight-ticket square or circle at the head of the party column. By 1972, the first year for which the Council of State Governments published data on the subject, barely half the states, or twenty-six, made it possible to vote for a party's entire slate in a presidential election by marking one box on the ballot or pulling a master lever on the voting machine. Eight years later, the number had declined to nineteen.[7] At least one state, Virginia, even went so far as to eliminate party identification from the ballot altogether,

6. The vagaries of the electoral college could still produce a split result between the presidency and the House, as in 1876. Even though the Senate was insulated from the presidential balloting by virtue of staggered terms and election by state legislatures, the opposition controlled the Senate after a presidential election only in the one instance cited (after 1884) in the century ending in 1954.

7. Council of State Governments, *The Book of the States, 1974–75*, p. 35; *1982–83*, p. 104. One of the nineteen, Oklahoma, had separate straight-ticket boxes or levers for each level of government.

leaving it to party workers outside the polling place to remind voters of the identity of a party's candidates.

Even as political parties were losing the committed allegiance of reform-minded progressives, their hold on their traditional supporters was weakened also, through the loss of patronage. Civil service merit systems, introduced in the 1880s, spread to encompass more and more jobs at all levels of government, denying those posts to party loyalists and so weakening one of the incentives for loyalty itself. Meanwhile, the boom in the private relative to the public sector was reducing the value and appeal of those jobs that remained at the disposal of party organizations. And the informal welfare functions of parties—the traditional ton of coal and Christmas basket for the needy—gave way, after the 1930s, to public welfare.

As ticket-splitting became both mechanically possible and morally acceptable—even virtuous—it would appear whenever voters found themselves out of sympathy with their party's candidate for president or the program he espoused. Thus Theodore Roosevelt as a third-party candidate for president in 1912 could attract millions of voters who remained loyal Republicans in state and local contests. Alfred E. Smith as the Democratic candidate in 1928 could impel millions of southern Democrats to scratch the top of their ticket while steadfastly supporting the rest of the party slate. With the realignment of the 1930s came massive ticket-splitting among northern Republicans backing Franklin Roosevelt's New Deal and southern Democrats opposing it.

The bonds of party were clearly attenuating, but their weakness was concealed as long as the Democrats, installed by the New Deal realignment as the country's majority party, were able to elect their president. So Roosevelt and Harry Truman succeeded in doing what every twentieth century president before them had accomplished; they carried into office with them majorities of their own party in both the Senate and the House. Journalists and political scientists who for years had accepted the "president's coattails" as one of the immutable phenomena of political life, guaranteed to assure every president a sympathetic Congress during his first two years, saw no reason to reverse their judgment. Nor did they after the 1952 election, when a Republican president brought a Republican Congress to Washington with him.

But in 1956, the frayed and tattered state of the presidential coattails was dramatically exposed. In that year, President Eisenhower won 41 of the 48 states and 58 percent of the two-party vote but his party still lost both houses of the Congress. The GOP lost 11 of the senatorial elections in the states that Eisenhower won—or 42 percent— and nearly the same proportion of House seats in the districts Eisenhower carried. The voters who gave the president 58 percent support gave the Republican House candidates only 49 percent. Yet even this extraordinary degree of ticket-splitting was exceeded in Richard Nixon's landslide reelection in 1972. The president carried every state but Massachusetts, with a popular vote margin 4 points higher than Eisenhower's—62 percent of the two-party vote—but lost the Senate and House by even greater margins. Democratic candidates won exactly half the Senate races in the states that Nixon carried, 16 of 32, and about half the House seats in districts Nixon won. The president's 62 percent fell off to 47 percent for his party's House nominees.

These elections displayed the pattern of ticket-splitting that has prevailed for thirty years. The Democratic party remains the country's majority party, holding most of the governorships, most of the state legislative seats, and most of the city halls and county courthouses in populous areas most of the time. Democratic party loyalty has extended to congressional elections as well, giving the party control of the House continuously since 1955 and the Senate from that year to 1980. But, most of the time, enough Democrats have preferred the Republican candidates for president—Eisenhower, Nixon, and Reagan—to give the GOP the White House, and thus divide the government. In 1980, the presidential coattails proved somewhat stronger; Republican candidates lost in 11 of the 31 senatorial contests in states carried by Ronald Reagan—or 35 percent—but since most of the seats in those states were held by Democrats the GOP was able to capture control of the Senate for the first time since the first Eisenhower landslide. But the results of House elections made clear that the political system has by no means returned to the pre-1956 years. Republican House candidates still polled only 49 percent of the two-party vote, lagging 6 percentage points behind Reagan, and the Democrats emerged with a 51-seat margin—enough to enable them to organize that body and chair all of its committees, even though they lacked the votes, and perhaps the will, to defeat the Reagan economic program during the honeymoon year of 1981. In

1984, the number of states with split results between the presidency and the Senate returned almost to the halfway mark, as Democrats won in 15 of the 32 races in states carried by Reagan and a Republican won in Minnesota, the only state supporting the Democratic candidate, Walter Mondale. Of the 371 congressional districts carried by President Reagan, Democrats were elected to the House in 191, or 51 percent.[8]

If divided government with its inevitable interbranch conflict and deadlock are to be forestalled, how can the trend of recent history be reversed? Four approaches to a remedy are discussed below. One would proceed directly to the point, by simply making ticket-splitting impossible. The second and third would employ less drastic methods, relying on a change in the ballot format and in the electoral schedule to encourage straight-ticket voting. The fourth would assure the president a congressional majority by arbitrarily assigning his party enough additional Senate and House seats to outnumber the opposition.

One point bears on the feasibility of any of these solutions. Any measure that held real promise of bringing about a reduction in split-ticket voting would be anathema to the incumbent members of the Senate and the House. The reason is simple; members of Congress are the direct and personal beneficiaries of ticket-splitting.

Of the 100 members of the Senate in 1985, 93 had had personal experience running for the Senate or the House, or both, during a presidential election year. Of those 93, 50—or more than half—had saved their political careers by separating themselves from their party's candidate for president; they had managed to survive through ticket-splitting—usually reflecting the power of incumbency—in a year when the presidential candidate failed to carry the legislator's state or district. And more than half the others, or 23, had run stronger than the presidential candidate in one or more elections, by margins ranging as high as 23 percentage points. Thus, nearly three-quarters of the Senate's membership—73 of the 100—had been in a race where they found their party's presidential candidate to be at least a drag on the ticket, if not a sure loser from the start.

Similarly, of the 435 members who organized the House in 1985,

8. *National Journal*, April 20, 1985, pp. 854–57. One district carried by Mondale, in New York City, reelected a Republican representative, making a total of 192 districts with split results.

at least 50 percent—or 218—had won in a year when the presidential candidate of his or her party had gone down to defeat in the member's district. This included 79 percent of the 253 House Democrats, or 201, of whom 186 had survived a 1984 Reagan victory in their districts. On the other hand, only 17 of the 182 House Republicans, or fewer than 10 percent, had won when a Democratic presidential candidate carried their districts—a few of these results going back as far as 1964—but many of the others had had the experience of running stronger than their party's nominee for president.[9]

Under these circumstances, a Democratic member of Congress would have to believe very deeply in the abstract principle of straight-ticket voting to see merit in any reform that linked his fate more closely to that of Walter Mondale in 1984, or to Jimmy Carter or George McGovern in earlier years. And a Republican senator or representative could anticipate the danger of someday being found on a ticket with a presidential candidate as weak as Goldwater proved to be in the North in 1964 or Gerald Ford in the South in 1976.

The Presidential-Congressional Team Ticket

The most direct and effective, but most arbitrary, way to end ticket-splitting between candidates for president and Congress would be simply to prohibit it. Each party's candidates for president, vice president, senator, and representative could be bound together as a slate—or team ticket, as it has been called—with the voter casting a single vote for the team of his or her choice.

The team ticket would be less than a foolproof protection against divided government, to be sure. Since only one-third of the Senate seats are filled in each presidential election, a lopsided Senate

9. Michael Barone, Grant Ujifusa, and Douglas Matthews, *The Almanac of American Politics, 1972* (Gambit) and *1980* (Dutton), and Michael Barone and Grant Ujifusa, eds., *The Almanac of American Politics, 1984* (National Journal) contain presidential election returns for most congressional districts from 1968 to 1980. *National Journal*, April 20, 1985, pp. 855–57, presents results for all districts, if one accepts the estimates of the *Journal's* writer, Richard E. Cohen, for nine districts for which calculations were not complete. For the missing districts in the earlier elections, I relied on presidential election returns by counties (or big city wards). In the very few cases where there were no detailed data, I tried to err on the side of minimum ticket-splitting in dividing a county's or ward's presidential vote between congressional districts. Hence the "at least" phrase in the tally of House elections.

majority—such as the Democratic majorities of the 1960s—would not be overturned in a narrow presidential election won by the opposition candidate (assuming that the system of staggered six-year terms is not altered, a possibility discussed in chapter 5). And even in the case of the House, where all the seats are at stake in each election, a slim mathematical possibility would exist that in a close election the winning presidential candidate might not carry a majority of House districts. Nevertheless, the prospects for unified party control of the government would be tremendously enhanced. Divided government following a presidential election would become the kind of rarity it was during the first century of Republican-Democratic competition.

Beyond that, the team ticket would have a profound effect on the conduct of politicians of the majority party in office. Throughout a president's first term, the chief executive and legislators of the winning party would recognize that when reelection time came around they would stand or fall together. Congressmen of the president's party would be at pains to enhance the president's success, since they as well as he would be dependent on the public's acceptance of his record in office. Would this produce a Congress too docile, too subservient to exercise its responsibility to oversee, and where necessary investigate, the executive branch? Certainly—at least until a president was reelected and entered his lame-duck second term— the congressmen would lose a measure of their independence, as is the case in parliamentary countries where members are forced to run on the party record. Members would no longer be free to score political points in their home states or districts by opposing, and embarrassing, a president of their own party. They could no longer denounce their leader and reject party discipline altogether, as leading senators and representatives have done so often in the past, reducing their party's program to a shambles. They would have to accept the president's leadership, like it or not, as long as he remained the party's likely nominee for reelection.

Nevertheless, in their own interests, individual legislators would be forced to oppose the president where his policies and programs appeared likely to undercut support for the party in a particular state or district. Their incentive to make the president's record look good would extend to the prevention of mistakes, and their oversight and investigative powers would still be important for that end. If the

president persisted in a locally unpopular course, dissenting legislators would have the recourse always available in any democracy
when party discipline becomes intolerable—to bolt the party and
either join another party or form a new one. The likelihood of splinter
parties, such as Strom Thurmond's States Rights Democratic (Dixie-
crat) party of 1948 or George Wallace's American Independent party
of 1968, might be increased somewhat.

While the pressures for accommodation and harmony within the
governing party would weigh most heavily on the legislators, it
would be felt to some degree by the president as well. The threat of
third-party challenges would be one source of pressure. But short of
that extremity, a president would be aware that in each presidential
election, the party team would be dependent not only on the
president's record in office but on that of the legislators, too. A
president would have to attend to building their reputations, and
records, as well as his own. To that end, patronage and local projects
would be of prime importance; the "pork barrel" would lose none
of its current significance. But the president would have reason to
accommodate the legislators' viewpoints on his legislative program,
too. At both ends of Pennsylvania Avenue, the culture of individualism, of "every politician for himself or herself" would give way, to
some considerable extent, to an ethos of teamwork.

Crucially affected, also, would be the presidential nominating
process. As a precondition to accepting the team-ticket idea, the
legislators would surely insist they have an effective veto over the
selection of the presidential and vice presidential nominees to whom
they would be bound. Some device such as a bicameral nominating
convention, as discussed in chapter 7, would be in prospect.

The Challenge to Tradition

The idea of a team ticket has one notable precedent. Since the
formation of parties in the United States, candidates for president
and vice president have been bound together; the voter casts a single
ballot for a slate of electors committed to one or another party's
presidential–vice presidential team. No one has been heard to advocate a right for voters to split their ticket for those two offices.

Nevertheless, to further restrict the voter's right of choice would
do violence to a tradition that has been cherished by the American

polity ever since progressive reformers introduced the secret ballot. One may anticipate the response of typical southern ticket-splitters in 1984 had it been suggested that, in order to support President Reagan for a second term, they be required to vote to oust their friendly and effective Democratic congressman. Or if they wanted to retain their congressman in office, that they be forced to accept Walter Mondale and Geraldine Ferraro. And these southern voters have their counterparts in every region, who split tickets in both directions and would defend vehemently their right to do so. If those voters had thought about divided government at all, they would be apt to see its adverse consequences as remote and speculative—and of a kind that could be averted if only the responsible officials would put aside partisanship and do their duty in the national interest—while the restriction on their freedom to vote as they please would be immediate, clear, and personally felt.

Moreover, they might not see divided government as an evil at all, but as a boon. In at least one poll, taken by Louis Harris in November 1972, more respondents felt that to have a president of one party and a Congress controlled by the other—a circumstance the voters had decreed that very month—was good for the country than believed it to be detrimental. Of the sample, 36 percent believed divided government was better for the country, 21 percent thought it worse, 36 percent suggested it made no difference, and 7 percent had no opinion. The respondents, wrote Mr. Harris, believed divided government "keeps both the President and Congress in line." Yet this poll was taken at the time members of Congress were beginning to demand an investigation of the president's role in the Watergate scandal, and the timing may have influenced the public view. In August 1976, a similar Harris poll found a slight plurality in favor of divided government, 40 to 38 percent, but three months later—after the election—the balance had shifted to a 45 to 39 percent margin in favor of single-party control. Yet during the 1984 campaign, two Harris samples showed 55 and 60 percent believing the country would be "worse off" if the voters gave President Reagan "a Republican-controlled Congress that would pass nearly everything he wants."[10]

10. Louis Harris and Associates, *The Harris Survey Yearbook of Public Opinion, 1972,* p. 17; Austin Ranney, "What Constitutional Changes Do Americans Want?" *This*

Respect for the freedom of the individual voters might suggest that the electorate should be free, in any presidential election year, to decide whether it preferred united or divided government. As in other matters, it might appear, the majority should rule. But it is fallacious to argue that, when divided government occurs following a presidential election, that is because a majority of voters positively desired split control. Only a minority of voters will have so expressed themselves. To begin with, divided government is determined, in the case of the House, by a minority of the nation's 435 congressional districts. In the recent elections with the most ticket-splitting, those of 1972 and 1984, only 192 of the 435 districts in each case turned in split results; the other 243 supported presidential and House candidates of the same party. And within most of the split districts, a minority of voters—and possibly a very small minority—determined the results. In 1972, while Nixon ran 15 percentage points ahead of Republican House candidates, on the average, that proves only that as many as 15 percent of the voters split their tickets between the presidential and House candidates (disregarding the impact of those who may have voted for only one of the two offices). Assuming that 5 percent of the voters split their tickets in favor of George McGovern— a generous assumption—while 20 percent split in Nixon's direction, for a net of 15 percentage points, the ticket-splitters would still amount to only 25 percent. The results for 1984, when Reagan's percentage of the presidential vote was 12 points higher than the Republican share of the aggregate House vote, indicate that the proportion of ticket-splitters may have been less, and was certainly not much higher, than in 1972.

Divided government therefore results from the behavior of a minority of voters in a minority of districts. In the case of the Senate, divided government after a presidential election may be the consequence of the carryover of an opposition majority from earlier elections. Insofar as the division is produced by ticket-splitting in the most recent election, that is similarly the result of the action in a minority of states. On no occasion have as many as half the states with both presidential and senatorial elections split in favor of the

Constitution: A Bicentennial Chronicle (Winter 1984), reprinted in Donald L. Robinson, ed., *Reforming American Government: The Bicentennial Papers of the Committee on the Constitutional System* (Westview Press, 1985), p. 286; Harris Survey, news release no. 98, November 2, 1984, reporting polls of September 21–25 and October 26–31, 1984.

winning presidential candidate and the senatorial nominee of the opposing party.

It would be equally fallacious, of course, to assert that the majority of voters has any steadfast interest in, or desire for, united government as such. Confronted with an abstract question as to the merits of united government, the reply of the typical Democrat or Republican would no doubt be: "By which party? If you mean, by my party, I'm in favor of united government. If you mean, by the other party, I'm against it." This attitude seems clearly enough demonstrated, in the case of the Democrats at least, by the results of recent midterm elections. In 1954, 1958, 1970, 1974, and 1982, a majority of the voters preferred Democratic control of the House of Representatives—or at least did not consider it undesirable—at times when they knew a Republican president would be in office two more years. In three of those five elections, the electorate also increased the number of Democratic senators. But it can be doubted that the voters deliberately sought divided government, or that the advantages or disadvantages of such an outcome entered into the consideration of very many of them when they made their electoral decisions. Whether united or divided government eventuates from any election, it is the unanticipated, and not necessarily desired, consequence of voting choices made for other reasons.

Clearly, proponents of the team ticket will have an enormous task persuading typical voters that giving up their freedom to split their tickets will be good for the country, and for them. The Democrats who had no fear of divided government in five midterm elections, and who may even have preferred it, will have to be persuaded that unified control by the Republican party will somehow produce better government. Few partisan Democrats, surely, would admit to such a probability—least of all the party activists who have contributed the leadership, the effort, and the money to press for Democratic congressional victories while a Republican president was in the White House. The argument can assuredly be made that, with united Republican control, one party could be held indisputably accountable for the exercise of power, and that that would be healthy and beneficial for the political system as a whole, and hence good for everybody. But to make the argument is not to predict that many Democrats would be persuaded, or that the party would abandon its campaign. And Republicans are no more likely to yield to the logic of the claim. When Democratic presidents have been in office, there has been no evidence of slackening in the desire of Republican partisans to regain control of the Congress at midterm.

If the party activist and the rank-and-file partisan voter would be difficult to persuade, the average member of Congress, as noted earlier, would be even more so. For every winner in general elections, of course, there is a loser. For every incumbent senator or representative who survived only because of ticket-splitting, there is a candidate of the other party who would have been elected if the practice had been forbidden. Southern Republicans, for example, should find great merit in the team-ticket idea. Indeed, if the scheme had been in place over the past thirty years, the entire Republican party would have benefited, for it would have been the majority party in the Congress during many of the years when it was in fact consigned to what seemed to be perpetual minority status. That assumes, as seems likely, that the support given the team ticket would have come closer to that accorded its presidential candidates in 1956, 1968, 1972, 1980, and 1984 than to the much lower level of support given its nominees for Congress. Even if the Republicans had won the White House on only four of those five occasions (the 1968 election having been the only close one), they would have gained from having had the opportunity to enact their party program unobstructed by the opposition.

It is the incumbent members of Congress who vote, however, not the opponents they defeated. And those whose own political careers, or whose colleagues' careers, were saved by ticket-splitting are not likely to step forward quickly to outlaw the practice. Adoption of the team ticket would therefore depend, in all likelihood, on bypassing the Congress in the constitutional amendment process. That has never been done, but it can be. On petition of two-thirds of the state legislatures, the Congress must call a constitutional convention, which submits its proposed amendments directly to the states for ratification—and that method would have to be used to accomplish any of the changes discussed in this book that might be perceived by sitting members of the Congress to be against their interest (a possibility considered in chapter 9). However, the state legislators who would have to initiate such a convention have much in common with congressmen. Many of them, too, have survived through ticket-splitting in state elections, and their outlook might not differ greatly from that of their counterparts in Washington.

An electoral system should never be judged, of course, according to the degree of comfort and convenience it accords political candidates and officeholders. It should be measured by its effects on the performance of the political system as a whole. And from that perspective, and given the premises stated at the outset of this volume, the very features that discommend the team ticket idea to members of Congress are its merit. By requiring a party's presidential and legislative candidates to share a common success or failure at the polls, it would compel them to work together once elected. Inevitably, some members of Congress would be dragged to defeat by a presidential candidate unpopular in their states or districts. Occasionally, a presidential candidate might be dragged down, too. But one candidate's loss would be another's gain. And, if reducing conflict and averting deadlock would benefit the political system as a whole, the public at large would gain immensely from an end to divided government as the normal circumstance, and from the incentives to party cohesion and cooperation that the team ticket would provide.

The Effect on Third-Party Prospects

In all of U.S. history few third-party candidates have been elected, and no third party has ever waged more than one strong presidential campaign since the Republicans emerged as a new party in 1854. But a free and open political system must at least allow the opportunity for a Theodore Roosevelt or a George Wallace or a John Anderson to organize a party and make a try.

Under a team-ticket system, as observed above, party splintering and third-party attempts might very well become more common, because there would be less room for dissidents within the major parties. Conceivably, the tendency toward splintering could become so pronounced that the familiar American two-party system would at times give way to multiparty competition. If the minor parties were to gain enough strength to hold a balance of power, some of the advantages of the team-ticket scheme would be lost; coalitions would have to be formed and responsibility and accountability would be diffused. Such an outcome would not alter the American governmental system as fundamentally as might be supposed, however, for the same coalition-building that would have to be carried out across party lines in a multiparty system now has to take place within the governing party, even in a united government, before its programs can be enacted. It may be assumed, moreover, that third parties in this country would tend to have short lives under the new electoral system just as under the present one. Stable multiparty systems are associated, the world over, with proportional representation in parliamentary elections. Wherever representatives are chosen from single-member districts, no matter how tightly disciplined the parties may be, two strong parties usually dominate the scene. That is the case in Great Britain and in the nations formed from the British Commonwealth, including Canada. Even France, with its long tradition of multiparty competition and with the complication of a strong Communist party, appears to be evolving into a two-party nation.

If team tickets were required, a candidate for president who was running essentially as an individual rather than as the head of a genuine party, such as John Anderson in 1980, would be at a marked disadvantage. Without capable running mates for the Senate and House, he could hardly hope to compete on equal terms against team tickets with strong candidates for the legislative seats. If the object is to forestall divided government, however, independent candidacies—as distinct from third-party candidacies—should be discouraged, whether under the present electoral system or the team-ticket plan. If an independent were somehow to reach the White House, his or her hope of successful leadership would be dashed from the outset by the combined opposition of both the majority and minority parties in both houses of the Congress.

If a John Anderson were serious, under the team-ticket scheme, he would be forced to organize a full-fledged party, one capable of governing—and that would be all to the good. Any presidential candidacy would have to reflect, as it should, more than the individual ambition of a maverick politician. It would have to grow out of broad political forces—as, for example, the Populists in the 1890s or the Dixiecrats and the American Independent party (AIP) in the postwar South. And such solidly based parties would have probably as favorable a prospect in a team-ticket electoral system as they do now, for they should encounter no difficulty in recruiting capable and appealing candidates for Congress. That would be particularly the case if a legislative candidate were permitted under the plan to run on more than one team ticket, with his or her votes aggregated. The success and acceptance of the present New York method of totaling the votes of candidates running on more than one party slate suggests its adaptability to the national level. But even without such a device, the experience of the Populists suggests that any party with a depth of popular support can field a winning team. In carrying five states for its presidential candidate in 1892, the People's party elected three senators and eleven representatives. The Dixiecrats and the AIP did not attempt to field full slates, but there is no reason to think they would have found it difficult to do so.

Independent candidacies for the Senate or the House, on the other hand, would be virtually barred if the team-ticket idea were adopted. The number of independents in the Congress has been so negligible— there were none at all in the Ninety-ninth Congress (1985–86)—that this problem can probably be disregarded. In any case, independents in the Congress can contribute only to the disintegration, not the integration, of the government.

Two Simpler Approaches

Recognizing the radical character of the team-ticket solution, and the enormous practical obstacles to its adoption, those who decry the consequences of divided government have sought simpler, less drastic approaches that would stop short of compelling straight-ticket voting. Any reform that still permitted ticket-splitting would, by definition, be less effective than the team ticket as a safeguard against divided government. But any substantial reduction in the number of split ballots would help. The question is how much help could be expected—whether any measure lacking the element of compulsion would have sufficient effect to make its adoption worth the effort. To the extent it did hold promise of results, it would, of course, arouse the opposition of incumbent congressmen. And if its adoption depended on federal statute rather than constitutional amendment, the Congress could not be bypassed in the enactment process.

Change in the Ballot Format

If the elimination of the straight-ticket voting box on the ballot, or the master lever on the voting machine, in most of the fifty states has contributed to the rise in ticket-splitting, restoring that box or lever would presumably induce a decline. A return to the nineteenth century practice of open voting, with party-printed ballots, could not be seriously proposed, but within the context of secret ballot procedures voters in every state could be enabled to support all or a portion of a party's list of candidates by checking a single box or pulling a single lever.

For the purpose of encouraging unity in the national government, the opportunity for straight-ticket voting would need only to extend to a party's candidates for federal offices. A reform so limited would be a simple, minimal change in existing practices that could be accomplished by legislation in the thirty-one states not now providing the straight-ticket opportunity. Yet the slowness and uncertainty of a state-by-state approach suggests the desirability of national action, through an act of Congress, to make the reform universal.

Any suggestion that the Congress take responsibility for any aspect of the design of ballots on a nationwide scale would encounter a states-rights objection that so intimate a feature of the local election process is none of Washington's business. Yet the national government has regulated elections in many respects. It has set rules governing the financing of national campaigns. It has intervened to overrule state decisions as to who may vote—by prescribing Negro suffrage and woman suffrage, setting the minimum voting age at eighteen years, and abolishing the poll tax as a prerequisite for voting. In the Voting Rights Act of 1965, it outlawed discrimination at local polling places and authorized federal enforcement. Federal officials have been assigned as local voting registrars, and changes in the election laws of some states are subject to review and approval by the U.S. Department of Justice, which has on occasion invalidated a state statute. For the Congress to act on a related matter of clear national concern and interest should not appear as an unreasonable extension of federal power, assuming the regulation applied only to candidates for national office.

But if the thirty-one states that now do not provide the option to vote a straight ticket for president, vice president, senator, and representative with a single ballot mark were to do so, how many voters would exercise the option? Not many, if one may judge from a comparison of voter behavior in 1980 between the states that do offer the straight-ticket opportunity and those that do not. Of the thirty-three states that chose senators in the 1980 presidential election, fourteen offered the straight-ticket option, while nineteen did not.[11] In the fourteen, the average percentage-point spread between the proportion of the two-party vote given a party's presidential and its senatorial candidate was 8.2 points, the median 6.0 points. In the nineteen states not offering the straight-ticket option, the spread was only slightly greater, an average of 10.9 and a median of 8.6 points. The proportion of split outcomes was about the same. Seven of the nineteen states, or 37 percent, gave their electoral votes to a president of one party while choosing a senator of the other, while five of the fourteen straight-ticket option states, or 36 percent, did likewise. That Democratic Senators Dodd of Connecticut, Dixon of Illinois, Ford of Kentucky, Eagleton of Missouri, and Hollings of South Carolina all survived the Reagan tide in their states, despite the straight-ticket option, by running from 6 percentage points (Eagleton) to 21 percentage points (Hollings) ahead of President Carter as a candidate on the same ballot may be evidence enough that a change in the form of the ballot, standing alone, is unlikely to reduce significantly the likelihood of divided government in Washington. In 1984, the states with the straight-ticket option actually showed a higher proportion of split results in senatorial elections—seven of thirteen, or 54 percent, compared to nine of nineteen, or 47 percent, in states without it.

Separate Congressional Elections

A second relatively simple proposal would be to separate the presidential and congressional elections by a short interval—two weeks, say—so that when the voters came to choose their senators and representatives they would already know whom they had sent to occupy the White House. Then they would, it is suggested, be disposed to elect congressmen of the president's party, to help make successful the administration of the man or woman they had just

11. The nineteen states with the straight-ticket option as of 1980 were Alabama, Connecticut, Illinois, Indiana, Iowa, Kentucky, Michigan, Missouri, New Hampshire, New Mexico, Oklahoma, Pennsylvania, Rhode Island, South Carolina, South Dakota, Texas, Utah, West Virginia, and Wisconsin. Louisiana holds its senatorial and presidential elections separately, with the former choice made in its unique nonpartisan primary in September. Council of State Governments, *The Book of the States, 1982–83*, p. 104. The calculation for 1984 assumes that the same nineteen states have retained the option.

entrusted with the nation's leadership. This is what happened in France in 1981. Having just placed the Socialist François Mitterrand in the Elysée Palace, the French electorate in a separate poll five weeks later returned a substantial Socialist majority to the Chamber of Deputies.

The question, of course, is whether the American electors would behave as the French did on that occasion. Perhaps in some years they would be in the mood expressed in the Harris poll of 1972, when a 50-to-29 percent majority favored divided government to keep both the president and the Congress "in line." In that event, separating the elections would have the opposite effect from that intended. Perhaps at other times the voters would be in the mood of November 1976, when they felt that the president they had just elected deserved a Congress controlled by his partisan allies.

In guessing what the public response to such an appeal might be, in any future circumstances, the history of midterm elections may be relevant. Every four years under the present Constitution, the people in a separate congressional election have the opportunity to send to Washington a Congress that will support the president or one that will oppose him. Invariably, the president campaigns on behalf of his party's nominees and pleads with the people to elect them. The nominees in turn ask for election on the ground the president deserves support. But with monotonous regularity the president and his party are rebuffed. Only once in this century, in 1934, has the president's party increased its proportion of members of the House in the midterm election, and in only six of those twenty-one contests has it picked up Senate seats.[12] (The Senate, because the seats at stake in a given year may be preponderantly of one party or the other, is a less revealing measure of a president's persuasive power than is the House.) Woodrow Wilson's nationwide campaign for a Democratic Congress in 1918 was perhaps the most energetic such appeal to the electorate—and the most spectacular failure. To all these demonstrations of the absence of presidential coattails in the midterm elections must be added President Franklin Roosevelt's equally historic failure in 1938 to persuade members of his own Democratic party to "purge" senators and congressmen unsympathetic to the Roosevelt New Deal in favor of candidates pledged to cooperate with the party's leader.

12. Ornstein and others, *Vital Statistics, 1984–85*, pp. 32–35.

Granted, if the presidential and congressional elections were separated by a brief interval, the question of divided government might become the focus of the separate congressional election. One may then speculate as to whether that issue would create a bandwagon effect in favor of the president-elect's party or have the opposite result—more ticket-splitting—because the voters resented the interference of even a popular president-elect and rejected his advice, just as they have spurned the advice of sitting presidents. Or to make little difference at all, as the electorate continued to make its congressional choices as it does now, on the basis of many other considerations beyond a preference for, or an aversion to, divided government.

Perhaps the best prediction is that the voters would behave just about as they do now. Those who believe the president should have a cooperative Congress controlled by his own partisans have every opportunity now to vote a straight ticket—and do. Those who positively favor divided government, or for other reasons favor the opposing party's candidate for senator or representative, split their tickets. Only one factor would be altered by separating the elections: the voter would know the outcome of the presidential election. Yet why would this knowledge change behavior? Surely, the voters who supported President Eisenhower in 1956 expected him to be elected—almost everyone else did, too—yet enough of them voted Democratic for congressional candidates to deny the GOP control of either body. Similarly, the supporters of Richard Nixon in 1972 and Ronald Reagan in 1980 and 1984 must have been nearly as certain of the election outcome when they cast their ballots as they were the morning after. Yet, again, enough of them split their tickets to produce divided government.

The inevitable congressional resistance to any proposal that would lessen the electoral independence of the legislators would be compounded, in this instance, by an added circumstance—the falloff in voting turnout that could be expected between the first and second elections. Every member of Congress would ponder whether his or her chances would be helped or hurt by the lower turnout—would try to divine which party's supporters would be more likely to stay home in the second balloting—and would be influenced accordingly. If in doubt, members would shy away from change—after all, under the existing schedule of elections, they have been successful. And opponents of the dual-election plan would be given a persuasive argument: any scheme that would result in senators and congressmen being chosen by a reduced electorate would be demonstrably anti-democratic. Whether correct or not, the idea that a large voter turnout is a sign of high civic morale, and a low turnout bad for a democratic polity, is a national article of faith. If the Congress could be persuaded to experiment with separate elections, the experience would be illuminating. But whether the election outcome would be different—or different enough, at least, to warrant the cost and the nuisance of two elections instead of one—is doubtful. And any differences that appeared would be stigmatized as the result of an antidemocratic reduction in the size of the electorate.

Bonus Seats in the Congress

A direct and effective way of eliminating the possibility of divided government following a presidential election—although one with no precedent in American experience—would be to create additional seats in the Congress for the president-elect's party in a number sufficient to give it control of the Senate and the House.

If control were to be guaranteed, the number of additional seats awarded in some years would have to be substantial. To have provided President Nixon with Republican majorities after the 1968 election would have required the addition of 17 GOP senators, enlarging that body from 100 to 117, and 52 representatives, increasing the size of the House from 435 to 487. Precisely the same numbers would have been required after the 1972 election, and after 1984 President Reagan would have needed 72 added Republicans in the House.

The addition of bonus members, it has been argued, would not only assure the president's party of a majority (if only a one-seat margin) and so permit it to organize the Congress but also would bring to the legislative bodies a group of leaders who would approach their legislative duties with a national rather than a parochial per-spective and could, if properly selected, bring a wealth of experience and wisdom to congressional deliberations. It is this very prospect, of course, that would be sure to arouse the most intense opposition to the proposal from incumbent members, who would see some of their power and influence flow to a group of newcomers who might outclass them in stature and prestige.

This objection would be mitigated if the number of bonus seats were fixed at a small figure, but the effectiveness of the approach would be reduced to the extent that the number of seats was limited. If the additional House seats had been fixed at a number even as high as fifty, for example, it would have been insufficient to assure Republican House majorities in the 1956, 1972, 1980, and 1984 elections, all won by Republican presidents. To make the idea acceptable to incumbent members as an experiment would probably require reducing the number to the point where the prospect of preventing divided government at any given time would be so small as to make the effort hardly worthwhile.

In the case of the Senate, the proposal encounters a constitutional obstacle, for it could be interpreted to contravene the one unamend- able clause of the Constitution—the provision in Article V that "no State, without its Consent, shall be deprived of its equal Suffrage in the Senate." While proponents could argue that the bonus senators would represent the nation, and hence all states equally—and this could be specified in the language of the amendment—opponents would advance the plausible contention that whatever state was the home of a national senator would in fact have extra suffrage.

Leaving aside these practical and constitutional difficulties, one may speculate as to how a scheme for adding members to the Senate and the House could best be designed to serve the purposes that are sought. Much depends, of course, on the method of selection, and on this point a range of possibilities is open.

At-large candidates could be nominated by the party at its national convention, along with its choices for president and vice president. If the numbers were large enough to cover any need that could be reasonably anticipated—twenty candidates for the Senate and sev- enty-five for the House would be the minimum suggested by recent elections—each quadrennial party convention would be faced with an enormously complex task. Presumably, it would simplify its job by delegating the selection in fact to the presidential nominee, as it does now in the case of selecting its candidate for vice president. But that in turn would thrust an onerous and distracting burden on presidential candidates, who while engrossed in the contest for the nomination would have to find time to make judicious choices among the persons seeking places on the party list. In a hotly contested race, a candidate would have to delegate the selection process to advisers and assistants and would, to some extent, lose control. Whether the public would have confidence in a selection process that was in the hands of anonymous, behind-the-scenes negotiators is conjectural. Moreover, such a process would surely defeat the aims of those who see in at-large members the opportunity to place in the Senate and House a corps of the ablest, most nationally minded party leaders. The list-makers would be confronted with overwhelming pressures from all of the organized and unorganized groups and factions within the party—state and local party organizations, women, blacks, Hispanics, Asian-Americans, other ethnic and religious groups, liberals and conservatives, business and labor, and all the rest—for representation. Any group that could claim the allegiance of a few hundred thousand voters would make its demands, and would have to be heard. Group representatives, when elected, would hardly be nationally minded. They would be seen, and would probably behave, as the representatives of the interests responsible for getting them included on the slate in the first place.

If the number to be elected were uncertain, to be determined after the election by the need of the president's party for additional seats to attain its majority, all of the candidates would have to be ranked in order—as is done in some proportional representation systems of election in parliamentary democracies—which would compound the pressures for inclusion on the party list with jockeying for high positions on the slate. This suggests the desirability of fixing the number of at-large seats in advance. But any fixed number would necessarily turn out, in any given election, to be either too small to give the president's party the control sought or larger—perhaps much larger—than necessary for that purpose, and hence unnecessarily disruptive.

The rank-ordering could be done, of course, by the voters themselves. At the time of the presidential election, each voter could be permitted to cast a ballot for a specified number of persons listed on the slate of the party of his or her choice, and the candidates could be ranked according to the results. Whether an individual voter could obtain the information necessary to make an intelligent choice among eighty competing candidates may surely be questioned. That problem could be ameliorated if the choice were made by regions, from smaller lists, but it would remain. And a regional system would defeat the purpose of electing nationally minded members to the Congress.

Finally, for the voter to make the choice, on either a national or regional basis, would lead to a general election season in which candidates for the at-large seats would be campaigning against their opponents within their party, thus extending the primary season through the whole general election period, with all of the divisive consequences that hard-fought primaries can have. The Italian proportional representation system has been widely criticized within Italy for having that result.

These weaknesses and difficulties suggest still another alternative—that the at-large seats be filled *after* the election, by appointment. The responsibility could be vested in the president alone,[13] or in the president subject to confirmation by his party's members in the house affected, or even exclusively in the legislative body. The first of those methods would probably strike all concerned as giving the president excessive authority over the legislature, upsetting the balance between the branches. If the legislators chose their added colleagues, one may surmise that former legislators, including some retired by their constituents, would be chosen for many of the at-large seats, and that eminent, nationally minded statesmen likely to outshine the members who selected them would be scrupulously avoided. In fact, it might come to be understood, as a condition of appointment, that the at-large members would take no active role in the legislative process. The middle course—appointment by the president subject to confirmation—might well lead to an assertion by the legislative parties of the right not merely to confirm but to nominate some or all of the at-large members, just as senators now in fact nominate many of the presidential appointees who are subject to Senate confirmation, including judges, federal district attorneys, and many other officials who head regional and state offices of federal agencies.

If the at-large members were so selected, then, they might be mediocre party hacks, sure to vote as the party leaders dictated but otherwise committed to stay in the background, appearing in committee or on the floor only for the purpose of voting. But that at least would make for harmony within the Senate and the House. Any method of selection that in fact placed in the Congress experienced and eminent leaders would inevitably create tension and friction

13. The possibility of a president's appointing officials of the executive branch to the at-large seats, which would require repealing the constitutional prohibition against dual officeholding, is discussed in chapter 7.

within the legislative houses that would make those bodies even less manageable than they are now. The Senate and the House would be made up of two classes of members—those elected in the usual way, who shared a common outlook because they had survived the obstacle course of state or district electoral politics, and those who had achieved their status by one or another form of appointment. How committee and subcommittee chairmanships would be assigned, how seniority would be measured and recognized, how patronage and office space would be distributed—all these would be subjects of incessant antagonism pitting the two classes of legislators against each other.

There remains the question of what would happen after the first two years. Would the at-large members of the House be appointed for only the two-year terms that their regularly elected colleagues enjoy? Assuming they were elected in the first instance, would they run for reelection nationwide (or regionwide if originally chosen regionally)? Since they could not have competition from the opposing party (which would have no right to fill the at-large seats), would challenges by members of the same party be admitted? Would an election serve any real purpose in the absence of interparty rivalry? But if the seats were filled by appointment at midterm, the at-large members would lose any semblance of independence during the first two years. These complications suggest that whatever method of selection be used in the first instance, the at-large members be given four-year terms.

In the case of senators, six-year terms corresponding to those of the regularly elected members would appear inappropriate, for that would extend the term of a member appointed to give one president a Senate majority into the term of a president who might be of the opposing party. Four-year terms for at-large senators would pose no difficulty, except for setting them apart from their colleagues in one more way.

In no event, however, would appointments of any length made at the outset of a presidential term provide a safeguard against divided government after the midterm election, when the president's party normally suffers a setback. To provide that assurance would require the possibility of additional appointments at midterm. But such a provision would authorize the appointing authorities, in effect, to reverse the electorate's midterm decision—an idea so patently antidemocratic as to be surely unacceptable. In the absence of such a provision, would the at-large members remain in office the full four years even if the midterm election put them in the minority and so rendered them unable to serve the purpose for which they were elected or appointed? The midterm problem would be eliminated, of course, if the terms of House members were extended to four years, as discussed in chapter 5.

In the case of the House, a variant of the team-ticket scheme would avert the complications of at-large selection. The 435 House districts could be divided by the House into 87 groups of 5 districts each, with each party to nominate a candidate in the superdistrict who would run as a member of a curtailed team ticket with the presidential and vice presidential nominees. Where the superdistricts crossed state lines, the nominating process would have to be worked out through interstate agreements, which could be negotiated by the state party organizations within the terms of flexible authorizing legislation. Several objections to this proposition are apparent. In a closely divided election, the bonus seats would merely enlarge the House without giving the president's party assured control. The grouping of the House districts would create internal stresses within that body, with the opportunity of—and certainly the charges and countercharges related to—gerrymandering on a national scale. The organization of multistate nominating processes would encounter technical difficulties that, while not insoluble, would create conflict and dissatisfaction.

A corresponding process could be conceived for the Senate, with 25 bonus senators representing pairs of states or 10 chosen by 5-state regions. If the votes of individuals were weighted to give the states equal influence on the result, the requirement of equal state suffrage in the Senate would presumably be met. The bonus senators could be given four-year terms coincident with the president's. But the same objections that apply in the case of the House apply also to the Senate, plus the additional obstacle of devising a weighted voting scheme that would not strike everyone as illogical and undemocratic.

Effectiveness versus Feasibility

The problem of divided government, it is clear from this analysis, will not yield to ready resolution. Neither of the two schemes that would prove truly effective—the team ticket and the congressional bonus seats—could hope to garner significant support among incumbent members of Congress. And both would arouse strong public opposition as antidemocratic—the former by destroying the voter's freedom of choice and the latter by "packing" the Congress. The two more modest proposals—the requirement of a straight-ticket box on the ballot and the separation of presidential and congressional elections—would draw less hostility only because they gave less promise of making any real difference. To the extent that they appeared likely to succeed in their purpose—that is, to tie the fate of senators and representatives seeking reelection to that of their parties' presidential candidates—they would be fought by the same incumbent members, less vociferously perhaps but no less firmly, and would be likewise attacked as antidemocratic. The pervasive question of the feasibility of these and other approaches to consitutional reform is reexamined in chapter 9.

CHAPTER FIVE

Lengthening Terms of Office

Reviewing the outlook for the federal budget deficit in the spring of 1984, Budget Director David A. Stockman observed that "we only have one more chance: that is in the first six months of 1985." The reason? "In the cycle of the American political system, there is about a six or seven month window every four years when concentrated efforts need to be made to grapple with problems."[1]

The same prediction was offered four months later by Representative Trent Lott of Mississippi, the House Republican whip. Even assuming substantial Republican gains in the 1984 election and reestablishment of the conservative coalition of 1981, said Lott, "we'll have six months, and that's all."[2] Barber Conable of New York, about to retire as the ranking Republican member of the House Ways and Means Committee, was more generous. He thought "the window of opportunity" might last for the entire congressional session of 1985— but not beyond.[3] After his election in late 1984, Senate Majority Leader Robert J. Dole, Kansas Republican, made the same estimate.

This view that little can be accomplished except in the first year— or half year—of any presidential term has been something approaching accepted doctrine in the Washington political community for a long time. President Lyndon Johnson, an old Washington hand,

1. Speech to the United States Chamber of Commerce, Washington, D.C., *New York Times*, May 24, 1984.

2. *New York Times*, September 17, 1984.

3. *Congressional Quarterly Weekly Report*, vol. 42 (October 22, 1984), p. 2786; *Washington Post*, October 28, 1984.

justified his frenetic attempt to pass a controversial measure in 1965—the first year after his election—on the ground that "this was the only chance I would have." In 1966, he said, members of Congress would "all be thinking about their reelections. I'll have made mistakes, my polls will be down, and they'll be trying to put some distance between themselves and me." Johnson went on: "You've got to give it all you can, that first year. . . . You've got just one year when they treat you right, and before they start worrying about themselves. The third year, you lose votes. . . . The fourth year's all politics. . . . So you've got one year."[4]

Reviewing presidential policy leadership over two decades, Paul C. Light concluded that "speed is a key to presidential success in Congress" and "the first year provides the prime opportunity for legislative influence."[5] In the second year, as Johnson graphically observed, members of Congress are engrossed in staking out positions for the midterm election scheduled for that year's November, and serious issues tend to be deferred. And in that election the incumbent president's party is almost invariably dealt a setback. The president's ability to lead is impaired, and he—especially if he is running for reelection—and the members of Congress as well begin to feel the pressures of the coming presidential election. Difficult issues tend again to be postponed, political risks are sidestepped, and politicians await the new mandate from the people that the presidential election is expected to confer.

The first term of Ronald Reagan is a classic illustration of the one-year-in-four cycle. The president's achievements in reversing the unbroken trend of half a century toward the welfare state were massive and historic. But the breakthroughs came almost exclusively in 1981. After the initial year, the dismantling of governmental agencies and programs came to a halt. The president could lead the Congress no further in the direction he had set for it; indeed, the most significant movement in 1982 was a slight retreat, as the Congress forced the president to accept a tax increase he had not sought and initially resisted. In the midterm election, the Democrats added twenty-six seats to their House majority, and the government reverted

4. Harry McPherson, *A Political Education* (Little, Brown, 1972), p. 268. The measure that prompted Johnson's comments was one granting home rule to the District of Columbia.

5. *The President's Agenda: Domestic Policy Choice from Kennedy to Carter* (Johns Hopkins University Press, 1983), p. viii.

to its familiar stalemate. The president lacked votes to impose further sizable cuts in governmental spending and in taxes, but he had the power to block any significant initiatives by the Congress in the opposite direction. Meanwhile, the deficit, acknowledged on all sides to be dangerously high, remained out of control. The president and the Congress did manage to get together on a "down payment" reduction, but that was all; decisive action was deferred. And that measure and a bill to rescue the social security system (which had to be fashioned outside the regular legislative process by a special bipartisan commission and then ratified without alteration by the Congress) were the only major legislative achievements of Reagan's third and fourth years.[6] Not only was a concerted effort to cope with the deficit left for 1985; so too, for example, was action—likewise seen as a necessity by legislators and executive alike—to stem the flood of illegal immigrants across the Mexican border.

Three other periods comparable in legislative output to that of 1981 can be identified in this century, and all were at the outset of a presidential tenure. The first such period covered Woodrow Wilson's first two years, when the Federal Reserve Act, the Underwood Tariff Act, and other elements of Wilson's New Freedom were enacted. The second was the New Deal era, the longest of the four, lasting throughout Franklin Roosevelt's first term and into his second. The third spanned 1964, the first year of Lyndon Johnson's presidency, and 1965, the first year after his landslide reelection, when the Great Society was enacted. Of the four bursts of creative activity, including that of 1981, only the New Deal survived the first midterm election. Indeed, except for the years 1935–36 and the 1947–48 surge of bipartisan achievement in foreign affairs, it is hard to identify any major new governmental departures occurring after the midterm election in any administration in this century.

The setbacks to presidential leadership are numerous, and clearly

6. The National Commission on Social Security Reform, chaired by Alan Greenspan, was appointed by the president and the congressional leadership in December 1981 and reported its recommendations in January 1983. This method of overcoming policy deadlocks between the branches, used successfully on occasion in the past, was tried twice more during the Reagan first term. A commission on the MX missile, chaired by General Brent Scowcroft, made recommendations that were the basis of a bipartisan agreement that kept the missile program alive until after the 1984 election. But a commission on U.S. policy toward Central America and the Caribbean basin, headed by former Secretary of State Henry A. Kissinger, failed to establish its credibility and win support for its recommendations.

measurable. The election of 1906 cost the Republicans twenty-eight seats in the House and plunged Theodore Roosevelt's final two years into fruitless conflict with the Congress. William Howard Taft fared even worse; the Republicans lost ten Senate and fifty-seven House seats—and control of the House—in 1910. Woodrow Wilson's Democratic party lost fifty-nine House seats in 1914, and the spurt of progressive legislation known as New Freedom, for this and other reasons, came to an end; in Wilson's second midterm election, in 1918, the Republicans regained control of the House. Franklin Roosevelt's New Deal legislative achievements were effectively terminated by the Democrats' loss of seventy-one House and six Senate seats in 1938. Harry Truman's first midterm election, in 1946, gave the opposition Republicans control of both houses; in domestic matters, the only successful initiatives were those of the Congress, notably the Taft-Hartley Labor Relations Act, passed over President Truman's veto. Dwight Eisenhower's Republican party likewise lost control of the Congress in the midterm election of 1954, resulting in a stalemate on domestic legislation that lasted six full years—broken ultimately by the restoration of unified governmental control by the elections of 1960–64. After that, the Democrats' loss of forty-seven House and four Senate seats in 1966 brought a halt to Lyndon Johnson's Great Society—which had already lost its momentum in the previous year. And like Johnson before them and Reagan afterward, Gerald Ford and Jimmy Carter saw their parties' numbers in the Congress reduced at midterm. Of all the midterm elections in this century, only 1934 saw the president's party gain in relative strength in the House of Representatives.[7]

Yet if the "window of opportunity" is open for only six months to a year, at most, will a new president necessarily be ready with a program to thrust through that opening? Reagan was better prepared than most; he had a clear vision of the massive retrenchment of governmental operations that he desired to accomplish and he had a budget director in David Stockman who was extraordinarily well

7. Because Senate seats at stake in a midterm election may be disproportionately of the opposition party, the president's party has occasionally gained in the Senate while losing in the House. Six of the midterm elections in this century resulted in Senate gains for the president's party and one—that of 1982—in a standoff. Norman J. Ornstein and others, *Vital Statistics on Congress, 1982* (Washington: American Enterprise Institute, 1982), pp. 128–31, 41.

equipped—in background, in a zeal that matched the president's, and in ability to master budgetary detail—to translate the president's philosophy into specific fiscal decisions. The accomplishments of 1981 were legendary, yet before that year was over Stockman had drawn a vivid picture of the costs of haste:

> The thing was put together so fast that it probably should have been put together differently. . . . The defense numbers got out of control and we were doing that whole budget-cutting exercise so frenetically. In other words, you were juggling details, pushing people, and going from one session to another . . . and we were doing it so fast, we didn't know where we were ending up for sure. . . . In other words, we should have designed those pieces to be more compatible. But the pieces were moving on independent tracks. . . . And it didn't quite mesh.
>
> If you don't do this [social security reform] in 1981, this system is going to land on the rocks, because you won't do it in '82. . . . I was just racing against the clock. All the office things I knew ought to be done by way of groundwork, advance preparation, and so forth just fell by the way-side. . . .
>
> The reason we did it wrong—not wrong, but less than the optimum— was that we said, Hey, we have to get a program out fast. And when you decide to put a program of this breadth and depth out fast, you can only do so much. We were working in a twenty or twenty-five-day time frame, and we didn't think it all the way through. We didn't add up all the numbers. We didn't make all the thorough, comprehensive calculations about where we really needed to come out and how much to put on the plate the first time, and so forth.[8]

For a president who is less well prepared, more time is required to assemble a staff, analyze the issues, and define a program, and by the time the organizing and learning period is over, much of the first year may have passed. Even Richard Nixon, long experienced in Washington, failed to seize the opportunity. "The more we seemed to learn about the domestic system," a Nixon aide told Paul Light, "the less we could do. We had our best shot at the start of the term but didn't have the organization to cash in. By the time we had the organization, the opportunity was closed." Jimmy Carter had even more need for time to learn and organize; he was new to Washington and so were most of the members of his staff. So the first year was lost, and with it the chance for any notable achievement in the entire term. Light observes that in each presidency a "cycle of increasing

---

8. Quoted by William Greider, "The Education of David Stockman," *Atlantic Monthly* (December 1981), pp. 40, 43, 45, 54.

effectiveness" coincides with a "cycle of decreasing influence." "Regardless of the President's initial expertise and information," he writes, "the first year of the first term is characterized by a surprising level of confusion. As the President and the staff settle the chaos, the opportunities disappear. By the third and fourth years, the President and the staff are fully trained for domestic choice, but the agenda must be restricted."[9]

If the midterm election could be delayed, or even eliminated altogether, the "window of opportunity" would presumably be opened wider. A four-year term for House members, as proposed by President Johnson in 1966, would allow the representatives two full years before the next election loomed as close as it does now on the day each member is sworn in. If the window is now six to twelve months, it would become thirty to thirty-six months. A midterm election would still choose one-third of the Senate, however, unless senatorial terms were either shortened to four years or extended to eight, with one senator from each state elected in each presidential year. Since the latter would clearly be more acceptable to senators, whether or not more desirable on its merits, what has been called the four-eight-four plan (four years for president, eight for senators, four for representatives) represents one approach for those who believe a too-soon midterm election schedule contributes to the debilitation of the government.

Elimination of the midterm election would not in itself, of course, assure harmonious cooperation between the branches. If the House and half the Senate were chosen on the same date as the president, they could be as hostile to the executive as, say, the Democratic-controlled Congress chosen in 1972 was to Richard Nixon; their feud began long before the election and continued afterward, with a bitterness that only intensified until the day of the president's resignation nearly two years later. All that can be said is that the Congress elected in the presidential year is somewhat more compatible with the president, usually, than the one elected at the midterm. Eliminating the midterm ballot would simply prevent relations from getting worse, as they are now bound to do whenever the opposition party scores its normal gains. To assure that they are harmonious at the outset of a presidential term would require attention to the

9. Light, *The President's Agenda*, pp. 36–38.

problem of divided government, discussed in chapter 4, and other measures directed toward encouraging cohesion within a united party government, considered in chapter 7.

For those who pause at the prospect of waiting four full years before rendering an electoral verdict on the course of government, a three-year term for House members represents an intermediate solution. This would appear to depend, however, on extending the president's term to six years, in order that congressional elections would occur in each presidential election year. The six-year term for presidents is currently being advocated on its own merits, quite independent of any accompanying adjustment in House terms, usually with a proviso that the president would be ineligible for reelection. If the presidential term were so changed and the House term set at three years, a six-six-three pattern would result. This, it will be noted, would not eliminate the midterm election, only delay it. And after the midterm setback, the normal period of stalemate would last three years instead of two.

The Four-Eight-Four Plan

The case for short terms, for any elective office, rests on the contention that frequent elections keep officeholders "close to the people" and hence more responsive, more representative, more accountable. In a word, short terms are more democratic. Those who advocate longer tenure reply that too-frequent elections are a burden and a distraction, that an elected officer in fact needs some distance from the people in order that he or she may concentrate on the responsibilities of office and have the freedom to act courageously without fear of immediate retribution at the polls. This issue of responsiveness and accountability versus freedom to act is as old as representative government itself. Granted, elected officials must submit themselves periodically to the voters. But, in the case of the House of Representatives, how frequently is too frequently? How often is often enough?

If one looks to other governments, the judgment there is that every two years is unquestionably too frequent for legislators. A British parliament sits for five years, or until whatever earlier date the government of the day may designate. Nations of the British

Commonwealth have continued this tradition of long tenure. Some European countries elect for shorter terms, but three years appears to be the least; no other advanced country gives its legislature only a two-year life. These models must be considered with a caveat: constitutions are designed by politicians, usually by the legislators themselves, who can be expected to prefer long terms, and what is most convenient for the legislators themselves is not necessarily best for a nation. If it were, all terms should be for life.

Responsiveness versus Freedom to Act

A four-year term for the House of Representatives was not considered at the 1787 convention—a time when annual elections were the vogue—but in its first decision on the matter the framers did approve a three-year term. Too-frequent elections, contended Daniel of St. Thomas Jenifer of Maryland, rendered the people indifferent "and made the best men unwilling to engage in so precarious a service." James Madison seconded Jenifer's motion for a three-year term. One year, he observed, would be consumed in preparing for, and traveling, to the capital, and three years "will be necessary . . . for members to form any knowledge of the various interests of the States to which they do not belong." Elbridge Gerry of Massachusetts made the case for annual elections "as the only defence of the people against tyranny"; to him, a triennial House was as undemocratic as a hereditary executive.[10] After their initial defeat, Gerry and his allies continued to protest the three-year term as too great a departure from the current practice (only South Carolina elected legislators for more than a single year) and from the presumed expectations of the people who would have to approve the document that came out of Philadelphia. The obvious compromise was a two-year term. That was adopted on reconsideration, and the matter remained settled.[11]

Some of the arguments of 1787 in favor of the three-year term are now outdated. Madison's argument about time-consuming travel disappeared in the last century. And his contention that three years were necessary for a representative to gain sufficient knowledge for

10. Max Farrand, ed., *The Records of the Federal Convention of 1787*, 1937 rev. ed., 4 vols. (Yale University Press, 1966), vol. 1, pp. 214–15, June 15, from notes of James Madison.

11. Ibid., pp. 360–62, June 21, notes of Madison.

his job lost its pertinence when the early practice of rotating House seats among the counties making up a district, and thus assuring a House comprised largely of freshmen, was abandoned. In the 1985–86 House, only 39 of the 435 members—or 9 percent—were freshmen learning their jobs. More than 70 percent of the members had more than four years of experience in the House when the session opened.

The Jenifer argument that short terms discourage "the best men" from seeking legislative seats seems also to have scant validity today—even though Lyndon Johnson in 1966 reiterated Jenifer's position and repeated his very words. Frequent elections may be a nuisance, and an expensive one, but prospective candidates know that if they ever reach the House of Representatives their tenure is, in fact, likely to be long. In any event, while this judgment is necessarily subjective, the electorate in almost any district does not nowadays lack highly qualified and highly motivated candidates from whom to choose. Most of the House members and staff who discussed the issue at a 1966 meeting "either did not consider the two-year term harmful to recruitment or thought it played only a small role."[12] And the two-year term does not deter members from seeking to continue in the House, for few voluntarily retire after brief service. The eight members—fewer than 2 percent of the House—who had announced by early 1984 their intention to retire from the House, and from politics, at the end of that year (excluding those who were retiring to seek another elective office) averaged fifty-seven years of age and sixteen years of House service. A similar list for 1982 comprised twelve members, averaging sixty-two years in age and seventeen in service.[13] The average age for all twenty—sixty years—does not differ greatly from the typical retirement age of persons in other occupations who have early retirement options with generous pensions. The House average is under the average age of sixty-five at which half a dozen senators retired in those years, but the fact remains that most members end their House careers not voluntarily because of the strain and the cost of biennial elections but because of death, defeat, or the fear of it, or ambition for higher office. House members find their careers satisfying and attractive despite the two-year term.

12. Charles O. Jones, *Every Second Year: Congressional Behavior and the Two-Year Term* (Brookings Institution, 1967), p. 47.
13. *Congressional Quarterly Weekly Reports*, vol. 42 (February 25, 1984), p. 344, and vol. 40 (February 27, 1982), p. 352.

The language used by Elbridge Gerry in advocating the one-year term likewise does not ring true today, but if "defense . . . against tyranny" is translated into modern phraseology—defense against "lack of responsiveness," against "lack of sensitivity," against "arbitrariness"—his position still defines the central issue. Reviewing hearings and discussions that followed President Johnson's four-year-term proposal of 1966, Charles O. Jones summarized the position of the opponents this way: "The House of Representatives . . . was intended to be close to the people. It is the job of representatives to stay in touch with their constituents so as to reflect their needs, wants, and changes in attitude. It is highly unlikely that members will do this job if they are elected for longer terms. The only way to assure that they will stay close to the people is to force them to come home frequently so as to be reelected."[14]

But, to repeat, how frequent is frequent enough? Senators, blessed with six-year terms, commonly describe their attention to their constituents as cyclical. In the first two years, they stick to their business in Washington and go home only occasionally (the frequency influenced by the distance of their states from the capital); in the next two, they appear in their states more frequently, looking for occasions to make speeches and greet constituents; in the last two, they go home at every opportunity and campaign as assiduously as members of the House. The latter, if given a four-year term, would surely behave similarly. In their final two years, they would visit their districts as often, and follow the same campaign schedules, as they do now. It is the first two years that would be different; the representatives would stay in the capital more, spend less time in their districts.

But the argument that representatives should stay "close to the people" applies least forcefully to those first two years. During the election campaign, they have been constantly and intensely in touch with their constituents. They have listened to thousands of them. They have presented their platforms, explained and defended policy positions, and received approval. Their mandate to fulfill their campaign promises, whatever those may have been, is clear. Why should they have to worry during the next few months about whether their constituents have changed their minds? If they have, of course,

14. *Every Second Year,* p. 35.

the representatives are not likely to remain unaware of it. But beyond keeping informed, which they can scarcely avoid doing, there would seem to be every reason, from the standpoint of responsiveness, for the representatives to be kept free of campaign pressures—including the pressures of early and constant fund-raising—during their first two years so that they can devote themselves to responding through legislative activity to the promises they made to their constituents in the last campaign.

It is in the last two years that the real question arises. If the constituents by then have changed their "needs, wants, and attitude," the mandate of the last election will be obsolete and the member may be no longer representative. By that time, of course, the representative will be well aware of the next election and alert to every indication of opinion in the district. Will that suffice to assure responsiveness, or must the constituents have a chance to make their views clear by approving or relieving their representative and, in so doing, delivering a new mandate? That they may wish to do so is clearly shown by the midterm elections of 1946, 1954, 1958, 1966, 1974, and 1982, each of which revealed that a wide swing in public opinion had occurred since the preceding presidential election.

The difficulty is that the president elected two years earlier remained in office. Unless the president's term is shortened to two years—which no one has proposed—the midterm election cannot result in a clearly defined change in governmental direction anyway. All it can do is deadlock the government, or tighten an existing deadlock, as it did in each one of those cases. If a new direction cannot be decisively charted, would it not be wiser to permit the country to proceed along the old path a little longer, giving the governing party another couple of years to prove the merit of its policies? Sometimes, as in the case of Reaganomics, a policy that may look like a failure after only two years may appear much more successful after four. Especially when a new government introduces drastic changes, for the electorate to be obliged to render a verdict after only two years may be unfairly, and unwisely, premature. Stability and continuity of a government's policies are sacrificed, along with the opportunity for a sound test of the wisdom of those policies.

And, given the speed with which the midterm election bears down on governments, policies requiring political courage may not even be adopted. "I think that the four years would help you to be a braver congressman, and I think what you need is bravery," observed a representative during the 1966 discussion of President Johnson's proposal. Fair housing and situs picketing bills were cited as measures that were "too hot" for House members to be willing to consider that year with an election imminent. "If we had a four-year term," said another member, "I am as confident as I can be the situs picketing bill would have come to the floor and passed."[15] And those were not intricate bills. Complex measures that require an extended period for drafting or that require negotiation of differences among multiple conflicting interests are even harder to accommodate within the election cycle. The failure of the Congress to enact President Carter's energy legislation, for example, is often attributed to the haste with which the program was put together and sent to Capitol Hill without sufficient advance consultation with leading members of Congress or with interest groups. Carter hoped that an early start would enable Congress to act equally quickly, well before the midterm election. But on so complex and hotly controverted a matter, extensive negotiations were unavoidable; they dragged on into the election season, and the program was for the most part lost.

Immigration as a Case in Point

A more recent example of governmental inability to act has been immigration legislation—not the most important problem facing the nation but one that well illustrates the government's difficulty in concerting scattered powers. The need to check the flow into the country of illegal aliens, mainly Hispanic migrants who find their way across the Mexican border, is not seriously disputed; the Reagan administration has called for action and both the Senate and the House, responding to constituent concern, have passed separate immigration bills. Yet the three independent centers of power have been unable to reconcile their differences and enact any measure. Would a four-year rather than a two-year legislative cycle have made a difference?

A review of the chronology may be instructive. In 1981, Senate

15. Ibid., pp. 28–29. The situs picketing bill, which would have legalized "common site" picketing by labor unions at construction sites, was a key legislative objective of organized labor at the time, strongly opposed by the construction industry.

and House legislative sponsors—Senator Alan K. Simpson, Republican of Wyoming, and Representative Romano L. Mazzoli, Democrat of Kentucky—introduced their bills in March and President Reagan submitted his recommendations in July. Joint hearings did not begin until April of 1982—the midterm election year—but the Senate passed its bill on August 17. The House Judiciary Committee approved its version on September 22, but then the bill was referred to the Education and Labor Committee, where it languished until December 1, after the election. The Rules Committee cleared it for floor action on December 8 and consideration began December 16. But three hundred proposed floor amendments had been filed by opponents of the measure and, with Christmas approaching, the bill "died in the scramble to adjourn."[16] Even had the House taken final action, the bill would have drawn that epitaph, for there would have been no time to reconcile House and Senate differences.

Next year, both houses had to start over, but hearings were curtailed to a few days in each body and the Senate approved a measure on May 18. The House Judiciary Committee had its bill ready by July, but it was then referred to four other committees and amended by three of them. The chairman of the House Rules Committee summoned the four committee chairmen to a negotiating conference, but action was stalled into 1984 and the House did not pass its version until June 20 and then only by a five-vote margin. By that time, the issue had been plunged into the presidential campaign. Courting the Hispanic vote, Democratic presidential candidates had been vying with one another to see who could most enthusiastically endorse the Hispanic objections to the bill and, by the time of the Democratic convention in July, Walter Mondale and Geraldine Ferraro, the party's nominees, had both pledged to do everything in their power to kill the bill. Meanwhile, the White House had branded the House measure unacceptable.[17] After some weeks of speculation that the Senate and House conferees would not meet at all, they finally did convene, but broke up in a disagreement with President Reagan over an issue of the cost of the bill a week before the adjournment of the Congress in early October.

In both Congresses, final floor action was delayed until the second, election-year session, and the proceedings were dragged out until

16. *Congressional Quarterly Weekly Report*, vol. 41 (August 6, 1983), p. 1638.
17. Ibid., vol. 42 (July 28, 1984), pp. 1839–40.

insufficient time remained for action. Certainly, the coolness of House Speaker Thomas P. O'Neill, Jr., toward the Mazzoli bill, which reflected the bitter opposition of the House Democratic party's Hispanic bloc, contributed to the delays; he could have used various of his powers to expedite action had he chosen to do so. Yet, without the pressure of the midterm election and the December 1982 adjournment deadline, the atmosphere would have been calmer for sponsors and leaders to negotiate effective compromises. And whenever the bill came to the House floor the first time, whether in December 1982 or earlier or later, the opportunity to dispose of three hundred amendments would have existed—and, under those circumstances, no such number would have been offered, for their purpose was to obstruct the bill, not alter it. The conferees would then have had all of 1983 to reach agreement—a year that was devoted, under the existing cycle, to starting all over again and repeating the work of 1981. With luck, the issue could have been settled before election year politics enhanced the power of Hispanic organizations and other groups to get politicians committed to nonnegotiable stands in opposition to particular provisions of the bill.

All this is speculative, as is any guess as to how a particular problem would have been handled differently under a four-year rather than a two-year cycle. But a longer time horizon would surely work profound changes in attitude and behavior at both ends of Pennsylvania Avenue that would affect the outcome of many legislative issues. The wider "window of opportunity" would enable administrations to proceed in a more orderly fashion as well. Action that must be compressed into a single year could be extended over two or even three. Bills that now expire at the end of two years would survive for four. In some cases, the result might be simple procrastination. If there is no hurry, why exert oneself? Yet congressional committees would be under pressure from the president, from colleagues, and from constituents to get on with the work. The legislative traffic jam in both houses would be alleviated, making easier the orderly scheduling of members' time among the multiple committees and subcommittees on which they serve. And the number of required hearings would themselves be reduced. Now, any subject of legislative concern not disposed of by one Congress must be reopened by the next from the beginning, with wholly new hearings (although they are sometimes abbreviated).

In the discussion of the four-year term after the Johnson initiative of 1966, representatives who favored the longer tenure generally opposed election in the presidential year. Instead, they advocated staggered terms, with half the House elected each two years, or the election of the entire House at the presidential midterm. But neither of these schemes would eliminate the midterm election, lengthen the life of Congresses, or draw the executive and legislative branches closer together.[18] If those are the objectives to be sought in introducing the four-year term, only a term coincident with that of the president will serve the purpose; any variant would probably widen, not narrow, the distance between the branches.

The Eight-Year Senate Term

In the four-eight-four plan, senators would be divided into two classes rather than the present three, one member from each state chosen in each presidential election. With half rather than one-third of the Senate at stake in that election, a trend toward either party would have greater impact on the partisan makeup of the Senate, giving the president's party somewhat more seats and reducing to some degree the likelihood of divided government. Fifty rather than thirty-three or thirty-four senators would share the mandate of each election, and to that extent the Senate would be more rather than less responsive to the popular will at the outset of each presidential term.

The House term could be lengthened without altering the present six-year term for senators, resulting in a four-six-four plan. This would not satisfy those who would like to see the midterm election eliminated altogether, but retaining it only for one-third of one house would reduce its disruptive impact. The electorate of the thirty-odd states holding senatorial elections would be able to register a limited verdict on the course of government and by that means might bring about a modification of its policies without necessarily rendering it immobile. And if freedom from an immediate election can turn congressional cowards into heroes, two-thirds of the senators as well

18. The same applies to the variant, sponsored by Representative Richard J. Durbin, Democrat of Illinois, based on that state's constitution; members of the House would serve two four-year terms and one two-year term during the ten-year period following each reapportionment, with members divided into three classes for the purpose.

as all House members would be free to become statesmen— although those two-thirds would be under pressure from the one-third up for reelection.[19]

On the other hand, a four-six-four plan would surrender the advantages to be gained from extending the life of each Congress from two years to four. Theoretically, a four-year Congress could be introduced even without altering the terms of senators, by simply allowing one-third of the senators to take their seats at the midpoint. For a whole new class of freshman senators (usually from four to a dozen, but sometimes more) to enter at midpoint in each Congress would doubtless strike the Senate as awkward and incongruous— even though a few new senators and representatives selected to fill vacancies during each Congress now enter on their duties after the sessions have convened. To assure the benefits of a four-year Congress, the four-eight-four scheme appears more promising than four-six-four. Senators might be reluctant to initiate what would be attacked as a grab for power, but if the proposal were being pushed vigorously by House members and groups outside the government, their self-interest would clearly lie in acquiescing.[20]

Those who object that eight years is a term of excessive length for any elective office, even that of senator, have an arguable case. If the electorate makes a mistake in its initial choice, even six years is a long time to wait for the opportunity to rectify it. Yet an eight-year term would not alter the makeup of the Senate significantly. Few senators fail now to extend their service beyond six years. Of the thirty-two senators who left office during or at the close of the Ninety-sixth, Ninety-seventh, and Ninety-eighth Congresses (excluding one

19. A vote on May 1, 1985, vividly illustrates the effect of an imminent reelection contest on senatorial behavior. The issue was whether to support the agreement reached between President Reagan and the Republican Senate leadership to freeze cost-of-living increases for social security recipients as part of the deficit reduction effort. Republican senators not up for reelection in 1986 (including one whose term would expire who had announced his retirement) voted 24 to 8 to sustain the leadership. But Republicans facing reelection voted 11 to 9 against the party position. With only one Democratic senator supporting the freeze, the full cost-of-living increase was restored, 65 to 34.

20. One obstacle to the idea of a four-year House term has been the fear of senators, and governors as well, of challenges from representatives who could run against them in midterm without giving up their seats in the House. This objection has, however, been met in recent versions of four-year-term amendments by the inclusion of a simple proviso requiring House members to resign if they choose to run for any other office.

interim appointee who did not run for reelection), nine had served one term or less.[21] Five had served all or most of two terms; seven, three terms; eight, four terms; one, five terms; and two, six terms, for an average tenure of more than sixteen years. Clearly, the electorate is not appalled at the idea of long service for its senators; the number screened out after a single term, for whatever reason, is small, and extending the terms of those few senators by two years each would have a negligible effect on the makeup of that body.[22]

A four-four-four plan would, of course, remove this objection. While there has never been any significant adverse criticism of the present six-year term for senators, the voting public might well respond favorably to the notion of a shorter tenure. And if the entire Senate were chosen in each presidential year, the prospect for united party government would be enhanced. Yet the implacable enmity of a hundred senators is not to be lightly counted by advocates of reform—even if it were contemplated that the constitutional amendment would be initiated by a convention rather than by the Congress. Staggered Senate terms, moreover, are now embedded in tradition. Since extending the present six-year term would have so little effect on the actual makeup of the Senate, the four-eight-four plan appears to be the more promising of the alternatives.

21. The interim appointee was Nicholas F. Brady of New Jersey. One of the nine one-term senators, Paul Tsongas of Massachusetts, would have been favored to be reelected but retired because of illness. The three Congresses ran from January 1979 to January 1985.

22. The voters' behavior in reelecting their own senators contrasts sharply with their views, as told to poll takers, regarding congressional tenure in general. A 1982 Gallup poll showed 69 percent of a national sample favored a constitutional amendment that would limit the tenure of senators and representatives to twelve years, with only 25 percent opposed. Austin Ranney, "What Constitutional Changes Do Americans Want?" *This Constitution: A Bicentennial Chronicle* (Winter 1984), reprinted in Donald L. Robinson, ed., *Reforming American Government: The Bicentennial Papers of the Committee on the Constitutional System* (Westview Press, 1985), p. 284. The difference between the voters' professed views about tenure and their willingness to extend the service of their own representatives is even more striking in the case of House members, who are rarely removed by the voters after long service. In 1984, of 127 representatives who would have reached or exceeded the twelve-year limit at the end of that Congress, 114—or 90 percent—were returned for another term. Of the other 13, only 4 were defeated for reelection; the others retired voluntarily (although a few, of course, might have stepped aside in anticipation of defeat). This reflects the phenomenon commented on by Richard F. Fenno, Jr., and other students of the Congress that voters have a far higher opinion of their own senators and representatives than they do of the legislative bodies as a whole.

The Six-Six-Three Plan

Those who agree that two years is too short a time between national elections but worry that four years may be too long have an obvious compromise to consider—a three-year term, as initially approved by the Constitutional Convention. But unless presidential and Senate terms were changed also, House three-year terms would be incongruent with both. Half the time, the House election would occur in odd-numbered years. Only one House election in four would coincide with the presidential balloting. A national election would be held in three of every four years. Accordingly, the three-year term is not usually advocated except in conjunction with extending the president's term from four to six years and rescheduling senatorial elections so that half the Senate is chosen each three years. And since altering the president's term would be by far the most consequential of all these changes, the question of the three-year House term becomes subsidiary to the issue of making the presidency a six-year office.

The proposal for a six-year presidential term, in turn, usually incorporates a condition that the president be ineligible for reelection. And that provision is, indeed, the principal motivation for advocating any change at all—as it has been whenever the subject has arisen since Andrew Jackson's day. Much as in the Senate debate of 1913, six-year-term advocates consider that campaigning for reelection is a burdensome distraction for a president, and one that tends to reduce him from the level of statesman to that of politician and hence to corrupt the processes of government. But if reelection is to be forbidden, they argue, four years is too short a time for a president to accomplish the goals to which he committed himself in his original campaign.

The White House as Campaign Headquarters

Running for reelection does assuredly consume a president's time and energies, diverting him from attending to what may be pressing policy and administrative matters. "The public would be outraged if they knew, really knew, how much of the president's time is engaged in devising reelection strategy, which begins about 20 minutes after his election," writes Jack Valenti, who served as special assistant to President Lyndon Johnson. "Unhinge the president from the reelection process," Valenti urged, and thereby "increase his productive time in studying, learning, probing the economic riddles."[23] Johnson himself made the same point in his memoirs: "The old belief that a President can carry out the responsibilities of his office and at the same time undergo the rigors of campaigning is, in my opinion, no longer valid."[24]

And those rigors have been magnified in the two decades since Johnson campaigned. The proliferation of presidential primaries in the 1970s has opened the opportunity for serious challenge to an incumbent's renomination at his own party convention, as Gerald Ford learned in 1976 and Jimmy Carter in 1980. Campaigning for reelection now may have first call on a president's time not just for a few months but for more than a year. Ford, to fend off a challenge by Ronald Reagan, was a half-time campaigner during the entire period between the New Hampshire primary in early February and the close of the delegate-selection season in early June. In that eighteen-week period, he made nineteen trips to twenty-one states, spending a total of forty-two days on the campaign trail. Jimmy Carter made clear that, had it not been for the Iranian hostage crisis, he would have done likewise in his contest with Senator Edward Kennedy, but under the circumstances he chose a "Rose Garden strategy," confining himself to a single one-day campaign trip before the Democratic nominating convention. In both cases, of course, the incumbent presidents campaigned extensively during the traditional two-month electoral period that begins on Labor Day.

Even more important than the drain on presidential time and energy, in the view of those who would prohibit reelection, is the temptation for presidents and their subordinates to misuse the powers of their offices to win a second term. The Watergate burglary may be the ultimate illustration of governmental corruption to advance a president's ambition to remain in office, but surely every administration loses part of "its effectiveness for the public good" during the reelection campaign, as President Taft conceded after his own un-

23. " '6 Years in the White House?' You Bet," *Washington Post*, January 1, 1983.
24. Quoted by Foundation for the Study of Presidential and Congressional Terms, *Presidential and Congressional Term Limitation: The Issue That Stays Alive* (Washington: The Foundation, 1980), p.19.

successful effort to win a second term. Edward Tufte has shown that some presidents have sought to manipulate the economy to achieve a peak of prosperity in their reelection year, at the expense of more stable and desirable long-run policies.[25] And presidents try to manipulate public opinion as well. "During my administration," Richard Nixon wrote in his memoirs, "excessive euphoria built up around the 1972 Peking and Moscow summit meetings. I must assume a substantial part of the responsibility for this. It was an election year, and I wanted the political credit for what I believed were genuinely major advances toward a stable peace. . . . Euphoria is dangerous in dealing with the Soviets, or with any adversary."[26]

Finally, it is argued that presidents, like congressmen, would be more courageous if they did not have to worry about the effect of every action on their reelection prospects; they would rise above politics and make the "hard, tough, abrasive decisions"[27] that they now tend to put off. Cyrus Vance, secretary of state in the Carter administration, attested that in its last eighteen months the administration had lost "a great deal of the boldness and drive that we earlier had. . . . I am convinced that our handling of affairs in the Middle East, with regard to Salt II in 1979, and the situations that arose in the Caribbean would have been different had we not been in an electoral period."[28]

And when a president did act, his motives would be less likely to be questioned. As Jimmy Carter noted in endorsing the six-year term midway in his administration, "No matter what I do as President now, where I am really trying to ignore politics and stay away from any sort of campaign plans and so forth, a lot of the things I do are colored through the news media and in the minds of the American people by 'Is this a campaign ploy or is it genuinely done by an incumbent President in the best interest of the country without any sort of personal advantage involved?'" And because a president made ineligible for reelection would be given credit for acting in the national rather than his personal interest, his standing would be higher in the country and his influence in Congress would be greater.

25. *Political Control of the Economy* (Princeton University Press, 1978).
26. *The Real War* (Warner Books, 1980), pp. 266–67.
27. Valenti, "'6 Years in the White House?'"
28. Statement at meeting at the University Club, New York City, April 21, 1982.

"I think it would strengthen my hand with the Congress," Carter suggested.[29]

Lame Ducks, Influence, and Partisanship

The last point is the crucial one, for most hard and tough decisions require the acquiescence in some form of the Congress, and a courageous president will still be ineffective if the Congress is not willing to accept his leadership. And the traditional view has been the opposite of Carter's; it holds that once a president becomes a lame duck, ineligible for reelection—which a one-term president would be from the moment of his inauguration—he loses influence with the members of his own party in the Congress. "One of the strengths of the presidency is that the fellow will be around tomorrow," Lyn Nofziger, long a Reagan associate, told an interviewer. "And remember the threat of running again and being reelected is about the only party discipline we have in this country."[30] The same argument has been, and is, the core of the case against the Twenty-second Amendment, which makes every president a lame duck in his second term. "You have taken a man," said President Truman with reference to that amendment, "and put him in the hardest job in the world, and sent him out to fight our battles in a life and death struggle . . . with one hand tied behind his back."[31]

The opposing thesis, that a president ineligible for reelection would enjoy greater influence with the Congress, rests on the chain of reasoning that President Carter did not develop but, as suggested above, has been set forth by other proponents of the six-year term. Presidents who did not have to worry about reelection would behave differently from those who did, the reasoning goes. They would be less partisan. They would rise above the political battle. Set free from concern about their own political futures, they would think wholly of the welfare of the nation. Hence their motives would be respected.

29. "Interview with United Press International Advisory Board, April 27, 1979," *Public Papers of the Presidents: Jimmy Carter, 1979* (Government Printing Office, 1980), vol. 1, pp. 738, 739.

30. Ken Bode, "Reagan Runs Ahead," *New Republic* (February 18, 1978), p. 14; quoted in Foundation, *Term Limitation*, p. 17.

31. Paul B. Davis, "The Results and Implications of the Enactment of the 22nd Amendment," *Presidential Studies Quarterly*, vol. 9 (Summer 1979), p. 290.

They would gain stature and influence in the country at large, and that would be reflected in the Congress.

The question becomes, then, how much would presidential behavior really change? One test can be found in the record of two-term presidents who, in their second terms, were in fact lame ducks, either because (in the cases of Eisenhower and Nixon) the Twenty-second Amendment was in effect or, before its adoption, they had renounced any ambition to extend their service.

No two-term president, in this century at least, passes the test of rising above partisan political activity in his second term. Senator Borah, in the 1913 debate, contended that Theodore Roosevelt had exerted as much effort to win the nomination for Taft in 1908 as he had shown in seeking his own renomination four years later. Woodrow Wilson in the midterm election of his second term campaigned vigorously for a Democratic Congress. In 1952, President Truman spent twenty-six days of "whistle stop" campaigning in twenty-seven states to win the election of Adlai E. Stevenson as his Democratic successor—and in doing so to vindicate his own record. This comes close to the thirty-five days spent in campaigning for his own return to the White House in September and October of 1948 (although Truman had spent another fifteen campaign days in sixteen states in June of that year). Dwight Eisenhower, the only president until Reagan to be made ineligible for reelection by the Twenty-second Amendment, spent nine campaign days on behalf of Richard Nixon as his successor in 1960, which again comes close to the twelve days he spent on political tour to win his second term four years before. In Richard Nixon's case, reelection did nothing to dampen his intense partisan ardor. He entered his second term determined to confront and master the Democratic Congress; he "threw down the gauntlet" to them, as he said in his memoirs. Freed of concern about ever having to campaign again, he appeared to consider himself relieved of the need to be conciliatory. But when rising above politics leads to departing from the norms of political behavior in interinstitutional relationships, it does not make for a successful presidency.

Among the two-term presidents, Nixon and Truman were unusually intense partisans. But surely Eisenhower would not be so characterized. Yet even a president with nonpartisan inclinations cannot attain his office without fighting the partisan battle as nominee of one political party and opponent of the other. And in that fight he depends on his party for support, develops loyalty and emotional attachment to it, and acquires obligations to it that he cannot lightly cast aside. Moreover, if his party is repudiated at the polls when his term ends, he will see it as a personal repudiation; by the same token, its victory becomes his. Any president elected for a single six-year term, therefore, would be far from indifferent to the interests of his party and of its candidate for election as his successor. Assuming that he retained his public popularity, he would speak at party rallies, as he does now, and would be photographed with his party's candidates for Congress. He would insist that the national chairman of his party be a person acceptable to him. And he would, probably, take steps to make sure that the party's candidate for the next six-year term would be someone who would carry on the policies he had initiated. In short, he would not become a political neuter. That being the case, he would still face the temptation to use the powers of government for partisan advantage. And he would still be under public suspicion that his actions were politically motivated—perhaps not to the same degree that President Carter said his motives were suspected, but certainly to some degree.[32] And what is true of presidents is true of their political appointees; those who are not yet ready to retire from public life will be using their influence on behalf of their party's nominee, as President Taft acknowledged his own appointees did. Before the nominating convention, some will be backing various candidates. Their zeal may be somewhat less than if their president were himself running, but it will still exist. The difference in impact on the government will be of degree, not of kind.

Whether or not President Eisenhower behaved differently in his second term, there is little in his experience to support the Carter view that a president ineligible for reelection has a stronger hand with the Congress. Eisenhower, it is true, had to contend in his last six years with a Congress controlled by the opposition Democratic party, but divided government, as noted earlier, has become virtually

32. President Carter suggested that "there could be some appropriate constitutional prohibitions against trying to be a kingmaker and being involved in choosing one's own successor." Such a prohibition applies, he said, in Venezuela. "Interview, April 27, 1979," p. 739. But one may question both the theoretical wisdom of trying to remove a political party's chosen leader from participation in the party's affairs and the practical enforceability of any such provision.

the normal state of affairs in Washington. In any case, Eisenhower and the Congress were deadlocked on domestic policy issues throughout that six-year period. Relations were, if anything, worse in the second term. The Congress rejected virtually every presidential initiative as too timid and ineffective on domestic matters and he in turn vetoed a long series of Democratic bills as too far-reaching and too expensive. In 1959 he disapproved two housing bills, two public works appropriations bills, and a farm bill, and in 1960 bills to assist economically depressed areas, to raise federal pay, and to expand construction of sewage treatment plants, all on the spending issue.[33] In foreign and military affairs, the Democrats generally supported the president in his second term, but they had done so in his first term also. The tabulation by *Congressional Quarterly* of Democratic congressional votes cast for or against Eisenhower's position on individual measures shows no significant change as between the two terms. In the four Congresses, Eisenhower was supported by 45, 50, 51, and 41 percent of the Democratic votes, with 40, 37, 35, and 44 percent in opposition.[34]

As for the effect of President Eisenhower's second-term lame-duck status on his own party, the *Congressional Quarterly* figures show some deterioration of support among congressional Republicans. Republicans in the two houses voted with the president four times as often as they opposed him in his first Congress, 72 percent to 18 percent. In the following Congress, the ratio fell to 67 to 22 percent, or about three-to-one. But in his second term, Eisenhower fared measurably worse than in his first. The ratios for both Congresses are only a little better than two-to-one, at 61 to 27 percent and 66 to 30 percent, respectively.[35] These presidential-support "box scores" are far from a definitive measure of presidential influence; they do not attempt to distinguish between crucial votes on issues where presidential interest was intense and votes on questions of little importance where the president had announced a position but exerted

33. James L. Sundquist, *Politics and Policy: The Eisenhower, Kennedy, and Johnson Years* (Brookings Institution, 1968), p. 428.

34. *Congressional Quarterly Almanac, 1955*, p. 66; *1956*, p. 107; *1958*, p. 101; *1960*, p. 107. The sharp decline in Democratic support in the final Congress, that of 1959–60, is probably less a reflection of a stiffening of partisan attitudes than the change in composition of the Democratic party in the Congress with the increase in its ranks of 15 senators and 49 representatives following the election of 1958.

35. Ibid.

no pressure. But whatever they are worth, the figures lend more support to the Truman-Nofziger contention that a president ineligible for reelection loses influence in the Congress than to the opposing view that he gains.

It remains dubious, then, that a single six-year term would significantly alter presidential behavior and, in so doing, enhance presidential prestige and influence. But to gain those speculative benefits, the people would have to give up three rights they now have—first, to retain a successful president for eight years instead of six; second, to retire a failed president after four; third, to force a president seeking reelection to respond to the mood and policy views of the electorate.

Fifteen of the twenty-nine presidents who sought a second term after serving a complete or near-complete first term were adjudged successful and returned to office—Washington, Jefferson, Madison, Monroe, Jackson, Lincoln, Grant, McKinley, Theodore Roosevelt, Wilson, Franklin Roosevelt (for third and fourth terms also), Truman, Eisenhower, Nixon, and Reagan. Except for Lincoln, McKinley, and Nixon (and predictably Reagan), all served for more than six years. In some of those cases, what the president had to offer was given fully in his first six years, and two more added little luster to his name, while in others, the president's leadership was undiminished in the final years of the second term. Not more than one or two of the eleven full second terms, however, could be fairly called a failure, and some of the presidents were so successful—as was eventually demonstrated with Franklin Roosevelt—that they could have had a third term for the asking. On the other hand, of the fourteen presidents who sought reelection and were rejected, whether by their own party or by the country at large—John Adams, John Quincy Adams, Van Buren, Tyler, Fillmore, Pierce, Andrew Johnson, Arthur, Cleveland (after his first term), Benjamin Harrison, Taft, Hoover, Ford, and Carter—how many would have been effective leaders if their terms had continued for two more years? Some, like Andrew Johnson and Hoover, had been discredited and reduced to futility long before their single terms had ended, and had even aroused such hatred that two more years of inept leadership might have brought violence, with its threat to every institution. In many cases, the country could hardly wait to admit its mistake and send packing the president it had chosen at the last election. In the absence of any mechanism for removing presidents who have failed but remain innocent of any "high crimes and misdemeanors" that justify impeachment (a subject discussed in chapter 6), a four-year term presents more than sufficient risk. Six years for an incompetent, erratic, or listless president would have been disastrous on at least several past occasions—and could be again.

Moreover, a president facing a reelection contest is forced to remain in touch with, and be responsive to, the people. That, of course, is precisely what advocates of the single six-year term are seeking to avoid. They seek to insulate the president from popular pressure so that he may act with courage. Certainly the Supreme Court, heading the branch of government that is wholly insulated, has been able to enunciate policies—school integration, for example—that the executive and legislative branches could not muster the courage to adopt. Cyrus Vance, Jack Valenti, and others are surely right in contending that a president protected from popular reprisal would be able to act more courageously in the face of either adverse public opinion or the hostility of politically influential pressure groups.

But a president protected from public opinion is also a president unrestrained by it. If he is free to act in the national interest, as six-year-term proponents insist, that national interest will be as he defines it. And will his definition be superior to the one that is hammered out, under the current system, in the heat of a reelection contest? It is significant that Richard Nixon did not throw down the gauntlet to the Washington establishment until his second term, when he could disregard the hostility that he might—and, as it turned out, did—arouse. In his case, lack of restraint led to disgrace and resignation, but another president might pursue policies equally unwise and, with greater luck, survive a full term of office unrestrained in those areas of national policy where the Congress lacked the means to take control.

President Reagan's 1984 campaign for reelection illustrates the power of the voters both to moderate and to stiffen an incumbent's policy positions during the season when he pleads for their support. In response to public opinion polls showing that many, or even most, voters considered him too belligerent toward the Soviet Union, he dropped the harsh and condemnatory language from his vocabulary and adopted a tone of conciliation. Goaded by the charge that he was the first president since World War II not to meet with the Soviet leadership, he met with the Soviet foreign minister and reopened communication on disarmament and arms control. Under pressure from the nation's elderly, he was pushed into a categorical commitment not to propose reducing social security benefits. Seeking to exploit the antipathy of most voters to increased taxes, he pledged never to raise taxes except as a last resort, which would prevent any such action for at least a substantial period after his second inauguration. Perhaps with an eye to Hispanic voters, he participated in killing the bill to control illegal immigration. Entering his second term, the president held to his reelection campaign positions and cited his pledges in opposing tax increases and social security benefit cuts.

In these five cases, each person will have his own judgment as to whether the shift in President Reagan's position reflected the national interest. Democratic theory holds that, ultimately, the people must control and direct the government; as Gouverneur Morris said in 1787, the hope of reelection is "the great motive to good behavior." But democratic theory also finds room for institutions like the Supreme Court, which are removed wholly from the electoral process. A judgment on whether popular restraint on presidents through the requirement that they face the electorate after four years is good or bad depends on one's view as to where lie the greater promise and the greater risk—in submitting the president to public pressure through the reelection process, in the interest of presidential responsiveness to the mood of the electorate as a whole and to organized interests within the polity, or in insulating the president from such pressure, in the interest of presidential courage and decisiveness.

Finally, while the life of the Congress under a six-six-three plan would be extended from two years to three, thus delaying the midterm election and widening the "window of opportunity" at the outset of a presidential term, whenever the midterm election rebuffed the president and deadlocked the government—as history shows it usually does—the deadlock would last for three years instead of two unless some new method of breaking deadlocks were adopted. That question is reserved for chapter 6.

Repeal of the Twenty-second Amendment

The Twenty-second Amendment has made no difference, so far, in determining who actually occupies the White House. The only president so far denied a possible third term by the amendment has been Dwight Eisenhower, and surely he, with his history of serious illnesses and his belief that no man over seventy should serve as president (he reached that age just before his second term expired), would never have considered another race. Most other presidents would also voluntarily retire after eight years in the absence of the amendment, if the past can be taken as a guide. Only Franklin Roosevelt, of the ten presidents who completed a second term before the amendment took effect, even considered seeking a third consecutive term. The importance of the amendment is not its bearing on who occupies the White House, but its effect on the behavior of politicians when they know for certain that any president's second term must be his last. Harry Truman expressed one view with characteristic simplicity: with a two-term limit, the president would enter battle in his second term with one hand tied behind his back. The evidence from the Eisenhower years suggests that the president is not as critically handicapped as Truman's language portended, but that he does lose influence over the Congress to some degree. The president's party in both the executive and legislative branches becomes less cohesive, as candidates for president emerge and contest for power. If that is the case, repeal of the Twenty-second Amendment would tend to strengthen the president as party leader and hence improve cooperation between the executive and the members of his party in the Congress.

Even a lame-duck president, as Eisenhower himself pointed out, still possesses great power, and strong and active presidents have managed to maintain their influence as party leader to the end—as Theodore Roosevelt, for one, demonstrated in mobilizing the GOP in support of William Howard Taft as his successor. So while logic might suggest that the Twenty-second Amendment was unwise, both in denying the people a free choice of leaders, particularly in a time of crisis, and in depriving the presidency of one element of its power, its adoption does not appear to have had major consequences, nor is it likely to. Meanwhile, the existence of the amendment does provide reassurance to those who still worry now, as many did in the 1940s when the amendment was adopted, that the presidency has grown so strong that an unscrupulous leader could sustain himself in office indefinitely through the abuse of power. Now that one president has been forced to resign his office as the consequence of abuse, that concern is less credible today than forty years ago, but the presence of the amendment may contribute in some small measure to public confidence in the presidential office and hence in the constitutional system as a whole.

Eliminating the Midterm Election

Those who advocate a single six-year presidential term make a convincing case that, if that reform were adopted, presidents would suffer less distraction and some—though not necessarily all—would "rise above politics" and display more courageous leadership. But leadership to be effective depends on effective followership, and the two-year political time horizon for all members of the House of Representatives and one-third of the Senate would still leave the legislative branch in a state of perpetual distraction; and if a president is less than courageous with a four-year term, what can be expected of representatives who must face the voters every second year? With a two-year life, moreover, each Congress adjourns in a crush of hastily drawn and ill-considered legislation and leaves behind a mass of unfinished business. True, the midterm election does give the voters an opportunity "to send Washington a message" whenever they are discontent with the performance of their government, but they can do that only by strengthening the opposition party and driving the government as a whole toward, or deeper into, deadlock.

The six-year presidential term, however it might improve presidential behavior, would not improve to a corresponding degree the workings of the *whole* government because it would alter only one element of that whole. It would set back the date of only one election—the presidential—without recognizing that for all of the elements of the government the midterm election is the one that comes too soon. While the six-six-three plan delays the midterm test by one year—which is an improvement—it compensates for that gain by extending to three years the period of deadlock that commonly follows each midterm election.

In contrast, either the four-four-four or the four-eight-four plan confronts the problem of the midterm election and extends the time horizon of all three elements of the governmental structure. Both provide more time for deliberation, and more time for courage, not just to the president but to representatives and senators as well. As to the choice between the two, the difference in the practical effect is so slight that the question can be decided on the basis of feasibility. By that criterion, four-eight-four would appear to hold the greater promise.

Neither, of course, would resolve the problem of divided government discussed in chapter 4, but either would help. Despite the rise of ticket-splitting, presidential coattails still have some effect. The party of the winning presidential candidate normally gains strength in the Congress, as the 1980 Republican capture of the Senate so dramatically demonstrated. The probability of united government would be enhanced to some degree with a four-year House term (which, of course, lessens its appeal to incumbent congressmen). And the incentive to intraparty cohesion would last for the full four years, as members of Congress knew that in the next election, as in the one just past, they would be running not on their own but as a part of their party's presidential ticket. The force of this incentive would be even stronger, during a president's second term, if the Twenty-second Amendment were repealed.

In the event, however, that the presidential election produced an ineffective government—because of divided government, failure of presidential leadership, or whatever reason—the opportunity that now exists for the voters to change at least a part of the government after two years would be lost. Not that the midterm election now provides a cure for ineffective government; as noted earlier, reconstituting just one branch of such a government is liable only to make matters worse. While a four-eight-four or a four-four-four proposal tends to draw attention to the question of what the country can do about a failed government, the question is no less pertinent if official terms remain unchanged. That is the subject of the next chapter.

CHAPTER SIX

Reconstituting a Failed Government

All governments descend into periods of ineffectiveness, when for any of a wide range of causes leadership fails, public confidence is lost, and conflicts within the government deepen and remain unresolved. When this occurs, parliamentary systems possess a safeguard; their governments can be dissolved at any time and new elections can then install new leaders with a fresh mandate from the people. Or weak leaders can be replaced with stronger ones even in the absence of new elections, without provoking a constitutional crisis—as Neville Chamberlain was forced to give way to Winston Churchill following British defeats early in World War II.

The United States, in contrast, is in bondage to the calendar. The nation's leader is elected for four years, and no matter what his failures the office is his as a kind of property right until his term's scheduled expiration—with two exceptions. He may be removed under the impeachment clause of the Constitution if he is convicted of "treason, bribery, or other high crimes and misdemeanors." He may also be relieved of his duties under the Twenty-fifth Amendment, adopted in 1967, if the vice president and a majority of the cabinet declare him to be unable to perform the functions of his office and, in the event the president disputes that finding, two-thirds of both houses of Congress confirm his incapacity.

Eight of the nation's thirty-nine presidents have died in office, but only one has failed for any other reason to complete his term— Richard Nixon. But Nixon's case, perhaps more than any other, illustrates the hazards of the American system. When he resigned after serving nineteen months of his second term, the universal reaction was one of relief that "the system worked," rescuing the country from the final twenty-nine months of a presidency that had hopelessly collapsed. Yet a review of the events of 1973–74 suggests that the outcome was fortuitous.

For more than a year, from the time that the Watergate scandal began to unfold in 1973 until Nixon's resignation in August 1974, the country was in the throes of a constitutional crisis. Most Americans agreed that the president had flagrantly abused his powers, had presided over and tolerated, if not connived in, outrageous and widespread crime. Yet there was a grave question as to whether anything could be done about it, under the Constitution. Nixon and his supporters contended that for a president to be "hounded" out of office would establish a precedent that would damage the presidency and destabilize the constitutional system. His opponents had only one recourse under the Constitution—impeachment—and removal would require that the president be convicted of criminal activity. Some argued that the "high crimes and misdemeanors" clause was intended to have a broader meaning, but because conviction and removal would require the assent of two-thirds of the Senate, the interpretation of the clause in any impeachment trial could not ultimately be any broader than any minority of thirty-four of the one hundred senators would permit—and Nixon had more than that number of solid backers. Luckily, on August 5, one more tape was discovered, which contained incontrovertible evidence of the personal, indictable crime—obstruction of justice. Nixon's support vanished, and four days later he resigned.

But the episode laid bare the weaknesses in the impeachment process, and the need to consider alternative means for removing unfit presidents. What would have happened if the final tape had never been discovered, or if the crime had not been recorded on tape at all, or if the tape had been destroyed? Surely, no future president will preserve the evidence of his own malfeasance. In any of those events, the House Judiciary Committee would have gone ahead with its impeachment and the country would have been embroiled in the bitterest of debates about whether a president should be convicted and deposed on circumstantial evidence alone. Because crimes were committed by the president's closest associates, he must have "approved, condoned, and acquiesced in" them, the committee charged, but would sixty-seven senators ever agree to that?[1] If they did not, a discredited president would have every right to remain in office unable to lead and govern the country. And in any case, the whole world would witness the United States government immobilized while its president sat figuratively in the dock being tried as a common criminal in the glare of television cameras. No one knew whether the trial would last three months, or six, or even longer. And what of other crises that might well up for attention in the meantime?

Criminal activity is only one circumstance that can render a president unable to lead and govern. Andrew Johnson enraged the country not by flirting with common crime but by pursuing unpopular policies and then defying an act of Congress designed to restrain him by what he contended were unconstitutional means. A House majority impeached him and the Senate failed to convict by only a single vote. While the trial was in progress the government was incapacitated, and long before it was over, Johnson's presidency was destroyed. But a century ago the country could survive without a government better than it could today. Moreover, the trial occurred only a few months before the 1868 election, when a new executive reflecting the views of the Congress and the country would be chosen.

Other longer periods of governmental ineffectiveness can be identified, if one uses as the criterion the public judgment at the time. The clearest recent case is the three years that elapsed between the stock market crash of 1929 that precipitated the Great Depression and the inauguration of Franklin Roosevelt in 1933. Herbert Hoover clearly failed to give the country the leadership it was demanding, as evidenced by the Democratic gains in the midterm election of 1930 and even more emphatically by Hoover's personal repudiation in 1932. To cite a case is to invite argument as to whether the public judgment was correct. After all, the people delivered Harry Truman a similar rebuke in the midterm election of 1946 but changed their mind and gave him a new term two years later. And the Democratic tide in the 1982 election suggests that the voters at midterm had adjudged Ronald Reagan's policies a failure—a judgment which, if made, was clearly reversed in 1984. But however one may feel about a particular case, whether that of Hoover or someone else, it can hardly be disputed that a president *can* fail, that he can early in his

1. Article I, Obstruction of Justice, adopted by House Judiciary Committee, July 27, 1974, reprinted in *Congressional Quarterly Almanac, 1974*, p. 884.

term be shown up as inadequate to lead the country and fulfill the heavy responsibilities of his office. That is a hazard of human nature that applies to the occupant of any job, exacerbated in the case of the presidency by the almost superhuman demands of the office and the anything-can-happen process by which those who hold it are originally selected.

In other large organizations, no matter how carefully their chief executives are chosen, it is taken for granted that the power of removal in case of failure must exist. A corporate board of directors may remove its chief executive officer, a school board its superintendent, a university board of trustees its president, a city council its city manager, and so on, and in the case of private organizations there is no necessity even to show cause. A parliament may similarly remove its prime minister, at any time and for any reason. The United States government, and the state and city governments modeled after it, are virtually unique among all the world's organizations in possessing no true safeguard against executive failure.

One can identify five categories of circumstances in which a president would lose his capacity to lead the country yet could not be removed from office under the Constitution.

First, a pattern of criminal conduct that clearly stems from the president's office yet cannot be traced to the president personally. In other words, the president covers his tracks—which Nixon so conspicuously failed to do.

Second, a pattern of abuse of power for personal or partisan ends that is corruptive yet not specifically in violation of any criminal statute. A president could be exposed and even impeached, but if one-third plus one of the Senate insisted that the impeachment clause required criminal culpability he would be sustained in office.

Third, the mental or emotional breakdown of a president that is not clear and provable enough to be grounds for declaring him disabled under the Twenty-fifth Amendment. Under its terms, for a president to be relieved of his duties against his will requires a kind of palace coup; the initiative must be taken by the vice president, invariably a presidential loyalist nowadays, and a majority of the cabinet, all presidential appointees. The presidency is the country's very symbol of solidity and certitude, so one shrinks from even admitting the possibility that a president might gradually, or suddenly, break under the strains of office and become erratic or impulsive in his judgments, or lethargic and indecisive, or suffer delusions of grandeur or persecution or the early stages of senility. But it *could* happen. It has happened to prime ministers of other countries, to governors, to members of the Congress, to cabinet officers, under far less severe stress than that to which a president is subjected almost every day.

Fourth, a general and irremediable loss of public confidence in the president, for reasons other than any of the above, as was the case with Herbert Hoover.

Fifth, a systemic deadlock between the executive and legislative branches so severe as to cripple the capacity of the government to cope with crisis. This could happen to a healthy, competent, and assertive president, but one unable to lead a Congress controlled by an opposition that was solidly organized and equally determined. The Andrew Johnson case is the clearest illustration of executive-legislative deadlock, but the later years of Richard Nixon's administration and all of Gerald Ford's demonstrated that the president and the Congress can be so hopelessly at odds on both foreign and domestic policy that the country can have no coherent policy at all. In any period of a government divided between the parties, the government can come perilously close to that condition.

Whatever the desirability of an easier method of removing failed presidents elected for four-year terms, the issue becomes considerably sharper if extending the president's term to six years is contemplated. The country can survive short periods of ineffective government, but with a six-year presidency a failed leader could remain in office for as long as four to five years after his failure was established. That would be more than inconvenient. It could well be intolerable.

Similarly, if congressional terms are lengthened in such a way that the present midterm election is eliminated, the question of an additional safeguard against prolonged deadlock gains pertinence. The present midterm election has not in fact proved to be a serviceable mechanism for resolving deadlocks; it tends instead to intensify conflict and reinforce any executive-legislative impasses, by increasing the strength in the Congress of the party in opposition to the president. But it at least gives the electorate an opportunity to express a judgment about the course of government and, if it chooses, deliver a forceful mandate. A four-eight-four plan, as discussed in chapter 5, would protect the Congress as well as the president from public retaliation for a full four years. To free elected officials from the pressure of a

certain new election after only two years of a new presidential term
has the potential benefits outlined in the earlier discussion, but it
increases the danger that a failed government could remain in place
too long.

Special Elections as the Remedy

Were governmental failure always the consequence of presidential
sins of commission or omission—the first four of the five sets of
circumstances listed above—the remedy could be sought in some
additional method of removing the chief executive from office.

The simplest approach would be to broaden the impeachment
clause of the Constitution by adding to "treason, bribery, or other
high crimes and misdemeanors"some broad term such as *maladministration* (the word suggested by Mason and Gerry at the convention).
At first glance, such a change might appear to place the president
too much at the mercy of the Congress, subjecting him to removal
for petty, partisan, even whimsical reasons. But the barriers to
improper use of a broadened impeachment power would remain
formidable. Since two-thirds of the Senate would have to concur in
the removal action, it could not be taken without some degree of
bipartisan support. The opposition party would always lack the votes
to act alone; it has never held as many as two-thirds of Senate seats
in the modern era of two-party competition.

Even in the face of certain defeat in the Senate, a House controlled
by the opposition would have the power to impeach a president as
a partisan maneuver to embarrass him, because only a majority vote
is required there (a requirement that could, of course, be raised). But
the very gravity of the action would hold the legislators back; one
recalls the agitated faces and agonized words of the House Judiciary
Committee members in 1974 as they were making their fateful decision
to impeach Richard Nixon, fearful that they might be toppling not
just an individual president but the presidency itself. In a parliamentary country, a vote of "no confidence" only changes the government-
of-the-day while the chief of state—a monarch or a figurehead
president—remains as the symbol of stability. In this country, removing the president deposes the chief of state himself, even though
the vice president succeeds immediately to that office. Legislators

would also be deterred by the risk of the voters' retribution if they were perceived to be acting precipitately or from petty or partisan motives. In a parliamentary government, again, the prime minister is selected by the legislators rather than directly by the people, so if they remove that officer they are only changing their own minds. But for an American Congress to remove the president would be to reverse the decision of the people themselves, as expressed in the last election. Presumably, the voters would not look kindly on legislators who acted hastily, without compelling reasons, or out of crass partisanship, to upset the judgment of the electorate. One may guess that they would do so only under overwhelming and sustained public pressure. In this century, probably only Nixon, and perhaps Hoover, aroused mass hostility on the scale necessary to provoke a reluctant Congress, had it possessed an unrestrained removal power.

Whether or not a broadened impeachment power might be over-used, however, it would be an undesirable mechanism for other reasons. It would remain a judicial process, with the chief justice of the Supreme Court presiding, members of the House as prosecutors, and the president on public trial. Whether that process is any longer appropriate even when the grounds for removal are limited to crime may be questioned. One may ponder what would happen to the position of the United States in world opinion if the president were subject to a long proceeding, reported breathlessly each day to the global audience through its television news, even if like Andrew Johnson he were ultimately acquitted. One may worry, too, about the consequences of immobilizing the government for the duration of the ordeal. A reevaluation of the suitability of the existing im-peachment process in the modern age is needed in any case. But if the grounds for removal were extended to cover maladministration or any other of the many possible forms that presidential failure may take, the impeachment process is clearly inappropriate, for the decision becomes a matter for political judgment rather than judicial proof. Finally, were the president to be removed through trial and conviction for some form of noncriminal conduct or incapacity, the vice president might not be a suitable successor. He might be associated with the acts and policies that destroyed congressional and public confidence in the president, and so be equally discredited.

For all these reasons, a simple system for calling a new presidential election would appear to be preferable to modification of the impeachment process. The verdict on removal of the president could then be left to the people, assuming that the president sought vindication and could win the nomination of his party, and whether he or his opponent won, the new president would have a fresh mandate from the country.

The Bingham, Green, and Reuss resolutions introduced during the Watergate crisis (and discussed in chapter 3) all provided for new elections. All placed the initiative for calling the elections in the Congress, and all predicated the action on a vote of "no confidence." Action under the Bingham plan, which would simply authorize a special election to be called by statute, would require a two-thirds vote of both houses—a barrier greater than that embodied in the impeachment process itself—assuming that the president would use his veto to reject the derogation of his record. The Green resolution similarly called for a two-thirds vote of both houses. In contrast, Representative Reuss lowered the necessary congressional majorities to 60 percent but he introduced another inhibition to hasty congressional action; his resolution required that every seat in both houses, as well as the presidency and vice presidency, be filled in the special election. Those elected under any of these resolutions would serve the unexpired terms of the officers whose seats were vacated.

It is understandable that in the Watergate period concern focused on the presidency. It was not difficult then to locate the source of governmental failure—in the character flaws of Richard Nixon. But in the five sets of circumstances listed earlier that can destroy a government's capacity to govern, only the first four represent presidential failure. The fifth circumstance is deadlock between the branches on fundamental policy, which can render even a strong and wholly competent president unable to lead the nation. That was the problem that worried the reformers of an earlier generation, in the 1930s and 1940s. They saw the legislative branch as the source, or potential source, of governmental incapacity. Admirers of Franklin Roosevelt and Harry Truman, they feared that wise and progressive presidents would be prevented by reactionary and parochial legislators from doing necessary things. Some of them, therefore, proposed a power in the executive—the president or a presidentially designated premier—to dissolve the Congress, or one house of it, and order new elections.

The problem appears, therefore, in a broader context than that of simple presidential failure. Governments can fail for other reasons, too, and any amendment to the Constitution establishing a mechanism for special elections as the means for reconstituting a government incapable of governing should be broad enough to deal with the whole range of circumstances that can result in failure.

Designing the Special Election Mechanism

In countries with a pure parliamentary form of government, every national election has the character of a special election. It is called by the government in power, on short notice, at any time of the year. Campaigns are short, and the parties select their candidates and formulate their programs in advance to be ready to run whenever the starting gun goes off. But in this country, the opposite tradition has developed. National elections occur rhythmically and automatically on specified calendar dates—with the sole exception of the occasional by-elections called to fill vacancies in the House of Representatives. And the same is true of state and local elections, with the additional rare exception of recall elections that some state constitutions provide for. From the principle of calendar elections has evolved the whole system of candidate selection. Having unlimited time to prepare and conduct their campaigns, the parties have established extraordinarily complex and elaborate processes for choosing nominees. In recent years, serious candidates for the presidency (except incumbents) have felt compelled to begin full-time campaigning at least two years before the date on which they hoped to be inaugurated. Delegates to the national nominating conventions are selected in primaries and caucuses that extend over a four-month period beginning nearly a year before the inauguration day. Campaigns for Congress may be as long as those for president, and the formal nominating process in some states begins as early.

If a provision for calling special elections on short notice were to be introduced into the American political system, the parties would have to be prepared to conduct brief campaigns and to devise anticipatory or simplified processes for nominating the presidential and vice presidential candidates who would compete in the special balloting.

Designing a special election provision also requires selection from

a range of alternatives on each feature of the system. Who would
have the power to call the special election and what offices would
be filled? Would those elected serve fresh terms or only the unexpired
portions of the original terms? Could the special election be called at
any time or only at specified times?

The answers to these questions depend on the range of circumstances for which the special election mechanism is intended to be
available. An assumption that the governmental failure arises from
a divided, deadlocked government may lead to one design, while an
assumption that the problem is presidential failure at a time of unified
government—for any of the reasons listed at the outset of this
discussion—may lead to quite another. Ideally, the mechanism should
be flexible enough to serve all the circumstances in which a government may fail. But the more flexible the system the more often,
presumably, it would be utilized. That leads, then, to still other
questions. How often would special elections need to be held, and
in what circumstances? And if the process were designed for only
the gravest of emergencies—once or twice a century, say—how can
it be limited to just those situations? Whether special elections are to
be encouraged or discouraged affects the design of the mechanism
at every stage.

Calling the Election

Some of the proposals advanced in the past have placed the
initiative for calling special elections in only one branch of the
government. They were conceived as measures to permit the president
to dissolve the Congress, or for Congress to bring about the removal
of a failed president, but not both. However, if the cause of the
governmental failure were systemic deadlock between the branches
(as distinct from an impasse on a specific policy issue, for which a
referendum device, discussed in chapter 8, might be appropriate),
either the president or the Congress should have authority to initiate
the election that would be intended to resolve the crisis.

If the power were so lodged, either branch in a period of government futility could challenge the other to a showdown, with the
people to decide. Both the Congress and the presidency would
therefore have to be at stake in the special election. To fully ensure
that control of the Congress could be reversed by the election, not

just some of the House and Senate seats but all of them would have to be submitted to the people's verdict, as in the Reuss resolution. If the president were vindicated, presumably the voters would give him a Congress of his own party that would follow his leadership. Conversely, if the opposition were upheld, the voters would presumably replace the president with the candidate of the other party and solidify its control of the legislature.[2]

In a provision empowering the Congress to call a new election, should an extraordinary majority be required? There is solid precedent for such a standard. For the Congress to declare a president unable to discharge his duties under the Twenty-fifth Amendment, over his objection, a two-thirds vote by both houses is required. For a president to be removed under the impeachment clause, a simple majority of the House can vote to bring the executive to trial before the Senate, but a two-thirds vote by that body is required for conviction. In the Bingham resolution providing for special elections, a two-thirds vote of both houses would again be required unless the president concurred, because the election would be called by statute.

The essential consequence of a two-thirds rule, as noted earlier, is that the decision becomes bipartisan. Such a rigorous requirement might be appropriate if the special election were always to be conceived as a punitive action against the president as an individual; a broad bipartisan consensus should underlie any action that drives a president from office in disgrace. But if the purpose is to enable the electorate simply to choose between opposing parties when their conflict is so deep as to vitiate the powers of government, a requirement for a bipartisan consensus would be self-defeating. To serve that purpose, either party should be in a position to initiate the showdown, whether or not the other concurred. Indeed, even the 60 percent standard in the Reuss amendment would not enable the congressional majority to act in most circumstances of divided government. Of the eight Congresses since World War II in which both houses were controlled by the party in opposition to the

2. The word *presumably* is key, however, for it is entirely conceivable that the president and the congressional majorities, given the power of incumbency, would all be returned, with no mandate other than to resume their quarrel. Such a result might discredit the new procedure, but it might also focus attention on the need for revision of the election system along the lines discussed in chapter 4, to forestall the partisan division of the government.

president, only two—the Eighty-sixth, following the election of 1958, and the Ninety-fourth, following 1974—were held by majorities of 60 percent or more. If the provision is to be usable whenever it is needed, the Congress must be able to act by, at most, a vote of a constitutional majority—that is, a majority of the total membership. In instances where the minority gave the action no support, the majority party would have to achieve near unanimity, for a few dissidents could block the election simply by absenting themselves or by abstaining. But if it was fully unified and prepared to take the risk, it would be able to put before the people its case against the president.

A proposal to entrust the power to so small a majority would inevitably arouse fear that the special election mechanism might be overused, that it might be employed by either the president or the Congress in instances where the disagreement was in no sense fundamental but where either party might see the opportunity to capitalize on a transient public mood to improve its partisan position. A special election called in such circumstances might not in fact be undesirable, from the standpoint of effective government. As a general rule, when the government is under split partisan control the sooner a new election is called to avert, or resolve, the inevitable deadlock the better. Yet even if the Congress were free to act by no more than a constitutional majority, a powerful deterrent would exist in the provision that all of the seats in the Congress as well as the presidency would be subjected to the decision of the voters. The members of Congress who called the new election would be foreshortening their own tenure and putting in jeopardy their own careers as well as that of the chief executive.

That would cause no great risk, and perhaps not even any inconvenience, in the case of members of the House, assuming that the two-year term is continued. The special election could well be scheduled to coincide with the regular midterm election when House members would be running anyway. But it would involve both risk and inconvenience for most senators, one-third of whom, at any given time, have assured service of four to six years ahead of them, and another third from two to four more years. Only the final third are scheduled to face the voters at the next election. Two-thirds of the Senate, then, would have strong reason to resist acting to dissolve the Congress under any but the gravest circumstances. For this and other reasons that were discussed earlier, a special election would not be called by the Congress except when the incapacity of the government became so palpable that public clamor made a new election inescapable. If the Senate terms were extended to eight years, with two classes, the disincentives would be even greater, for half the Senate at any time would be assured of tenure for more than four additional years.[3]

The president, however, would not be subjected to quite the same restraint. Each four years, the presidency is at stake in a national election, along with the entire House and one-third of the Senate. As that election approached, a president would have reason to reflect on the makeup of the Senate and, if a majority of the holdover senators were of the opposition party, consider the prospect of gaining additional seats for his party by dissolving the Congress and requiring the entire Senate to be chosen. It is difficult to see a president's taking such action, however; the cries of outrage from holdover senators of his own party would be deafening. Again, the initiative for a new election would be likely only in response to an irresistible demand from the people—in which case, the Congress might act first or the two would proceed in unison.

If it is deemed necessary or prudent to devise additional restraints on the president, however, several may be considered. Elliott's suggestions for resolving deadlocks, discussed in chapter 3, would limit the president to exercising his dissolution power once in a term, and for the remainder of his term he would lose his veto power, leaving the Congress free to establish policy. The former restriction would be of little import, since it is hardly conceivable that any president would want to dissolve the Congress more than once in

3. Donald L. Robinson has suggested that, for purposes of continuity, half of the Senate might be left in place. In that case, the carryover senators opposed to the verdict of the special election (assuming the verdict is a clear one) might have the numbers to block the program of the new administration and the House majority and so perpetuate the deadlock. As Robinson argues, they too would probably respond to the election returns—at least during the new president's honeymoon period—just as congressional Democrats largely went along with President Reagan's program in 1981. But they might not, and to that extent the utility of the special election mechanism would be reduced. The argument of a need for continuity does not appear to be a strong one, for far more than half the incumbent senators would surely be reelected (see chapter 5). And to so limit the special election would significantly reduce the deterrent effect of requiring all of the legislators who vote to call the election to place their own tenure at risk.

four years, and it may be questioned whether outright suspension of the veto—although that would have some deterrent effect on presidents—would be desirable under any circumstances. The principal purpose of the veto, as the founders saw it, was to enable the president to defend his powers against congressional encroachment, and at a time of intense conflict between the branches—which would always be the case during a dissolution crisis—the veto power would be more than ever important for that purpose.

A second suggestion is that the president be empowered to call the election only with the concurrence of either the House or the Senate. This plan presents a certain symmetry. The government's three policymaking centers—presidency, Senate, and House—can deadlock in any of three ways, with any two combined against the third. Any two, therefore, should be able to initiate the new election. Such a plan would appear singularly appropriate for the circumstance of the Reagan years, when a Republican administration and a Republican Senate confronted a Democratic House. But it can be doubted that a requirement for Senate concurrence would add any real restraint to what would exist if the president possessed the power to act alone. In the latter case, he would surely not act without the wholehearted support of his party members in the Senate anyway. And requiring the concurrence of one house would strip the president of the power to deal with the kind of situation that developed during the second term of Franklin Roosevelt, when the president's program was blocked by a conservative coalition that controlled both houses, or in the administrations of Presidents Eisenhower, Nixon, and Ford, when Republican presidents and Democratic Congresses continually thwarted and frustrated each other. If, under those circumstances, neither house were willing to submit its membership to new elections—which they might anticipate would result in popular endorsement of the president—the constitutional amendment that was designed to provide a means for breaking deadlocks would prove inadequate.

A corresponding case can be made for placing authority in just one house of the Congress to call the special election. If the deadlock occurred at a time when the opposition party controlled only one chamber, as in the Reagan years, the president and his party in the other house might anticipate defeat in the new election and hence be reluctant to act. Ideally, it was suggested earlier, either party during a continuing impasse should be able to challenge the other to a showdown by asking the voters to make a choice between the two parties and their respective programs. Logically, then, the opposition-controlled house should be able to initiate the election on its own.

Even so liberal a mechanism would not suffice, however, in the case of a governmental failure at a time when one party controlled both branches and neither the president nor his majority in either house—all fearing repudiation at the polls—was willing to risk a special election. This is a common complaint about parliamentary government in countries such as Britain; since a government holds office for its full term (five years in Britain) unless the ruling party chooses to call an election at an earlier date, the country has no means of dislodging a failed government barring a split within the governing party itself. A parallel situation can, of course, develop in the United States. Perhaps the Hoover administration in 1930 can be accepted as an example, but for those who reject that illustration any number of hypothetical cases can readily be constructed. What would have happened, for instance, if President Franklin Roosevelt, like Neville Chamberlain, had proved totally inadequate as a leader in wartime and was leading his country to defeat, at a time when his party had full control of both houses of Congress? He would have been entitled to his office, as a kind of property right, while the war was lost. The midterm election, it must be repeated, provides no safeguard against presidential failure, for the presidency is not at stake. If the special election mechanism were to be available for the entire range of circumstances, authority to call the election would have to be placed somehow in the minority party—perhaps by vesting that power in 40 or 45 percent of the members of both houses. And even a number that small would not enable the minority, in a time of lopsided congressional majorities, to act without the aid of at least a few members of the majority.

Carrying the logic to this extreme leads to the fundamental question posed earlier. If a mechanism is to be available for the gravest of emergencies, should its use be limited to those occasions? And, if so, how can it be?

Some of those who have considered these issues answer the first question in the negative. They find the advantages of special elections, as against elections fixed by the calendar, to be so great that they would maximize their use by empowering a minority of the two houses, or even of one house, to initiate the action. The reduction in the duration, strain, and costs of campaigning, they argue, would be a boon, and if elections were frequently called on short notice, the parties would be compelled to have their leaders designated and their programs defined, in order to be ready. The indirect consequence, then, would be greater party cohesion, which would make whichever party was the victor better prepared to govern.

But making the special election so readily available would open the way to political gamesmanship. If the minority party in the Congress were empowered to call the election, it would have an incentive to do so whenever the public opinion polls showed that a majority of voters disapproved of the president's performance. Five of the nine postwar presidents, according to the Gallup poll, have experienced that high a rate of disapproval at some point before the expiration of their terms—Truman in 1946 and again in 1951–52, Johnson in 1967–68, Nixon in 1973–74, Carter in 1979–80, Reagan in 1983. But these were sometimes temporary; Truman was rebuffed in the 1946 election but recouped in 1948, and Reagan was set back in 1982–83 but recovered by 1984. One of the arguments for longer terms, discussed in chapter 5, was that a longer time horizon gives officeholders a chance to be statesmen and take actions that are unpopular in the short run but to the country's—and their—longer run advantage. Enabling the minority party to initiate an election whenever a president's popularity suffered a drastic drop would work in the opposite direction. It would make presidents more cautious than they are now. They would be even more preoccupied with politics, running hard for reelection not just in the last two years of their first terms but throughout those terms and during much of their second terms as well.

To prevent the minority party from being able to call an election capriciously, with a what-do-we-have-to-lose attitude, some have suggested that some form of referendum be interposed, giving the people rather than the minority party the opportunity to decide, by a vote or by petition of a specific proportion of the electorate, whether a special election were in order. But if the contention in chapter 5 that midterm elections now come too soon has any merit, adding a midterm referendum on a special presidential election would compound the present problem. The object should be to relieve the

Congress from the burden of an always-imminent election, not to subject the president to that same strain.

If one concedes this point, then a governmental failure at a time of united government could be solved only by the majority itself. If the present midterm election is retained, that provides a safeguard, for the electorate could give the opposition control of at least one house, which could then invoke its power (if the amendment permitted one house alone to initiate action). If the midterm election were eliminated, however, the American people would be in the same position as the British; they would have no recourse if their leaders were not disposed to move. Yet the power of public opinion should not be discounted. Chamberlain did, after all, relinquish his office, and so at a later date, under pressure from his own party, did Anthony Eden. Richard Nixon's resignation set a useful precedent in this country. If the public outcry against a failed president and a leaderless governing party were loud enough, revolt would surely stir in the party's congressional rank and file. The fact that either house of the Congress possessed the power to call a special election would have a profound effect. By threatening to join with the opposition to provoke such an election, a minority of the majority party in either house could in some cases bring about a presidential resignation. If it failed, and if the situation in the country were bad enough, it could carry out its threat.

On balance, placing the authority to call the new election in either the president or a constitutional majority of either house of Congress would provide a mechanism that would be available in cases of deadlock and—through the pressure of public opinion—in most other cases of failed government as well. To make the mechanism available for every conceivable case, by empowering the minority to act, would have a destabilizing effect so great as to outweigh the advantages of going to that extreme. The remainder of this discussion assumes that the authority to call the special election would be limited to the president or a Senate or House constitutional majority.

Full or Unexpired Terms?

On the face of it, if the nation is to be put through the trauma and turmoil of a special election for the president and the entire Congress, more should be at stake than just the unexpired terms of the current officeholders. The new election would presumably reconstitute a failed government and give the nation a fresh team of leaders. They would enter office eager to carry out their mandate, and the electorate would expect them to do so. It would appear both unnecessary and undesirable to give them less than normal full terms; to do so would thrust them at once into preparing for the next election and would force the country to go through its electoral ordeal twice within a single four-year span.[4]

But the question again arises as to whether, if full terms were to be awarded, politicians would be encouraged to maneuver for personal and partisan advantage. Might the process be invoked unnecessarily or even frivolously, in circumstances for which it was not intended, at times when governments were successful? If a united government were riding high in the public opinion polls, might it choose to go to the electorate for bigger majorities and a reinforced mandate rather than wait for the next regular election when its standing might be lower—much as governments in parliamentary countries strive to schedule their elections on the most advantageous dates?

The Twenty-second Amendment adds a complication here. Under its terms, a person may be elected president only twice, so a hostile Congress could be certain of curtailing a president's tenure by calling a special election. If it were scheduled during the president's first term, he would serve less than eight years even if he were reelected, and if the Congress scheduled such a vote during his second term, he would be ineligible to run. On the other hand, if the amendment were modified to exempt special elections from its provisions, a president could circumvent the present limitations on his tenure (eight years plus up to two years of the unexpired term of his predecessor) by calling a special election at whatever time seemed

---

4. If the Senate terms continue to be staggered—either as at present, with one-third of the Senate elected each two years, or as discussed in chapter 5, one-half chosen each four years—any constitutional amendment providing for election of the entire Senate to new terms would have to provide for dividing the Senate into classes with varying terms. That could be done simply, by providing that the class with the shortest time remaining at the time of the special election would have the shortest term, and the class with the longest time remaining the longest. As used in this section, the full-term option means new terms of two, four, and six years for the Senate classes (or four and eight years for the two classes in the four-eight-four plan) but full terms for the president, vice president, and representatives.

most propitious for his purpose. With artful language, the new amendment could set limits corresponding to those now in effect. Thus, if a special election were held during the last half of a president's first term or the first half of his second, the president if reelected could be made ineligible to run again when the new term expired; and if the election were held after the midpoint of his second term, he could be barred from competing in that race. That would give a hostile house of Congress the means to shorten the term of the president it opposed, and it would present an ambitious president with a way to extend his term. But neither the curtailment nor the extension could be for more than two years, and neither the legislators nor the president would be likely to gamble on the electorate's approval for a stake so small.

But even if political gamesmanship appeared to offer some potential gain for a president or his party, the self-interest of senators (and House members too, if their terms were lengthened) would impose the severe inhibition discussed earlier. If the opposition party held a majority in one or both houses, it might find some incentive in the opportunity a special election would offer it to capture the White House (and the other chamber, if controlled by the president's party). Similarly, a majority of the president's party in one house might see a chance for their partisans to capture the other house as well. But the individual legislators, as well as the president, would have to weigh a conjectural gain for the party as a whole against the certain, premature risk to their own careers. They would vacate their offices and undergo the expense and strain of an early election, with no recompense except a renewed tenure in the seats they occupied already. House members could, of course, escape an extra contest (assuming congressional terms remain unchanged) if the special poll were scheduled to coincide with the present midterm election, but two-thirds of the Senators would find everything to lose and little to gain. And if House terms were extended to four years, the representatives would find themselves in the same position.

True, the slight extension of a senator's hold on his office if he survived the special election would provide a correspondingly slight incentive. A senator with five years remaining in his term would enter on a new six-year term, one with three years a four-year term, and so on, assuming the present structure of six-year staggered terms. With an eight-year term, the incentive would be somewhat greater, for a senator with five, six, or seven years remaining could win an eight-year term, and one with one, two, or three years left to serve could get a new four-year stay.[5] But even this mild incentive would be removed if the election were for only the unexpired terms of the offices being vacated. The question in that case would be whether the special election mechanism would be utilized in the circumstances for which it was designed—to reconstitute failed governments—or whether it would never be used at all.

Only the most intense public pressure, surely, could induce legislators to give up their seats and call a special election with no reward at all beyond being allowed to finish the term to which they were already entitled. The electorate would have to be so aroused that a majority of one house (or the president, but he would surely be sensitive to the attitudes of the legislators in this matter) would reappraise where their self-interest lay and conclude that to resist a special election would imperil them more than would yielding to it. One can identify perhaps a couple of times in this century when public hostility toward governmental leaders might have reached that degree of intensity. If the special election process is to be designed, and reserved, for only such occasions, then the unexpired-term option would be suitable. But it would be unavailable as a method of reconstituting governments whose failure has produced deep public frustration, alienation, and disgust but not yet driven the voters to the edge of revolution.

The full-term alternative would raise the incentive for politicians to act in these kinds of circumstances. Would it, then, lift the stakes too high and lead to overuse of the new mechanism? Public opinion would again be the key. If it could compel a special election in the most extreme situations under the unexpired-term alternative—and even that is less than certain—it could assuredly restrain any initiative at other times, even if full terms were the winners' reward. At every stage, the fear of an adverse public reaction would be a powerful inhibition on those who held the power to initiate the new election. Since they would be required to submit themselves to the verdict of the voters, they would not be likely to risk the voters' judgment that

5. This assumes that senators with short tenure remaining would not challenge their colleagues for the longer term. Traditions of comity would discourage such behavior, as would the greater risk involved in challenging an incumbent. But the possibility might well act as another factor discouraging the calling of special elections.

they had acted precipitously or for narrow, partisan purposes. The governmental failure would have to be patent and compelling, not only in the eyes of the politicians but in the judgment of the electorate at large. In other words, the public itself would have to be the true initiator, with the politicians in the posture of reluctantly responding. And the public could surely be counted on not to clamor for an extra, unnecessary election. Only a plain collapse of governmental leadership and competence would put the country in the kind of mood that would command the response of the Congress, or the president, or both. That would be true under either the full-term or the unexpired-term option, so the advantages of the former may as well be incorporated in any special election scheme.

Timing the Election

Any special election process would be designed for emergencies and, by definition, emergencies cannot wait. Governments may fail abruptly, and once that failure is established, the sooner a new, invigorated government is put in place the better. The parliamentary model suggests itself—elections to be called at any time, held promptly, and the fresh leadership installed in office as soon as possible after the votes are tabulated. In Britain, an interregnum lasts not much longer than a month.

If the newly elected officials in this country are to serve full terms, however, complete flexibility in scheduling the special election would encounter some difficulties. The first is psychological. If a special election were called for March, say, and the new government installed in May (which is probably as quickly as American tradition would allow), the new terms would also expire in May and the next regular election therefore would be held in March. And so would subsequent national elections, until another special election initiated another series on another date. True, irregular elections do not upset the electorates of other countries, and a few American states and cities elect their leaders in the spring. Until a few decades ago, Maine held its national election in September. Nevertheless, it is argued, November as the proper month for choosing presidents is implanted in the national psyche by two centuries of ritualization; the fixed rhythms of politics are as reassuring as the unvarying, predictable movements of the sun, the moon, and the planets, and to remove the certainty of calendar elections would unsettle and alienate the electorate.[6]

The psychological problem would be compounded by a series of practical ones. If the national election were held in March, every stage of the nominating process would have to be rescheduled accordingly. Assuming that the present nominating processes were left essentially unchanged, the national party conventions would have to be held in midwinter rather than midsummer, and the presidential and congressional primaries now held in the spring would have to be rescheduled in the autumn. A large body of legislation, and an even vaster congeries of political habits, would have to be recast.

These objections could be met very simply, for the most part, by adjusting the full terms by a few months. The amendment could provide that the new full terms would expire in the January that came closest to the date that they would otherwise expire. At the next regular election, then, the familiar November date would be reinstated, although not necessarily in a year divisible by four.

Alternatively, the amendment could provide that special elections would be permitted only on the usual November date. As a further concession to tradition, the opportunity could be limited to the midterm even-numbered year. This could be defended on the ground that the first year after a presidential election would be too soon to ask the electorate to reconsider its decision of the previous autumn and by the third year the country could bear to struggle along until the regularly scheduled presidential balloting. And it could be presented—somewhat deceptively, to be sure—as a minimal, incremental change. All the reformers would be proposing would be to expand the scope of the familiar midterm election a bit, to include the presidency and vice presidency as well as legislative seats.

But while such a plan would meet the practical tests better, it would serve the theoretical ends less well. A president who became discredited early in his term would remain in office for a full two

6. The extent to which the public is attached to November elections as such may have been overestimated. The Gallup poll reports that a majority of its sample responded favorably to the suggestion that the presidential elections be moved forward to September, in order that the president would have more time to prepare for the opening of Congress in January. George Gallup, Jr., "Americans Favor Major Overhaul of Electoral Process," *Dallas Morning News*, December 6, 1984.

years, unless following the Nixon precedent he could be persuaded to resign. In the country's interest, two years might be too long. But, what is more likely, the governmental incapacity would not become clearly enough established to create a public demand for action until the deadline for calling the midterm election had passed. If that deadline were fixed as September 1—and practical considerations would probably lead to choosing an even earlier date—a new government would have only nineteen months to demonstrate its incapacity.

Once it survived that short period, it would be assured of continuance for its full four years. The crucial year for the people to decide whether a government should be turned out of office before its time is either the later part of the second year or the third. If the decision must be made somewhere near the middle of its second year, the procedure would be unavailable when it would be likely to be needed most. The purpose of the amendment would be vitiated. Whenever governmental deadlock or failed leadership becomes intolerable and a special election imperative, the remedy should be available for immediate application without the necessity to wait for what might be an entire tense and wasted year until the next November comes around.

If the special election process is worth adopting at all, then, the principle of flexible timing needs to be accepted and the psychological objections to elections in unaccustomed months and odd years confronted and somehow overcome. And the political parties would have to face the necessity of designing special nominating processes for use if and when a special election were called.

Adjustment of Nominating Procedures

Whoever called the special election should be granted some degree of discretion as to how soon the voting would take place. In the gravest of emergencies, the special election would need to be held, then, as soon as possible, but in any case the normal nine-month span for the entire nominating and electing process would have to be compressed. The parties would have to be ready at any time to nominate their candidates and present their cases to the voters in a period of weeks rather than, as is now the case, of months.

In the case of congressional candidates, existing nominating processes could be preserved in their essentials, by simply expediting each step of the procedure. The one casualty might be the runoff primaries, which would probably have to be suspended by the few states that still conduct them. But a single primary would be feasible. If the special election were called on March 15, say, and set for sixty days later, on May 14, states would have time to organize primary balloting on April 23, with three weeks left for the general election. Candidates could be required to file for nomination within a week, by March 22, which would allow more than a month for arranging the mechanics of the election. So brisk a schedule would be a radical departure from the leisurely pace to which American politicians and election officials have become accustomed, but precedents do exist. Special elections to fill vacancies in the House are held within a few weeks after the vacancies occur, and in states that hold runoff primaries the interval between the first and second primaries is usually three weeks but in South Carolina has been only two.

The presidential nominating process is, however, another matter. The present elaborate series of events, beginning with the first primaries and caucuses in midwinter and ending with the national convention extravaganzas in midsummer, followed by a general election campaign of nearly three months, obviously could not be compressed into a sixty-day period—or even a June–November period if November elections were maintained—without fundamental alteration.

One approach would be for the Congress by law, or the parties by their own rules, to prescribe a national presidential primary to be held concurrently with those for House and Senate. The massive party convention would be regretfully abandoned on this occasion, and its functions beyond nominating the president otherwise assigned. The most important of those duties would be the nomination of a candidate for vice president, but that would be scant loss; vice presidential selection has not always been performed satisfactorily by conventions anyway. In most instances, the convention simply ratifies the hasty choice of the presidential candidate, and that ministerial act can be as well left to the party's national committee as to a convention. On the other hand, if the choice is to be made in a more considered fashion, the procedure of the Twenty-fifth Amendment could be invoked, with the new president appointing his vice president, subject to confirmation by the Congress, after taking office.

A second function of the convention is to write a platform; this duty could be entrusted to the national committee, or the party policy could be left to be enunciated and defined by its presidential candidate, whose pronouncements always carry considerably more weight anyhow than party platform declarations. Finally, the convention is the party's plenary rule-making body, but the national committee acts for the convention between its sessions. The calling of a special election would not generate a need for new rules that could not be met by the national committee.

The national primary has other features, though, that affect its suitability as the mode for nominating party candidates in a special election. Most versions of the primary that have been advanced have suggested a runoff feature in the event no candidate gets more than a specified proportion of the vote—usually 40 percent—in order to assure that the winner in a multicandidate contest is the choice of more than a small minority. Allowing eighty rather than sixty days for the entire election process would be sufficient to accommodate a runoff primary—if those designing the process were willing to risk the reaction from an electorate asked to vote three times at intervals of two or three weeks (or four times altogether, if a referendum is included in the scheme). Two alternatives to the runoff primary are available, however. One would be to delegate a preliminary screening responsibility to the national committee, or to that body augmented by some or all of the party's membership in Congress and its governors; it would select two candidates to be presented to the voters. A second alternative would be a theoretically appealing but virtually untried procedure called "approval voting" in which each primary voter could vote for as many of the candidates in a multi-candidate primary as he or she considered suitable to lead the party in the general election. The candidate acceptable to the largest number of primary voters would be the nominee, with probably a reasonable chance that he or she would have the approval of a majority.

But while a national primary would appear to be feasible, its desirability is a separate question. It has always been a ready alternative to the present convention process but has never achieved enough support to bring it into serious consideration, despite the widespread and vociferous criticism of the existing system. One objection is that it would give too decisive an advantage to the candidate or candidates with the greatest name recognition or access to the most copious financial resources, or both. The possibility that now exists for a relatively unknown candidate with limited resources—such as Senator Gary Hart in 1984—to burst upon the political scene by making an impressive showing in the earliest caucuses and primaries would probably be eliminated. A second objection is that even at the present time too many states hold primaries and the aim should be to reduce rather than increase the number.[7] The proliferation of primaries in the last two decades has placed the choice of each party's nominee in the hands of ten to twenty million rank-and-file voters in each party, but those voters must base their judgment of a candidate's leadership capacity on what is essentially a casual impression, gained mostly over television. What is needed, it is argued, is a return to the balanced nominating process that prevailed as late as the 1960s, when the various candidates could test their public appeal in a few primaries but the party's leaders—those who had worked with the candidates most closely and knew them most intimately—could make sure that the nomination did not go to one who, however popular he proved himself in the primaries, was unsuitable for the presidential office. That hazard would be avoided if, as suggested earlier, two candidates were nominated by the national committee (preferably augmented for the purpose) to run in the national primary.

If, even with that adjustment, a national primary seems undesirable, another alternative suggests itself. That is for the party to establish a much smaller nominating convention, consisting of only a few hundred people who could be assembled on a few days' notice in a prearranged location. The delegates to that convention could be selected during the first year of a new president's term, though that would appear to be an unnecessarily elaborate arrangement since special elections would surely prove to be rare events. Once again, a convention made up of the party's national committee plus its members in Congress and its governors would be both representative and knowledgeable as a nominating body.

To suspend the present nominating process in a time of crisis would inflict no permanent injury on the political system. If the result would be restoration of the faith of citizens in their government,

---

7. In 1984 there were thirty for the Republicans and twenty-nine for the Democrats, excluding four and five states, respectively, that held nonbinding, advisory primaries.

that would well justify the temporary disturbance of normal party practice. Moreover, on the positive side, one experience with a quick and relatively inexpensive process of choosing new leaders might show the way to improvements in the interminable, exhausting, and excessively expensive political ordeal that the country now suffers each four years.

The Need for a Safety Valve

How to provide a "safety valve" when governments fail is a conundrum for constitutional designers in any democratic system. The objective is clear enough. When a government proves incapable of leading the country and loses the people's confidence, for whatever reason, the people should have the opportunity through a new election to replace it. But no country has a constitution that guarantees that opportunity.

In theory, parliamentary systems offer the people a recourse, because those who administer the government must maintain the confidence of a parliament made up of the elected representatives of the people, and if they fail to do so they can be removed at any time. When a prime minister fails, he can, like Chamberlain, be replaced. But that is not the same as giving the people a fresh choice. The members of parliament remain in office, the same majority party in that body still governs, and the new prime minister comes from that same party. If the party as a whole has lost the public confidence, it remains in power for its full term—or until it decides voluntarily to call an election—just as surely as a president remains in office for his full four years in the United States.

The difficulty in Britain and other parliamentary countries is that the party or parties that control the legislature must make their own decision as to whether and when their government should relinquish its authority. In a two-party parliamentary country, the governing party usually clings most tenaciously to power when it has the least public support, for it can always hope to restore itself if the election is delayed. In a multiparty system, where government is by coalition, a new election is more likely to be called, because in case of governmental failure the coalition will come unglued and there may be no way to restore it short of fresh elections. But coalition governments are characteristically weak and unstable, and are hardly to be taken as a model.

The framers of the U.S. Constitution sought their safety valve, for the legislative branch, in the biennial election of the House and one-third of the Senate. As for the executive, he would be chosen very carefully, by an electoral college composed of prudent and knowledgeable citizens or by the House of Representatives, and if by chance he proved traitorous or criminal, he could be impeached. The framers considered broader grounds for impeachment but rejected them to ensure the independence of the chief executive from too tight congressional control.

But with the democratization of the presidential selection process and the growth of executive power, the fixity of a president in office for four full years, no matter how incompetent he may prove to be, is a weakness in the American system that can, in a time of grave emergency, be perilous. For a president to be merely nontreasonous and noncriminal is no longer enough, if it ever was. The president today must be the country's leader in every respect, its chief legislator as well as chief executive, its moral preceptor and its commander in chief, and nowadays the leader of the whole free world and chief strategist and tactician in the global competition between freedom and Soviet communism. And in none of these roles will he be effective if he has discredited himself beyond recovery and so lost the confidence of the people he is to lead. In an electoral system that permits divided government, moreover, even a competent president can be rendered ineffective if he is forced to contend with a hostile Congress. And in such situations the biennial election turns out not to be a safety valve at all; history tells of no instance when a midterm election resolved a deadlock between the branches, but of many instances where it intensified conflict and immobilized the government.

An attempt to design a provision for special elections as the means to reconstitute a failed government encounters at once the dilemma that has faced constitution-makers in other countries. If a governmental entity itself must decide when a new election is needed, it may refuse to act no matter how patent the governmental failure and how loud the public outcry demanding action. On the other hand, if the power of decision is located somewhere outside the control of the elected officials who exercise responsibility—in the congressional minorities, perhaps subject to approval by the people themselves through some form of referendum—the stability of government will be undermined and responsible elected officials will suffer the continuous distraction of imminent elections. Neither solution is fully satisfactory, but on balance, the former seems preferable. In the interest of stability, the danger of rigidity has to be risked, and public pressure relied on to prevent the one from degenerating into the other.

But because so much of governmental failure in the United States is due to partisan squabbling and deadlock between the branches, any one of the three elements in a deadlock—the president, the Senate, or the House (the latter bodies by constitutional majorities)—should be able to initiate the election. In order that the deadlock can in fact be broken, all elective offices in both branches should be declared vacant and filled in the election. Ideally, the election should be callable at any time and the newly elected officers should serve new, full terms. But on these points, if concessions have to be made in order to preserve the country's traditional political calendar, at least some new flexibility could still be introduced into the constitutional system.

For all the reasons discussed earlier, the inhibitions to calling a special election—in any of the forms the new mechanism might take—would be so great that the procedure, if added to the Constitution, might never be used. But the very existence of the authority would operate subtly to prevent the kinds of deadlocks that the provision would be intended to resolve. In times of conflict between the president and a Congress controlled in whole or in part by the opposition, the hand of a strong and popular president would be greatly strengthened. If he felt confident that public opinion was behind him, he could challenge recalcitrant legislators to yield to his wishes—or else. The result would be greater cohesion among the elements of the government, even when they were controlled by opposing parties. Theoretically, members of the Congress could threaten the president as well, if he were unpopular in the country, but they would be less credible. The Congress is so pluralistic, its power so diffused, the authority of its leaders to impose discipline so limited that it can rarely stand united and steadfast in any battle with even a weak president. But in a circumstance where the problem was one of presidential incapacity and failure, the Congress would at least have an ultimate sanction to force the president from office. To maintain the confidence of the Congress and forestall any such eventuality, a president could not ignore and afford to defy the legislators and provoke conflict, as presidents have sometimes done. He would be forced to seek a close relationship. Yet if in the end he failed and sensed that he would lose in a showdown—probably anticipating that his own party might well deny him renomination— the chief executive would be likely to follow the useful precedent of resignation established by President Nixon in just such a situation.

A constitutional provision for special elections could, in sum, be written in a form that would make it safe from abuse, because the electorate could readily penalize the politician or party who abused it. It would be a spur toward cooperation between the branches— with a shift in influence from the Congress to any strong and popular president but to the legislature from a weak and unpopular one. And it would provide a safety valve for the country in any of the many varied circumstances that can lead to an inept, failed, and debilitated government.

CHAPTER SEVEN

Fostering Interbranch Collaboration

No one would ever expect to find perfect harmony, for long, between the executive and legislative branches of the American government, even when they are controlled by members of the same party chosen at the same election. Nor is an absence of conflict necessary for the government to function. Indeed, some degree of conflict is not only inevitable but desirable. Legislators must respond to presidential initiatives with a degree of skepticism and assert their independent views; otherwise, the legislative branch could be dispensed with altogether. And the president must review congressional initiatives with a corresponding independent outlook. But the problem arises when skepticism deepens into distrust and outright hostility. Then the power of each branch to check the other can lead to deadlock and immobility, and the government cannot muster the degree of unity necessary to enable it to act.

The problem of deadlock is reviewed in chapter 4 in the context of a government divided between the major parties. But while the most severe and debilitating impasses between the branches in recent decades have come during periods when Republican presidents have confronted Democratic Congresses, stalemate is by no means confined to such periods. Every Democratic president from Woodrow Wilson to Jimmy Carter has had his clashes, too, with Congresses at least nominally controlled by his own party. The quarrel over Franklin Roosevelt's "court-packing" plan, and its ultimate defeat, which brought an abrupt end to the whole New Deal reform era, was probably the most divisive of the Democratic disputes. But Democratic governments were devitalized by disputes over preparedness in Woodrow Wilson's time, over civil rights and civil liberties in Harry Truman's, over Vietnam and inflation in Lyndon Johnson's, and over energy policy in Jimmy Carter's. Real power in the Congress was often wielded not by the formal Democratic party structure in alliance with the president but by an informal coalition of conservative southern Democrats and Republicans. And in the pre-FDR era, when the Republicans normally held congressional majorities, GOP presidents and Congresses had their differences, too. Theodore Roosevelt was hardly on speaking terms with the conservative GOP congressional leaders by the time his second term ended, William Howard Taft fell out with those same leaders over the tariff, Warren Harding and the GOP legislators took opposite views on the World Court, and Coolidge twice vetoed Republican-written farm bills with blistering denunciations. In Ronald Reagan's first term, Senate Republican leaders upset the president's fiscal policy as early as 1982, when they forced him to accept a tax increase he did not want, and they scrapped his military spending buildup in 1985—but in these instances the president graciously accepted his defeats and went along.

Even with united government, then, presidential honeymoons with the Congress are often short. Writing in 1940, at a time when Democrats had controlled both branches for nearly a decade, Harold J. Laski could observe that the Congress "is always looking for occasions to differ from" the president, "and it never feels so really comfortable as when it has found such an occasion for difference. In doing so, it has the sense that it is affirming its own essence."[1]

Accordingly, those who have sought a greater degree of unity and cohesion within the government have sometimes attempted to design institutional changes that would somehow force the president and his party leaders in the Congress to collaborate, whether they were so inclined or not, or that would at least encourage harmony by creating countervailing pressures against the tendencies toward divergence that arise from the separation of the branches. These schemes can be divided into two categories—those that would formally modify the separation of powers by structurally interrelating the branches, and those that would seek their goal through strengthening the informal institution that binds the president and the congressional

1. *The American Presidency: An Interpretation* (Harper, 1940), p. 123.

majorities together in times of united government. That institution is, of course, the political party.

Modifying the Separation of Powers

Proposals to modify the separation of powers necessarily take the form, as Stephen Horn has pointed out, of either putting legislators in the executive branch or officials of that branch—usually cabinet members—in the legislature.[2] If the congressmen or cabinet officers who move across branch lines are to serve only in an advisory capacity, the constitutional separation of powers is not breached and the arrangement can be made through statute or simply by voluntary agreement. But if any official of either branch is to share authoritatively in the exercise of *power* in the other branch, the "incompatibility clause" of the Constitution stands in the way. That is the clause in Article I that declares that "no person holding any office under the United States shall be a member of either House during his continuance in office."

The clause originated, as noted in chapter 2, not out of a concern for dual officeholding as such but out of worry about preserving the independence of the Congress from presidential power. If the president could dangle the prospect of attractive patronage appointments, he could bend the legislators to his will, it was argued. Underpaid, part-time legislators in those days could presumably be easily seduced by the award of full-time offices that would enable them to settle their families in the capital. But much of the antipatronage purpose of the clause was vitiated, even for eighteenth century government, when the original language was modified to permit a legislator to accept an appointment (other than to a new office or one whose emoluments had been increased during his term) simply by resigning his seat. For modern government, the clause is even less significant, since membership in the Congress has become a full-time job with pay and prestige superior to all but the highest posts in the executive branch—cabinet posts, top White House staff positions, or major ambassadorships—and with, normally, a much longer tenure. Unless a member is ready for retirement from the Congress anyway, rarely

2. *The Cabinet and Congress* (Columbia University Press, 1960), p. 211.

does he or she resign to accept an executive branch position. When President Reagan formed his administration, only one member came from the Congress—Representative David A. Stockman of Michigan, who became director of the Office of Management and Budget. Whether the clause is useful in modern times depends, then, on whether the dual officeholding that it prohibits might, in some form, contribute to more harmonious relationships between the president and the Congress, without creating more serious problems than those it helps to solve.

Congressmen in the Cabinet

A Constitutional amendment proposed in 1979 by Representative Henry S. Reuss, Democrat of Wisconsin, represents one version of how the executive and legislative branches might be linked through dual officeholding. Reuss proposed to amend the incompatibility clause to permit as many as fifty legislators to serve in the executive branch. The Congress by statute would designate offices eligible to be filled by its members, and the president each two years would submit his list of nominees for those posts, whether members or nonmembers. They would be voted on by each house en bloc. If either house rejected the slate, it would be revised by the president until he obtained concurrence. The appointments would then be made, subject to individual Senate confirmation in the usual manner, with the legislator to receive a single salary—that of the executive branch position.

"Executive-legislative stalemate is a luxury we can no longer afford," Reuss said in offering his amendment. The change, he said, "would put the emphasis on cooperation" as well as "bring a 'home town touch' to federal agencies now too often isolated in Washington," "make service in Congress more attractive," and "give the President a wider choice of executive leaders, now denied him."[3]

The first question to be raised relates to the last of these claims. Who would in fact put together the slate of up to fifty candidates? The Congress, either house having the power to reject the slate, could enforce a demand that *its* slate be nominated by the president. In Britain, the queen appoints the ministers of the crown but she

3. Memorandum, Office of Representative Henry S. Reuss, July 29, 1979.

does not in fact choose them; that power was seized by the House of Commons long ago when it informed the monarch that it would not give a vote of confidence to any cabinet except that of its own selection. The same practice has been applied in this country to offices that are governed by the rule of "senatorial courtesy"; because the Senate as a whole defers to senators representing the state in which the office is filled, they are in effect empowered to reject any presidential appointee except the one they insist the president appoint. Such de facto senatorial selection does not apply now to cabinet posts and other positions of high rank, although powerful legislators have on occasion come close to dictating lesser appointments as the price of cooperation with the executive branch. Yet, under the Reuss proposal, when the Congress wrote its statute containing its list of offices, powerful elements within the legislature would surely be developing their own ideas as to which legislators should fill which of the designated posts. Fierce competition would surely ensue, and would the legislators prefer to bargain their way to their own solutions or leave the executive free to pick and choose among them? The former, in all likelihood. It would be an extraordinary example of self-restraint if a Congress that—like the House of Commons—had the clear power to impose its will on the executive did not find formal or informal ways of doing so.

This would seem the probable outcome not merely because of the ambition of members of Congress but because of the difficulty—even unworkability—of the alternative. If the president were left truly free to make his own selections, he would have to decide in the first instance how many legislators to put on his list and then whether to appoint the most senior and powerful members of the Congress or more junior members who might be more compatible with him. The objective of enhancing cooperation between the branches would appear to oblige the president to go in the former direction and seek as appointees the senior members who would have the greatest influence with their legislative colleagues. This is the theory of dual officeholding in parliamentary governments. The foreign secretary also manages legislation and leads debate on foreign policy issues in the British House of Commons, the chancellor of the exchequer on budget and financial issues, and so on. The cabinet is at the apex of both branches, leading both and in so doing keeping them fully coordinated.

Representative Reuss, in presenting his proposal, did not contemplate that pattern. "It would not be wise," he said, for the president to appoint committee chairmen to the cabinet, "because that would present a real conflict of interest, which would carry us, in my judgment, too far away from the Presidential system, which I certainly don't want to displace."[4] For that reason, he said, a wise president would not, for instance, appoint as secretary of the treasury the chairman of the House Ways and Means Committee. But, to pursue this example, if the chairman wanted the job, for the president to pass over him and appoint some other member of Congress or someone from outside the legislative branch would hardly be conducive to improving cooperation between the branches. The chairman would have to possess an unusually benign and forgiving temperament not to make life difficult for the secretary now and then, just to prove the president wrong in his judgment. Perhaps this particular chairman would be totally free of jealousy and vindictiveness, but most would not be. Staff assistants of the passed-over members and the preferred appointees would fan the jealousies. Moreover, even in cases where selection of a junior member affronted none of his seniors, he would be apt to lack the stature and influence required to enable him to become *their* leader in the legislative process. He would have to win their assent to his measures by persuasion, with no notable advantage over cabinet members selected under the current practice from outside the Congress, and the potential advantage of dual officeholding would not be realized.[5]

On the other hand, if the president were determined to select senior and influential members, he would still find it awkward to exercise free choice among that limited group. The bicameral structure of the Congress, in particular, would put the president at peril. Could the president find a person who would be influential in one house who would not become a liability, because of institutional jealousy, in the other? As ambitious members of the House and Senate competed for the president's favor, it would become increasingly

4. *Political Economy and Constitutional Reform,* Hearings before the Joint Economic Committee, 97 Cong. 1 sess. (Government Printing Office, 1983), p. 336.

5. The prospect would be even less promising in a time of divided government. There is little reason to think that cabinet members appointed by a Republican president from the House Republican minority would be more effective in dealing with the Democratic majority than would officials selected from outside the Congress. The discussion in this section therefore assumes unified party control of the two branches.

clear that for every member of one house he nominated, he would make at least one enemy in the other house, who would be in a position to do daily damage to his program. If many senior members were offended, the whole slate of nominees might be in danger of rejection. Presidents might eventually conclude that the only way to achieve harmony would be to allow the Congress itself to assign its own members to the jobs.

But this presents its own range of problems. The majority party that organizes each house of Congress has found that assigning posts of power within the limited confines of the house itself is a divisive process, which is the reason that both houses, whether the majority is Democratic or Republican, have fallen back on seniority as the simple, harmonious way of filling their committee and subcommittee chairmanships.[6] For the few posts that have been necessarily exempted from seniority, such as party leadership positions, the competition to fill vacancies is distracting and always a threat to party harmony. For the two houses of Congress to attempt to divide between themselves and then respectively allocate up to fifty eagerly coveted executive branch positions would multiply manifold the strains and stresses that arise each two years from merely organizing the Congress. The legislators would undoubtedly fall back on some automatic and nondivisive process based on standing and seniority, assigning those entrusted with leadership in the Senate or the House in particular functional areas to the corresponding executive branch positions, and settling conflicts between the houses by lot.

That might satisfy the Congress, but it would hardly satisfy the president. It would give him a slate of appointees of whom a large proportion might be unsuited for executive responsibility—by virtue of temperament, lack of administrative ability or energy, or ideological incompatibility with the president. One recalls the feud during the Vietnam War between President Johnson and the chairman of the Senate Foreign Relations Committee, J. William Fulbright of Arkansas,

6. In the 1970s, House Democrats stripped the seniority principle of its previously absolute and automatic character, and the Democratic caucus has since violated the tradition on several occasions, as when it replaced Melvin Price of Illinois with Les Aspin of Wisconsin as chairman of the Armed Services Committee in 1985. Democrats on some committees have likewise departed from seniority on occasion in selecting subcommittee chairmen. But such departures are still rare, and seniority remains the normal and dominant mode of selection among House Democrats. Republicans in the House and both parties in the Senate still adhere to seniority as rigorously as ever.

but other examples can be brought to mind from any period. No president could weld an effective and cohesive administration from a slate of officials not of his own choosing.

There remains, finally, the problem of workload. Ambitious members of Congress have managed to make being a legislator, in the American system, a demanding, exhausting, full-time job. And few cabinet members would contend that their executive branch duties alone are not sufficient to consume their total energies. The two jobs as now constituted would impose a superhuman burden. Parliamentary governments have evolved solutions to the problem of workload that are largely alien to this country. On the executive side, ministers do not actually administer their departments; that is left to a corps of permanent, senior civil servants of a type that the United States has never developed and, given its traditions, would not easily tolerate. On the legislative side, ministers have duties of floor leadership but the committee responsibilities that absorb members of Congress do not exist, because committees on the U.S. model do not themselves exist; their work, for the most part, is done by executive departments under the ministers' direction. Ministers do not even have to devote much attention to getting reelected, because campaigns are short and senior members of parliament usually enjoy safe seats. The ministers do not have constituent service duties either, because that tradition has not evolved in other countries. Representative Reuss contends that much of the congressman's constituency service is "make work and busy work" on the part of members who do not have enough genuine work to do.[7] But much of the work has come to be expected, and a member who neglected it would be open to attack by political opponents. Reuss proposed to reduce the workload also by relieving executive branch appointees from committee responsibilities. But that would appear to defeat the purpose of the scheme, for it would be through his or her committee—preferably as chairman—that the executive official would have the greatest opportunity to bring about collaboration between the branches. Without his participation, the committee would have about as much inclination as it does now to go its own way in defiance of the executive branch.[8]

7. *Political Economy and Constitutional Reform*, Hearings, p. 334.
8. France has adopted a unique scheme for coping with the workload problem.

All these considerations weigh against the idea of prescribing a fixed set of positions to which members of Congress would be eligible for appointment. Yet there is merit in the objective of giving the president latitude to appoint one or more members of Congress to executive branch positions, entirely at his own discretion, without requiring the members to resign. Such an arrangement would broaden the range of talent available to a president when he assembles his administration. For every David Stockman willing to resign his seat to accept an executive appointment, there might be several others who would enjoy tours of duty as administrative officials if they did not have to give up their careers in the Congress. Such appointments could be made possible by a simple amendment that merely repealed the incompatibility clause. Then presidents would be free to experiment. They could appoint a chair of a small business subcommittee to head the Small Business Administration, or the chair of a veterans' affairs panel to head the Veterans Administration, and see what happened. A David Stockman could keep his congressional seat, and find out whether the workload was indeed insuperable. Authors of laws could be invited to take responsibility for their execution, for a time at least. Part-time jobs, including membership on advisory or supervisory boards and commissions, could be filled by legislators and even created for them. Congressional oversight of administration—one of the benefits of independent branches, when it is done well—would be sacrificed to some degree, but whether the gains from cooperation between the branches outweighed that loss would be tested. Each individual appointment would be reviewed through the normal process of Senate confirmation.

Once an executive post had been held by a legislator, and successfully, the Congress might lay claim to it and advance its candidates, much as would be the case under the Reuss amendment. But at the outset at least, the initiative would lie with the president. Presidents would undoubtedly proceed cautiously, and if a pattern

---

Each member of the Chamber of Deputies has an alternate who, when the member assumes duties in the executive branch, takes the member's seat in the legislative body. If and when the member leaves his executive post and returns to the Chamber, the alternate steps down. The member serving in the executive branch loses his rights in the legislature but presumably retains his influence. If a proposal such as that of Representative Reuss is seriously considered, an adaptation of the French scheme would be worth exploring.

evolved for such appointments, it would be based on a series of experiments.

Cabinet Members in Congress

Participation by executive branch officials in the deliberations of Congress, as a means of linking the separate branches, would require constitutional amendment only if the officials were in some sense made members of the legislature, with some or all of the privileges—such as voting—attendant on membership. That would require not only repeal of the incompatibility clause but also modification of those sections of the Constitution that define the membership of the legislative body concerned. And the body concerned might be only the House of Representatives, for to add to the Senate membership on any basis other than one per state would run afoul of the clause prohibiting any amendment that would deprive any state of its equal suffrage in the Senate.

On balance, the advantages of actual membership in the House for cabinet members would appear to be so limited that they would hardly warrant the disruption that such a step would cause. To have two classes of members, one elected and one appointed, would inevitably create divisions and jealousies that would threaten the cohesion of the House. The appointed members would lack seniority and would therefore, under House tradition, occupy the most junior positions on committees and subcommittees; they would lack authority to lead the Congress, yet could hardly denigrate their own cabinet offices by submitting to someone else's leadership. The only workable solution would appear to be the adoption of new rules that, revoking the hallowed tradition of seniority, would give the presidential appointees instant and automatic chairmanships. Yet, unless the right to chairmanships was somehow fixed also in the Constitution—a suggestion that would defy draftsmanship—it is difficult to see how the sitting members of the House who had won and retained their seats through the ordeal of election could be persuaded to write and adopt rules yielding their prerogatives to neophyte members who had gained their positions through presidential patronage. Thus, to make executive branch officials leaders of the Congress, they would have to be appointed from the Congress in the first place.

Yet if interbranch collaboration is to be fostered through participation of executive officials in congressional activity, full membership for those officials—with all the complications that would follow—is by no means crucial. Collaboration takes place not at the time that votes are taken but in the deliberations that precede the vote, and executive branch officials can be admitted to any stage of those deliberations under the Constitution as it stands. Each house can make its own rules in that regard, or, if the arrangement is to reflect a negotiated agreement between the president and the Congress, it can be formalized in organizational structures and written into law. All of the proposals seriously considered over the years to give the cabinet a legislative role, as reported in chapter 3, were in the form of statutes.

Yet all of these schemes foundered because they were recognized, by both presidents and Congresses, to be either unnecessary or unworkable. When the two branches are disposed to cooperate, formal arrangements are not needed. But when they are not so disposed, any formal requirement for collaboration is likely to be ignored or negated.

When the president and the congressional majorities are of the same party, responding to the same popular mandate, and intent on carrying out a common program, the existing mechanisms for inter-branch collaboration are quite sufficient—as they were in the brief periods of harmonious and fruitful cooperation in the early years of the administrations of Wilson, Franklin Roosevelt, and Lyndon Johnson. At such times, presidents, cabinet members, and other executive officials participated informally, at every stage, in the deliberations of the Congress. Legislative agendas were established in meetings between the presidents and their Senate and House leaders. Legislation was drafted through give-and-take between administrators and legislators. In Wilson's day, the collaboration was formalized through executive participation in the House and Senate Democratic caucuses, but during the Roosevelt and Johnson years smaller, less formal meetings served as well. Cabinet members were sometimes present during subcommittee and committee meetings, but if they were not within the room they or their representatives were just outside the door available for instant consultation. They were also just outside the House and Senate chambers during floor debate. When the political mood calls for collaborative effort, infor-mation flows freely between the branches, facilitated by the congressional liaison staffs of the White House and the executive departments; administrators and legislators influence the thinking of one another, and the final legislation is truly a joint product. Even when relations between a president and congressional majorities of his own party become strained, as they always tend to do sooner or later, harmonious collaboration will continue in many areas of governmental activity, and nothing in the institutional structure stands in the way.

In other areas of activity, however—or in periods of divided government, in most or all areas—legislators and executive branch officials will find themselves in profound disagreement, each conscientiously intent on blocking the efforts of the other. In such circumstances, any requirement for collaboration that might be formalized in organizational structures and written into law—or into the Constitution—is certain to prove unavailing. Officials now may meet whenever they wish to; to compel any specified set of officials to hold meetings whether or not they may desire to confer, as in schemes for statutory joint councils or executive-legislative cabinets, would be to assure that the unwanted meetings would be brief, ill-attended, and unproductive.[9] Administration bills that have substantial support in the Congress are always introduced and considered; executive officials need not be in the legislative process to assure that that happens. Nor would any formal guarantee of the right to be heard in committee and floor proceedings be useful. Executive branch officials are now always given the courtesy of committee hearings whenever they desire to testify; to go further by guaranteeing the administrators access to committee rooms during deliberations when they are not wanted would not make them welcome or their advice more influential. Similarly, to give them the right of participation in floor debates would not bring them an audience they do not reach just as effectively through friendly members who expound the

9. For a review of proposals for joint councils, see James L. Sundquist, *The Decline and Resurgence of Congress* (Brookings Institution, 1981) pp. 469–71. Among the proposals were those advanced in the 1940s and 1950s by Edward S. Corwin and Louis W. Koenig, and endorsed by Thomas K. Finletter, for a statutory cabinet made up of legislative leaders that would have no administrative responsibility (to avoid the constitutional prohibition against dual officeholding) but would be advisory to the president and his department heads; the plan proposed by the Joint Committee on the Organization of Congress in 1946 for majority policy committees in the two houses to meet regularly with the president, an idea that was killed by House Speaker Sam Rayburn; and more recent proposals by Francis O. Wilcox and Senator Hubert H. Humphrey for a joint executive-legislative committee on national security affairs.

administration's views or through participation in public debate outside the halls of Congress.

To require officials to appear for questioning in the Senate or the House against their will would not contribute to harmonious relationships nor add significantly to the store of knowledge available to legislators. Any modification of the separation of powers principle that is to be effective, in sum, would require a constitutional amendment to permit dual officeholding.

Strengthening Political Parties

"For government to function," wrote V. O. Key, Jr., "the obstructions of the constitutional mechanism must be overcome, and it is the party that casts a web, at times weak, at times strong, over the dispersed organs of government and gives them a semblance of unity."[10]

Accordingly, reformers who are daunted by the theoretical and practical obstacles to altering the constitutional mechanism itself have been attracted to the notion that strengthening the party web may be an alternative means for attaining governmental unity. For this purpose, it is the party-in-government that counts—the political level of the administration, headed by the president, and the majorities of the House and Senate, fewer than five hundred persons in all. (For the party-in-government to be effective, of course, it normally needs to control not only the presidency but also both houses of the Congress, for a web that binds the presidency to a minority party in either house, or both, can hardly unite the organs of government.) While the party-in-government has a life of its own, to some extent its strengths and weaknesses reflect those of the party organizations in the individual states and districts and in the nation at large, for that is the political training ground of the individuals who rise to national office. Anything that would strengthen the party outside the government would therefore help to unify the governmental party. But there are no ready means to achieving stronger party organizations. If there were, they surely would have been adopted, for those who lead the Democratic and Republican parties assuredly

10. *Politics, Parties, and Pressure Groups*, 5th ed. (Crowell, 1964), p. 656.

desire to preside over more potent organizations. The barrier is that the American people have not wanted stronger parties. Quite the contrary, throughout this century—until the present time, at least— the people have distrusted party organizations and set out deliberately to weaken them.

The story of the decline of party is told in chapter 4. The Progressive movement that crusaded against public corruption early in the century found the root of the evil in party organizations. Not only were they riddled with graft and patronage, but they were undemocratic and hence unresponsive to the rising demand for governmental action to cure social and economic ills, and administratively incompetent. To reform government, party organizations had to be reformed first, and that meant that the old-style "machines," controlled by "bosses" and held together by the distribution of jobs, contracts, and other "spoils" of office, had to go. One set of Progressive reforms struck at the parties' patronage, through professionalization of management, civil service systems, competitive bidding on purchases and contracts, and public welfare programs. Another took away their control of the selection of elected officials, by instituting nonpartisan elections for municipal and some other offices and direct primaries for nominating candidates for partisan elections. Meanwhile, a newly independent press and civic reform organizations of every stripe lauded the concept of political independence. Educated, idealistic, and incorruptible voters would either choose the best individuals from the slates of candidates offered by the parties and by so doing cleanse and remake the party machines or, by organizing their own reform parties, they would defeat them. As the reforms and the attitudes spread, the old-style party organizations steadily withered. By now, they have all but vanished. In some places, they have been replaced by new-style party organizations that are open, democratic, and inclusive in their style and bound together by ideology and programmatic objectives rather than by patronage. In other places, the decline of the old-style machines has given way only to a politics of individualism, with candidates for office relying on themselves, their self-created personal organizations, and their skill in exploiting the mass media—especially television—to win their victories.

Members of Congress who arise from a political milieu of individualism carry their political style with them. Not accustomed to accepting party discipline at home, they are slow to recognize the need for it in Congress. If they had to defeat the remnants of old-style organizations in their initial races, they are likely to see merit in maintaining an antiorganization stance on Capitol Hill. As one benefit, they can be sure of gaining more media attention by challenging the established leadership in Washington than by meekly following it.

Since the party machines were destroyed by deliberate actions, taken in response to popular demand, to rebuild the old-style organizations would require a new popular demand, calling for reversal of a trend now nearly a century old. Yet, while an occasional voice is heard to suggest that such reforms as civil service be abolished in favor of a return to old-fashioned patronage, it is hardly conceivable that an attitudinal inversion on any significant scale could occur. More likely is the prospect that public sentiment may come to support the development and authority of the new-style party organizations, those that renounce the grosser forms of patronage and rely on ideology and programmatic goals as their unifying bond. There are signs that such organizations are indeed gaining strength, particularly in places where no old-style organization of consequence had to be displaced—for Republicans, in the once-solid Democratic South; for Democrats, in the formerly solid Republican northern tier of states. Yet the development and maintenance of such organizations cannot be legislated into being or otherwise created by anybody's act of will. Legal barriers to their activities can be removed—and this appears to be slowly happening, state by state and law by law—but otherwise their strengthening depends on their good behavior, by which they will earn and retain the public confidence.

Nevertheless, even if the new-style state and local parties gain in strength, that does not guarantee cohesive national party organizations, for the national parties are federations, and the organizations that compose them have always been diverse in composition and programmatic goals and even, sometimes, incompatible. The Democratic party in the 1920s, for example, was made up of locally powerful organizations in both North and South yet was never weaker as a national party, for its northern wing was urban, heavily Catholic, prolabor, more or less pro–civil rights, and wet, while its southern base was rural, overwhelmingly Protestant, proemployer, segregationist, and dry. The Republican party had a comparable East-West schism, with an agrarian bloc of progressives, or insurgents—

indelibly dubbed "sons of the wild jackass" by one of their senatorial
GOP opponents—pitted against a wing centered in the Atlantic
seaboard cities that reflected the economic views of industrialists and
financiers.

History may, however, be now on the side of more cohesive, more
nearly ideologically homogeneous national parties. As the result of
the political realignment of the New Deal era, which created a new
line of cleavage between a distinctly activist and liberal national
Democratic party and a staunchly conservative national Republican
party, ideology has been supplanting regional and religious–ethnic-
group traditions as the basis for party attachment. The movement to
the Democratic party of liberals who had been Republicans or who
came from Republican families was largely completed by the 1960s;
the once-considerable liberal wing of the GOP has all but died out,
and while conservatism has its factions that will vie for supremacy,
the party is no longer deeply divided, as it was from the time of
Theodore Roosevelt to that of Nelson Rockefeller, over fundamental
views about the role of government. The corresponding movement
of conservative southerners into the Republican party has lagged,
but in the last two decades has been proceeding at an accelerating
pace. There is no reason to think this trend will be reversed. When
the Democratic party is finally stripped of the southern conservative
wing that once held sufficient power in the Congress to thwart the
party's liberal presidents whenever it chose to do so, it will be reduced
to competing on equal terms with the Republicans for control of the
House as well as the Senate but it will be strengthened in ideological
cohesion and hence in the ability, when it does gain a majority in
either house, to concert its forces for legislative action.

The realignment has already made possible the strong and united
Republican party-in-government that was so strikingly evident in
1981 and that, had the GOP been granted control of the House as
well as the Senate, might have continued to be capable of decisive
government during the later years of the Reagan era. Perhaps the
need to foster improved collaboration between the branches—the
topic of this chapter—is no longer a Republican problem at all, but
that premise cannot be fully tested until such time as the GOP gains
undivided control of the government, a responsibility that party has
been granted only for one two-year period in more than half a
century. In any event, unity of the Democratic party-in-government

remains a problem, although realignment portends for it too a more favorable prospect if and as it is entrusted with governmental power in the future. While waiting for party realignment to exert its unifying influence, and recognizing that some degree of ideological hetero-geneity will always be found in both parties, the question is whether actions that might be designed to directly strengthen the web of the party-in-government hold promise both of effectiveness and of fea-sibility. Possibilities for such action fall into three categories—those that would alter the processes by which candidates for president and for Congress are selected, those that would strengthen the party organizations within the Congress, and those that would give national parties—and hence, in the case of the president's party, the presi-dent—stronger means for disciplining members of Congress.

The Presidential Nomination Process

The method by which the political parties choose their nominees for president has evolved through four stages. In each stage, the process that was employed had a profound effect on the relationship between the president and Congress.

As George Washington was completing his time in office, the Republican party that had taken form in the Congress under the leadership of James Madison sought a way to assure that the party's electors in 1796 would be mobilized to support the same candidates for president and vice president (a problem complicated by the fact that, before adoption of the Twelfth Amendment, electors did not vote separately to fill the two offices but simply cast two votes, with the presidency going to the candidate with the most votes, providing he had a majority, and the vice presidency to the runner-up.) They found the instrument, perhaps not unsurprisingly, in their own congressional caucus. The party members in Senate and House met and proposed Thomas Jefferson and Aaron Burr. Jefferson finished second to John Adams that year, but four years later the party was so well organized that the caucus nominees—again Jefferson and Burr—received the same number of electoral votes, and the decision had to go to the House of Representatives, which chose Jefferson. His successors, Madison and Monroe, gained the presidency as nominees of the Republican caucus. By then, however, it had become clear that this nominating process undermined the framers' concept of the separation of powers and the independent presidency. A president desiring reelection had to become the follower, even the creature, of his party's congressional wing; thus Madison, seeking renomination in 1812, had to acquiesce in the war with Britain that congressional jingoes, led by Speaker Henry Clay, were eagerly promoting. More important, the congressional caucus had earned the enmity of many state party leaders, who felt entitled to a role in the nominating process. Following the nomination of Monroe in 1816, therefore, it lapsed.

After a hiatus marked by the second occasion in which the presidential choice was thrown into the House, in 1824, a far broader nominating institution was invented—the national convention that every party has since conducted each four years. How the delegates were to be selected has been left to the individual states, but throughout the nineteenth century they were chosen, in one manner or another, by the state party organizations. A successful presidential candidate therefore had to cultivate the party elite, including its officeholders and its bosses, and he had to construct his administration from persons acceptable to them and distribute patronage according to their dictates. The elite was not monolithic, of course, and presidents had to contend with rivalries among ambitious party leaders in the states, but the party-in-government was invariably led by a man who was bred on an ethic of party regularity and discipline, enforced by patronage. Members of the Senate, selected by state legislatures, were organization men—often the party bosses themselves—and House members arose from the same milieu. The traditions of party regularity and deference to leadership bred in the state and local organizations were bound to be reflected in highly disciplined congressional parties, dominated in the House before and after the turn of the century by the Republican "czar" Speakers, Thomas B. Reed and Joseph G. Cannon, and in the Senate by a GOP oligarchy led by Nelson W. Aldrich of Rhode Island. Republican presidents had to deal with these powerful figures on equal terms, and relations were not invariably harmonious, but unity and decisiveness in government depended on the concurrence of only a few people who could easily be assembled in a small room.

Another invention—the presidential primary—carried the nominating process into a third phase, beginning in the first decade of this century and continuing through 1968. As the direct primary was introduced, state by state, in the selection of candidates for state office and for Congress, it was extended by some of those states to the choice of delegates to the national party nominating conventions. By 1920, twenty states had one or another form of presidential primary. After that, the number declined, fluctuating between fourteen and eighteen in the years from 1924 through 1968.[11]

Of these state primaries, however, some were preempted by favorite sons, whom serious national candidates usually did not risk challenging, and not all the candidates competed in all the others. In most campaign years, therefore, only a few states turned out to be true battlegrounds. In the 1960 Democratic contest, for example, Senators John F. Kennedy and Hubert H. Humphrey collided head-on in only two states—Wisconsin and West Virginia—and it was his triumphs there that clinched the nomination for Kennedy. In this kind of system, candidates had an opportunity to demonstrate their appeal to the voters, but the decision was finally made by a convention still composed predominantly of the party elite of professional politicians, officeholders, and leaders of interest groups allied with the party. All other things being equal, or nearly so, that elite preferred a candidate who was a proven vote-getter on a national scale, but if other things were not equal they were free to reject their most popular candidate—and often did. Thus, Theodore Roosevelt in 1912 campaigned for the Republican nomination in all twelve of that year's primary states and won nine of them, but the convention renominated President Taft, who carried only one. In 1920, Warren G. Harding's name appeared on the ballot in only two Republican state primaries outside his own Ohio and he finished last in both of those, yet won the nomination. In the 1940 Republican primaries, Thomas E. Dewey won nearly 50 percent of all the votes but lost in the convention to Wendell L. Willkie, who tallied less than 1 percent. And in 1952, Senator Estes Kefauver of Tennessee swept the Democratic primaries, losing only two states, one to a favorite son. Yet the convention rejected him in favor of Adlai E. Stevenson, who had not even sought the nomination before the delegates met.[12]

After the tumultuous 1968 Democratic convention in Chicago, however, the presidential selection process was revolutionized. The

11. Congressional Quarterly, *Guide to U.S. Elections* (Washington: CQ, 1975), pp. 309–49.
12. Ibid.

party that defied the anti-Vietnam demonstrators in nominating Hubert Humphrey yielded to them on their demand for more open and democratic processes in the future. A reform commission headed first by Senator George S. McGovern of South Dakota and later by Representative Donald M. Fraser of Minnesota devised new party rules to ensure proportional representation of women, young people, and minorities in each state delegation whenever the delegates were chosen by caucus. The complexity and rigidity of these requirements, as well as the continuing demand from the underrepresented groups for more participatory processes, led state after state to shift from caucuses to primaries. The Republican party was swept along in the reform tide and joined, usually, in drafting state legislation that established primaries for both parties. The number of primaries rose from fourteen states and the District of Columbia in 1968 to twenty in 1972, twenty-six in 1976, and thirty-five in 1980. From a total of 12 million voters in the 1968 primary (7.5 million Democratic, 4.5 million Republican) participation rose to 21.9 million in 1972 (16.0 million and 5.9 million), 26.5 million in 1976 (16.1 million and 10.4 million), and 31.4 million in 1980 (18.7 million and 12.7 million).[13] By that time, a large majority of convention delegates was selected in primaries, and even in the minority of states that still used caucuses, those meetings were required by party rules to be so open and well publicized that the party elite no longer controlled them either. The loss of influence of the party professionals was epitomized by the refusal of the 1972 Democratic convention to seat Mayor Richard J. Daley of Chicago. In the Democratic party, many party leaders, including a majority of the party's representatives in the Congress, avoided the risk of such humiliation by not seeking to be elected delegates. In 1980, only 50 of the 333 Democratic senators and representatives sat in the party conclave.[14]

In this fourth stage of the evolution of the presidential nominating process, the convention has been reduced from a deliberative to a

13. Ibid., pp. 343–45; Richard M. Scammon and Alice V. McGillivray, comps. and eds., *America Votes: A Handbook of Contemporary American Election Statistics, 1980,* vol. 14 (Washington: CQ, 1981), pp. 21–39.

14. Paul T. David, Ralph M. Goldman, and Richard C. Bain, *The Politics of National Party Conventions* (Brookings Institution, 1960), which analyzed the composition of conventions through 1956, found that 54 of 230 Democratic members of Congress served as delegates in 1948, 80 of 282 in 1952, and 99 of 280 in 1956. The average participation rate of 29.1 percent is almost double the 15.0 percent rate of 1980.

ratifying body, simply recording the decision made by more than 10 million party voters in primaries and caucuses. In an unusually close contest, the few delegates who were chosen uncommitted or who were committed to a candidate no longer in the race could, conceivably, wield the decisive influence, but since 1968 no contest in either party has been that close. Each four years, one candidate in each party has emerged from the delegate-selection season with enough votes to ensure his nomination. A candidate who dominates the primaries can no longer be jettisoned at the convention as was Roosevelt in 1912, Dewey in 1940, or Kefauver in 1952. The party elders no longer have the votes.

This has grave implications for the unity of the party-in-government. The party elite that includes the party's senators and representatives has lost the means to defend itself against the election of an outsider to the White House. The crucial qualifications of a presidential candidate now are his ability to raise money and to appeal to the public at large through television. Whether the candidate is acceptable to, and capable of working effectively with, the members of his party in the Congress and the other party leaders on whom he will depend for support has not been a criterion that the voters deemed important—or would have the information to apply if they did. Indeed, independence of the party elite can be a source of strength with the party's voters. Thus Jimmy Carter could win the Democratic nomination by proclaiming himself an outsider and boasting of his lack of association with the party's Washington establishment. After his failure in the presidency—brought on in no small part by his inexperience in national affairs and his lack of rapport with the party leaders in and out of Congress—important elements of the party elite were determined not to make the same mistake in 1984. So they rallied around former Vice President Walter F. Mondale, only to find that another outsider—Senator Gary Hart of Colorado—could come within an inch of victory by using their endorsements, particularly those of organized labor, as a club with which to bludgeon their favorite. On the Republican side, Ronald Reagan rose as an outsider like Carter, even mounting a powerful and nearly successful primary assault on the incumbent President Gerald Ford in 1976, but after his 1980 election he turned out to possess the political skills necessary to put together and lead a remarkably united Republican party-in-government. The Reagan experience shows, however, that the GOP is as vulnerable as the Democrats to the threat that an outsider might reach the White House by challenging and defeating the party establishment. And the next outsider might then turn out to lack the Reagan flair for leadership.

How, then, might the presidential nomination process be changed to assure the national party's leadership—and particularly its senators and representatives who with the president and his administration form, or would form, the party-in-government—sufficient influence to block the nomination of a candidate who is, in its view, unsuitable? At one extreme on the range of theoretical possibilities stands the 1796–1816 method of nomination by the party-in-Congress, but that was discarded as too cliquish and exclusionary even for that period and would surely be beyond the realm of possibility today. Yet if time cannot be rolled back that far, might it be carried back just twenty years? As late as 1968, the party elite had an effective veto power over the popular choice for president as expressed in the primaries, and unacceptable candidates could be, and often were, rejected. A working balance between democratic and elite influences protected the values of both. But that balance was struck by accident, not design. Responding to the reform spirit of the Progressive Era, some states introduced the presidential primary—but, as it happened, never more than a minority. Now, reacting to a new set of forces, an overwhelming majority of states has adopted that reform and the balance has been destroyed.

The answer appears simple, then. Reduce the number of states with presidential primaries to something like the former level. A trend in this direction may, indeed, be under way, but so far the results are modest. In 1984, only twenty-eight states plus the District of Columbia held presidential primaries, seven fewer than four years before, but the primary states still chose a large majority of delegates to both conventions and 17.8 million voters participated in the Democratic balloting, down less than a million from the 1980 total.[15] (In the Republican primaries, Ronald Reagan's renomination was uncontested.) The switch back to the caucus system by seven states was facilitated by a modification of the rigid quota requirements that had been adopted after 1968. But it may be doubted whether this trend will go much further or, if it did, whether it would in fact

15. *Congressional Quarterly Weekly Report*, vol. 42 (June 16, 1984), p. 1443.

restore the former balance between elite and democratic influences. The eruption at the 1968 Democratic convention released the pent-up frustration of many thousands of rank-and-file Democrats with their effective exclusion from the elite-controlled caucuses by which delegates had been selected. Women, blacks, and other minorities have been the beneficiaries of the new participatory processes, and so have antiestablishment Democratic candidates like Gary Hart and Jesse Jackson. In the Republican party, new groups, notably those of the New Right, have likewise moved in force into party affairs. All these newcomers to political power have a stake in blocking any move toward restoration of the old elite control. Their influence, in both parties, will surely hinder the development of any headlong trend away from primaries and back to caucuses. Yet, even if that trend continues, their influence will assure that caucuses are widely participatory, beyond control by any elite group. And they will be supported by national party rules that can hardly be rewritten to favor selection of delegates through closed, controlled processes.

If the balance of influence is not to be restored through a return to the pre-1968 model, the alternative must lie in altering the makeup of the convention itself. The Democratic party took a gingerly step in this direction after its 1980 defeat, by adopting a rule assigning 14 percent of its convention seats to unpledged delegates (who came to be known as superdelegates)—including 60 percent of the Democratic members of Congress, other elected officials, and party officers. Theoretically, in the event of a close convention contest, so large a bloc of uncommitted members of the party establishment could hold decisive power. But that prospect can easily be overestimated, because the superdelegates are not likely to be either a bloc or uncommitted. They will tend to split along much the same lines as the convention as a whole. True, a substantial majority of them in 1984 supported Walter Mondale, but by convention time his nomination had been ordained by the millions of primary voters. If Senator Hart had entered the convention with a majority, however slight, of regular delegates, the superdelegates might well have split more nearly evenly, out of reluctance to defy the will of the voters in their respective states or districts as expressed in primaries and caucuses. They might still have been somewhat more pro-Mondale than the convention as a whole, but a small bias among 14 percent of the delegates would not often decide the nomination in a convention where virtually all of the other participants were pledged to their candidates during the selection process.

If that proportion were significantly expanded, however, the chances would increase that the party establishment could exercise an effective veto over an unsuitable but popular candidate whose margin in the primaries and caucuses was less than overwhelming. And a greater participation of leaders and officeholders would strengthen party organizations by establishing closer bonds between the elite and the rank and file of party activists.

Another approach to altering the makeup of the convention has been suggested by Lloyd N. Cutler, a cochair of the Committee on the Constitutional System. Let the regular delegates be selected through primaries and caucuses, as at present, Cutler has proposed, but let them compose one chamber of a bicameral convention, the other chamber to consist of the party's nominees for Senate and House seats and its incumbent carryover senators. The two bodies, meeting separately but simultaneously, would each nominate a candidate. In the event they chose different nominees, each chamber would hold a runoff ballot between the two victors, and the nominee would be the one with the highest combined percentage, the two chambers having equal weight. Each chamber would also adopt a platform, resolving disagreements through a conference committee.[16]

This plan has appeal, as the means of giving the party's legislators and legislative candidates an opportunity to veto the popular choice of the party's voters while yet preserving the party convention as now constituted (minus the delegates who would sit in the new congressional chamber). A candidate who had to survive the screening of his party in the Congress would have to court the support of its members and make commitments about cooperation; Jimmy Carter, for one, would not have dared to run *against* the party establishment, including the party in Congress. And after taking office, a new president would have to continue to court his congressional party, lest it deny him renomination for a second term.

But a bicameral convention plan would encounter practical difficulties. It might place too much power in the congressional party, for the popular chamber might be narrowly divided while the congressional chamber would have a higher proportion of uncom-

16. Lloyd N. Cutler, "Getting Rid of Incoherent Government," *Washington Post*, March 27, 1983.

mitted delegates, some of whom would be receptive to leadership discipline to vote as a bloc. Since the 435 House candidates would outnumber the senators and Senate candidates in the congressional chamber by a ratio of six or seven to one, the Speaker of the House would hold a power far exceeding that of any other individual in the nominating process, if he chose to promise rewards and punishments in order to influence even a small proportion of his House colleagues.[17] He could become, conceivably, an individual kingmaker.

A party that adopted the bicameral convention scheme would, moreover, run the risk of crippling the candidacy of its nominee. If the two chambers agreed, of course, the candidate would be the beneficiary of two endorsements in two bursts of fanfare. But in the event they disagreed—and surely they would some of the time, if the change were worth making—the winner of the runoff election would go before the country, and be quickly branded by the opposition, as a loser, one who had been rejected, either by the people's representatives in the popular chamber or by his party peers in the congressional chamber.

Given the practical difficulties and risks, the more promising approach would appear to be that taken by the Democratic party in reserving seats for superdelegates at its 1984 convention. The number could well be increased to include all of the incumbent senators and representatives and nominees for those offices. But the unicameral structure would be retained, so that tensions between popularly elected and ex officio delegates would be kept submerged and easily resolved through regular convention procedures.

Strengthening the Parties in Congress

Just as the party is the web that unites Senate, House, and presidency as the policymaking triad, it is also the institution that brings coherence to the separate activities of each chamber of the legislature. It is through the party mechanism that a house organizes to conduct its business, elects its leaders, constitutes its committees,

17. The number would probably be increased by those running for the five non-voting House seats for the District of Columbia, Puerto Rico, Virgin Islands, Guam, and American Samoa, but minus a few districts that might have failed to nominate a candidate. Presumably, states whose nominees are now chosen in the autumn would advance their selection dates to the preconvention period.

develops a program insofar as it may have one, and schedules floor action. Whether the Senate or the House is efficient, productive, and creative depends on whether the majority party, which controls that body, itself possesses those attributes. That depends on whether it is unified enough to create strong internal institutions of leadership and disciplined enough to follow the leadership it has created.

But throughout the twentieth century, the unity and discipline of parties in the Congress have been steadily breaking down. In both houses, the rise of the western Republican insurgents early in the century split the majority Republican party. The House GOP rebels joined with the Democrats in 1910 to strip Speaker Cannon of his dictatorial powers, while in the Senate the authority of the Aldrich oligarchy gradually dissipated as its members retired or died.

For a brief period, in 1913–14, the Democratic party used its caucuses in both houses as an instrument of discipline. The measures that made up Woodrow Wilson's New Freedom were forged in party meetings, in which representatives of the administration participated. The House caucus then bound its members by two-thirds votes, and any member who violated the group's directive (unless an exception was made, which was possible under some circumstances) could be "read out of the party," with a loss of committee assignments and other perquisites. The Senate caucus was less authoritative but equally effective in enforcing discipline. But the procedure was vociferously denounced by the Republican opposition and by the reformist organizations and journals that flourished in the Progressive Era. Caucus coercion was undemocratic and tyrannous, they charged, destructive of the rights both of the Republican minorities as groups and of the Democratic members as individuals. The outcry contributed to the Democrats' decision to abandon caucus discipline after mid-1914, and except for a few measures in the early 1920s and the 1930s it has not been again attempted. The Republicans, having led the attack on King Caucus, even forsook the word, renaming their party meetings conferences. By Sam Rayburn's day, the Democratic caucus met only at the outset of each Congress to nominate its candidate for Speaker and elect the majority leadership; once installed, those officers saw nothing to be gained from further party meetings that could only attempt to restrict their freedom of action or otherwise embarrass them.[18]

18. Sundquist, *Decline and Resurgence*, pp. 168–76.

When Czar Cannon was dethroned and authority slipped from the leadership group in the Senate, the repository of power came to be the chairmen of the Senate and House standing committees, who gained their posts not by party preferment but by simple longevity, as beneficiaries of rigid seniority systems adopted by both parties in both houses. A strong majority leader like Senator Lyndon B. Johnson, the Texas Democrat who held sway in the 1950s, could sense the limits of what his chairmen would accept, develop and announce a program within those limits, and then maneuver most of it to passage. But his contemporary, the strongest House Speaker of modern times, Sam Rayburn, could not do even that. Rayburn was at the mercy of a coterie of committee chairmen who gained and held their positions by seniority—in particular, Rules Committee Chairman Howard W. Smith, a Virginia Democrat who possessed the power, and used it, to block legislation emerging from Democrat-controlled committees that did not accord with his ultraconservative individual views.

Eventually, the House Democratic party acted to destroy the arbitrary power of committee chairmen. The Rules Committee was enlarged in 1961 and, after Smith was defeated for renomination in his Virginia primary, the seniority system presently brought the first of a series of party loyalists to the chairmanship. The decisive actions, however, were those taken by the caucus to destroy the automaticity of the seniority system itself. When it deposed three veteran committee chairmen in 1975, it made clear that all chairmen held their posts at the sufferance of the party's House membership and must be responsive to it. But to make doubly sure, it adopted a "subcommittee bill of rights" that assured democratic procedures within committees.[19] Change in the Senate has paralleled that in the House. The majority Democrats in 1975 formally abandoned their rigid seniority system, and while no chairmen were dislodged, the rules

19. House Republicans formally renounced seniority as an absolute principle even before the Democrats did, but in practice they have adhered to the tradition in designating the ranking minority members of committees and subcommittees. Since the Democrats have organized the House and held all chairmanships continuously since 1955, and for all but two Congresses since 1931, the story of redistribution of power in the House is necessarily a Democratic story. How a Republican majority party in the House would proceed in organizing the chamber and managing its business can only be speculated about, but the same attitudes and influences that have led the Democrats to introduce the institutional changes discussed in this section have been clearly apparent on the Republican side as well, and one may surmise that GOP institutions and practices would not differ fundamentally from those of the Democrats.

change—and the example of the House—had its effect in democratizing committee operations. Once the Republicans gained control of the Senate in 1981, they adhered strictly to the seniority principle in assigning committee chairmanships, but no chairman gave evidence of relapsing toward the authoritarianism of earlier decades.[20]

The power held by autocratic committee chairmen was thus dispersed, to subcommittee chairmen and to the individual members of the majority party, who not only could assert themselves more effectively at the subcommittee level but also had the power to choose, and to unseat, subcommittee chairmen. Moreover, the steady growth in the number of subcommittees in the House from 119 in 1972 to 146 in 1983 introduced new opportunities for entrepreneurship, with groups inevitably competing for jurisdiction.[21] Accompanying these institutional changes—and, in the most fundamental sense, causing them—was what amounted to a cultural change in both the Senate and the House. A new breed of politicians had arisen from the individualistic politics that now flourished in the states and congressional districts where the old political machines had disintegrated, and they brought an ethic of individualism and egalitarianism to the legislative chambers that as late as the 1950s had been described as venerating seniority and experience. By the mid-1970s, Senate Majority Leader Mike Mansfield, Montana Democrat, was boasting that "nobody is telling anybody what to do" in the Senate and House Majority Leader Thomas P. O'Neill, Jr., Massachusetts Democrat, was noting that since machine politics was "dead" in the country it was dead in the House as well, making that body "extremely difficult to coordinate."[22]

Nevertheless, the destruction of the power of independent committee chairmen opened new opportunities for the majority leaders

20. But the tradition became a matter of serious concern to the Reagan administration and the Senate Republican leadership. In 1985, Jesse Helms of North Carolina would have been entitled to the chairmanship of the Senate Foreign Relations Committee on the basis of seniority, had he claimed it, even though his policies would probably have been in conflict at times with those of the administration. Secretary of State George P. Shultz and other foreign policy officials were relieved when Helms chose to remain as chairman of the Agriculture Committee and allow an administration loyalist, Richard G. Lugar of Indiana, to take the Foreign Relations post.

21. The House 1983 figure includes the task forces of the new Budget Committee. In the Senate, the number of subcommittees rose from 103 to 107 in the same period.

22. Other members and journalistic observers made similar comments, summarized in Sundquist, *Decline and Resurgence*, pp. 395–402.

to try to forge cohesive parties. Given the individualistic temper of the members, leaders had to move gingerly. Yet when they did move carefully, they met little resistance, for the members were in fact ambivalent. Each member valued his or her individual prerogatives, yet each was also concerned with the record of the legislative body as a whole, and members understood that if the legislature was to be productive, rampant individualism had to be restrained. The result has been a development of centralizing institutions that offsets to some degree the trend toward dispersion of power in the last two decades.

Most significant of these centralizing innovations has been the creation of a budget committee in each house with responsibility for recommending spending and revenue levels, which as amended and adopted on the floor—and reconciled between the houses in conference committees—establish a general fiscal policy to which individual pieces of legislation are then supposed to conform. In admitting this new element into the legislature's power structure, the authorizing and appropriating committees yielded a significant share of their autonomy and their policymaking power. Tension has continued between the old committees and the new, and the resolutions presented by the budget committees, and revised and adopted by the chambers, have not always been enforced. Yet in 1980 and especially in 1981, the budget process made possible the wholesale revision of laws that mandated expenditures, an achievement that would have been inconceivable under the former decentralized committee structure.

The budget committees, as bipartisan bodies reporting to their respective houses, have had their effect on *party* cohesion only indirectly, but in both houses the majority party leadership has been linked more closely to the budget committee than it has ever been tied to the older authorizing and appropriating committees. In the House, the linkage is institutionalized. By tradition, the House majority leader does not serve on committees, but when the Budget Committee was established an exception was made. Both Majority Leader O'Neill and his assistant, Jim Wright of Texas, were appointed to it, ranking just below the chairman, and when O'Neill became Speaker, Wright continued his service—the only member exempt from limitation as to the number of terms he may serve. In 1980, the Democratic leaders and budget committee chairmen of both houses, with other chairmen brought in for consultation, met in continuous session for more than a week to work out agreement on how to bring the budget into balance. The next year, when President Reagan presented his radical fiscal program to the Congress, the House majority leadership and the Democratic majority on the Budget Committee collaborated to produce a measure that could be identified as the party's alternative to the Reagan proposals. The Democrats suffered enough defections to defeat that alternative but the precedent was established solidly enough that in each succeeding year the party has had something that could be called a budget policy. Meanwhile, the Republican majority that assumed control of the Senate in 1981 emerged as a tightly cohesive group, both in support of the Reagan program, as in its first year, and in its own initiatives, particularly the tax increase bill of 1982 and its substitute for the president's budget in 1985. Because so many policy decisions are encompassed in the budget, the chairman of the Budget Committee, Pete V. Domenici of New Mexico, became a central figure in the Senate leadership structure.

The institutions that are designed explicitly to foster majority party unity are more important in the large, unwieldy House than in the more intimate Senate, and they have been gaining strength despite the rise of the culture of individualism. Since all of the instruments through which the party acts are created by, and responsible to, its caucus, the vitality of the instruments is likely to be no greater than the vitality of the caucus itself. No one in either party has suggested that a return to the binding caucuses of 1913 would be desirable or even conceivable, but the reformers who set out to democratize the House in the 1960s seized upon the caucus as their indispensable tool. They won an agreement from Speaker John W. McCormack, Rayburn's successor, that the caucus would meet not just biennially but every month. In those meetings, they carried out their successful attack on the entrenched seniority system, designed through a caucus committee the "subcommittee bill of rights," and then inevitably plunged the caucus into discussion of party policy on legislative issues—particularly the Vietnam War. By the 1970s, the caucus was giving specific instructions to the Democratic members of committees on what they must do in those bodies as "agents of the caucus." But this presumed a greater degree of unity than the party had achieved. Dissenters from the positions taken by the caucus majority, including some senior and influential members, vehemently protested the attempts at party discipline; the leadership retreated, enough of the dissenters boycotted the meetings to reduce attendance below a quorum, and the caucus fell again for a time into disuse.

During the Reagan administration, however, the caucus was revived as a discussion forum, and late in 1984 Speaker O'Neill agreed that during the next two years regular meetings would be scheduled on a biweekly rather than a monthly basis. He also expressed an intent to use the party's steering and policy committee more systematically in the development of legislative strategy, and he agreed to formalize a smaller, representative consultative group to meet with him biweekly.[23]

That centralizing institutions have evolved at all in an environment of equality and individualism reveals House Democrats' acceptance of party unity as a necessary and desirable goal, but the slow and sporadic character of the institutional evolution shows also that the tolerance of the members has limits that are easily transgressed. Those who would seek to strengthen the congressional party can offer no panacea for instant party unity—not, at least, any panacea that today's individualistic congressmen would find acceptable. Reformers can do no more than encourage steady experimentation with institutional devices by the majority party in each house and hope, perhaps, that a new generation of leaders emerging from the group that has demanded the revitalization of the caucus and of party committees may possess greater skill in using them to weld the disparate elements of the party into a more cohesive working body.

During the Reagan administration, of course, greater unity and discipline among House Democrats would have resulted in a lesser, rather than a greater, degree of unity in the government as a whole. Had the Democratic party been monolithic, the confrontation with the president and the Republican Senate would have been more forceful, deadlocks more rigid, and negotiations to break them more arduous. The decisive governmental actions of 1981 were made possible by Democratic disunity that permitted a coalition of Republicans and southern Democratic "boll weevils" to make the essential decisions in the House. What can be accomplished through the

---

23. Diane Granat, "Junior Democrats Gain a Louder Voice. . .Leadership Panels Will Serve as a Forum," *National Journal* (December 8, 1984), pp. 3054–55.

measures to strengthen parties within the Congress, then, will avail little in a time of divided government.

Money as a Means of Discipline

The ultimate disciplinary power that a political party can hold over a legislator is the right to deny him or her the party's nomination for reelection or for advancement to a higher office. In other countries, parties commonly possess that right, whether or not they exercise it. The direct primary is unknown outside the United States, and nominations are effectively in the hands of the party elite. Either the national party organization makes the choice, or it ratifies the selection of the party in the local electoral area—after, perhaps, having directly influenced the area nominating body in the first place. While it may be rare for a legislator to be read out of the party, the fact that an ultimate disciplinary power exists accounts in part for the power of the party whips to compel obedience on crucial votes in the legislature.

Before the invention of the direct primary, state and local party organizations in the United States exercised that kind of power, too. Although nominations might be made by conventions that were larger and involved wider citizen participation than those in other countries, they still were often tightly controlled by a boss or a small group of bosses who could deny renomination to a maverick legislator. And the results were reflected in the disciplined, party-line voting frequently recorded in state legislatures and city councils and the ready acceptance of party discipline as the norm in the Congress. Even after the primary replaced the convention as the nominating process in almost every state, the bosses in some places still retained a powerful influence, or even control, for a while, because their organizations could still dominate the relatively small turnouts in the party primaries. As the old party machines have disintegrated, a half dozen states have reintroduced the convention into the nominating process for senatorial (but not House) candidates, but usually as an endorsing rather than a nominating body. A candidate who loses the endorsement may still run in the party primary and the endorsed candidate does not always win.[24] With the exception of these few

24. In Colorado and Connecticut, a candidate must receive at least 20 percent of the convention vote in order to be eligible to run in the primary, and in Utah a candidate who receives 70 percent of the convention vote is declared the nominee.

states, then, and as a practical matter even in most of them, anyone who calls himself a Democrat or a Republican can enter the party's primary and, if successful—aided, perhaps, by the crossover votes of persons who are not even adherents of the party—carry its banner in the general election for Congress without the approval of that party's official governing body at the state level. And the national party organization has no ratifying authority whatever. Thus, Democrats and Republicans arrive in the Congress with all the rights and privileges of party members even though they may be wholly opposed to the party's philosophy and program. They take their place on the seniority ladder and, until the abandonment of the rigid seniority system by the Democrats and House Republicans, they could rise automatically to the chairmanship of major committees. A party in Congress is able to deny preferment to a member, as House Democrats have shown. But it cannot deny a member his right to run for reelection on the party's slate.[25]

In the absence of that ultimate sanction, however, the national parties—particularly the Republican party—have developed an alternative power that may turn out to be hardly less potent. That is the power of money. With television commercials now the dominant mode of communication of candidates to voters, campaigns have become, by any established standard, incredibly expensive. In 1982, a total of $190 million was raised for campaigns for House seats, or more than $430,000 per seat—almost three times the total of only six years earlier. The average of the seriously contested seats was, of course, much higher, approaching $1 million, or $500,000 per candidate. The corresponding total for thirty-three U.S. Senate races was $127 million, or nearly $4 million per seat and $2 million per candidate—again more than three times the level of six years earlier.[26]

Preprimary endorsement conventions are held in Massachusetts, Minnesota, and New York. Several southern states give parties the option of nominating by convention or by primary, but except in Virginia the primary has usually been chosen.

25. The national party headquarters of both parties have on rare occasions publicly repudiated a nominee for Congress, because of his identification with racism or communism or because of personal scandal, but they have not been able to deny the use of the party name. Some have suggested that parties could gain proprietary rights to their names under the copyright laws, but the suggestion has not been followed.

26. Federal Election Commission data, compiled in Norman J. Ornstein and others, *Vital Statistics on Congress, 1984–1985* (Washington: American Enterprise Institute, 1984), pp. 78–79. These figures exclude the funds raised and spent by candidates who lost in the primaries.

However able and ambitious, a candidate without access to large sums of money will, in most states and districts, be left at the starting gate. And the power to influence, or even to dictate, nominations that was once held by the leaders of party organizations has now passed in large measure to informal networks of money raisers.

This shift in power may have contributed, in some unmeasurable degree, to the decline of party discipline in the Congress. If the ultimate sanction—the capacity to grant or deny nomination and renomination—lies in money sources outside the party structure, it is they who have the power to impose discipline. To a great extent, the large blocs of outside money are in the hands of political action committees (PACs), which contributed about $80 million to 1982 Senate and House campaigns—more than three times the $24 million contributed by party organizations or spent by them on the candidates' behalf. Congressmen and PACs alike contend that campaign donations only buy the committees "access" to present their views on legislation, but journalistic exposés have produced solid evidence that money often directly sways votes. A quotation from Representative Mike Synar, Oklahoma Democrat, is typical of many: "I go out on the floor and say to a member, 'I need your help on this bill,' and often he will say, 'I can't do that, I got $5,000 from a special interest.' So I no longer lobby Congressmen. I lobby the lobbyists to lobby the Congressmen."[27]

The extent to which the power of money has flowed from the parties to the PACs may, however, be overemphasized, for the two are by no means divorced. Business PACs work closely with Republican party organizations, and labor PACs with Democratic, to determine where a concentration of campaign money is most likely to tip the balance in a close race. Spokespersons for both the Democratic and Republican national committees have described their function as "matchmaking" between their candidates and friendly PACs. Ronald Reagan himself made a plea in 1978 to business leaders

27. Mark Green, "Political Pac-Man," *New Republic* (December 13, 1982), p. 19. Green assembles an array of such quotations and other evidence of PAC influence. More extensive treatments of the persuasive power of PACs are Larry J. Sabato, *PAC Power: Inside the World of Political Action Committees* (Norton, 1984), esp. chap. 4; Amitai Etzioni, *Capital Corruption: The New Attack on American Democracy* (Harcourt Brace Jovanovich, 1984), esp. chaps. 3, 4; Elizabeth Drew, *Politics and Money: The New Road to Corruption* (Macmillan, 1983).

for greater support to the Republican party from corporate PACs.[28] And Representative Tony Coelho, the Californian who became chairman of the Democratic Congressional Campaign Committee in 1980, built his solid reputation in that job partly on his success in persuading business PACs that since the Democrats were likely to control the House for the rest of the century, the committees would be well advised to divide their funds more evenly between Democratic and Republican candidates.[29]

Since party organizations can help or hinder a candidate's appeal to PACs for funds, both new candidates and sitting members have an incentive to maintain good relations with party leaders, inside and outside the Congress. Nevertheless, if the funds were actually at the disposal of the party itself rather than the independent PACs, the party's control—and with it, its disciplinary power—would be still greater. Accordingly, those who seek to strengthen the party as the web that unifies the government have suggested reforms that would result in a candidate's getting a greater proportion of his or her total campaign funds directly from party committees. This could be accomplished by (1) lifting the limits on the totals that party committees may contribute to candidates; (2) adding from public funds to the total available to the parties for distribution to candidates; or (3) tightening the limits on PAC activity, thus increasing the relative importance of party organizations in campaign finance. These approaches are not mutually exclusive, and they would be most effective in combination.

The limits on PAC contributions were set in 1974 at $5,000 per House or Senate candidate in the general election (plus another $5,000 in the primary) and donations to House campaigns by a party's national committee or congressional campaign committee were treated as just another PAC contribution. The law permitted a $17,500 contribution by a party's senatorial campaign committee to each Senate race, plus direct expenditures of $8 million distributed among states by a formula based on voting-age population. Contributions to party committees were limited to $20,000 a year for individuals and $15,000 for PACs. The relative importance of party contributions

28. Sabato, *PAC Power*, pp. 141, 146.
29. Brooks Jackson, "How Money Matters: Democrats Credit Wins to Funding," *Wall Street Journal*, November 12, 1984.

would be enhanced if these ceilings on party contributions were raised or removed. They were, however, enacted by a Democratic-controlled Congress with the intent of preventing the Republicans from taking full advantage of their vastly superior capacity to raise campaign funds, and any proposal to remove them, or liberalize them significantly, would not be likely to attract bipartisan support.[30]

Public financing of congressional campaigns, with either a limitation or outright prohibition of private contributions, is an idea going back to the Progressive Era, but interest revived after the Watergate scandal and after the Congress authorized public funds for presidential campaigns. A bill to extend public financing to congressional campaigns passed the Senate in 1974 but failed by forty-one votes in the House, and a second bill limited to House races, actively supported by the House leadership and President Carter, died in a House committee in 1979.[31] Neither bill would have funneled the money through the parties, however; the public funds would have gone directly to the candidates on certification of their nomination and as they raised the required matching funds from small contributors, and single-issue as well as major-party candidates would have been eligible. Thus, opponents argued on the House floor in 1974 that the public financing provisions would actually weaken the parties. The Committee for Party Renewal, an organization consisting mainly of political scientists, urged in 1979 that the public financing bill be amended to channel the funds through political parties, with "rea-

30. In the absence of bipartisan support in the Congress for amendments to the campaign finance laws, it has been suggested that the Democratic party might unilaterally adopt party rules that imposed spending limits on candidates for national office, subject to acceptance by the Republicans of a challenge to do likewise. If the GOP declined to accept the limits, the Democrats presumably would gain politically from having issued the challenge, since the polls indicate the public favors limiting campaign expenditures. Proceeding by way of party rules would also circumvent that part of the Supreme Court's 1976 *Buckley* v. *Valeo* decision (424 U.S. 1) that invalidated those sections of the Federal Election Campaign Act that imposed limits on expenditures by candidates from their own resources. The Court held that these limits violated the free speech guarantees of the First Amendment, but that amendment applies only to statutes, not to party rules. No substantial support for this approach has yet developed, however, among Democratic party officials.

31. An account of the 1979 struggle is Gary W. Copeland, "The House Says 'No' to Public Financing of Congressional Campaigns," *Legislative Studies Quarterly*, vol. 9 (August 1984), pp. 487–504.

sonable discretion" as to their allocation.[32] But because public funding would reduce the Republican fund-raising advantage, this approach would not have bipartisan support either. And because it would fund challenges to incumbents, many sitting members of both parties—and any bill has to be passed by incumbents—are skeptical of this approach.

One of the simplest ways to divert PAC resources to the parties would be to amend the tax law relating to political contributions. At present, a limited tax credit is granted for contributions, including those made to PACs as well as to parties and candidates. If the credit were restricted to contributions to parties, and especially if the limit were then raised, the parties would gain a significant advantage in the competition for campaign funds. To reduce PAC influence, proposals have been made to lower the $5,000 limit on a PAC's contribution to individual candidates, or to put an aggregate limit on what a candidate may accept from all PACs. A $70,000 limit was approved by the House in 1979, but this approach is vulnerable to criticism as favoring incumbents over challengers, as favoring wealthy candidates who under the Constitution can spend unlimited amounts of their own money, and as likely to result in the PACs' spending the money directly to help the candidate.[33] At the extreme have been suggestions to outlaw PACs altogether or to require that their contributions be made to parties rather than to individual candidates.

As the number of PACs and their total expenditures and aggregate influence continue to grow, the clamor for further reform of congressional campaign finance is sure to mount correspondingly. Given the power that PACs now wield, any truly drastic reform—such as outright prohibition of the committees—is hardly likely, at least without another scandal on the scale of Watergate. But when reforms are considered, the possibility will exist to expand the share of a congressional candidate's total campaign treasury that comes from his or her party. It may be doubted that this would do much to remove the influence of money on legislative outcomes, in the absence of public financing, because the parties would be no less ready than

32. "Statement on Public Financing," *Public Financing of Congressional Elections*, Hearings before the House Committee on House Administration, 96 Cong. 1 sess. (GPO, 1979), pp. 392–93.
33. Sabato, *PAC Power*, pp. 173–75.

individual candidates to offer support for legislation in exchange for campaign contributions. But the purpose of strengthening parties would be served, because they could use the cash as a means of discipline.

If money is to be so used by the party leaders, a further question remains: which leaders? In the case of privately contributed funds, of course, it will be whichever leaders succeed in attracting the contributions. But if public financing of congressional campaigns were instituted, a public choice would have to be made. If the funds were appropriated to a committee controlled by the president, his power to dominate the Congress would clearly be enhanced. Congressional independence would be protected and even fortified, on the other hand, if the funds were appropriated to the Senate and House campaign committees made up of, and elected by, the parties' legislators. Then, assuming that those committees were granted the "reasonable discretion" suggested by the Committee for Party Renewal, the considerable increment of power would be gained instead by the leadership in the Congress.

Even if one accepts today's prevailing judgment that authority in Congress is too diffused and stronger leadership is needed, would centralized control of the congressional campaign treasury strengthen the leadership too much? Presumably, few would wish to recreate czar Speakers in the House or make the majority leader all-powerful in the Senate. Yet this seems but a faint possibility, whatever may happen in the realm of campaign finance. The authority to allocate campaign funds would be a step removed from the Speaker or majority leader, in the hands of a committee with its own chairman, chosen by the caucus by secret ballot and responsible to it. The culture of equality and individualism is so deeply embedded in the Congress that a campaign committee chairman could not discriminate blatantly without risking revolt within his own committee and eventually within the caucus itself.

Moreover, for campaign committees, the goal is victory. They are judged by the number of seats they win or lose in a given campaign year, not by whether they have successfully carried out ideological purges by denying funds to selected candidates. Traditionally, the committees have not used discretionary funds in that manner. A Republican candidate running a close contest as a moderate, or even a liberal, in a liberal district is therefore likely to be granted as much support as one who had regularly voted the party line, and Democratic committees likewise can be expected to give conservative candidates their share of party funds.[34] Nevertheless, a campaign committee chairman is in a strong position to help bring pressure to bear on wavering party members on crucial votes—even if he only hints at the possibility of penalizing disloyalty when campaign funds are distributed at some future date. No one can say how much the power of money may have been influential in helping the Reagan administration obtain near-unanimous party support in 1981 for its tax and spending reduction measures, but most observers would probably concede that it had some influence.[35]

On balance, a modest amount of public funds made available to the congressional campaign committees—perhaps, as has been suggested, in the form of a congressional broadcast fund—would be likely to be useful in promoting a greater degree of party unity without posing a serious threat that party leaders would once again attain the dictatorial power that the American people found intolerable three-quarters of a century ago.

The Obstacles to Improved Collaboration

Whatever can be done to strengthen political party organizations will serve to improve cohesion between the executive branch and the president's party in the Congress. The party is still the web that

34. In 1980, the Republican National Committee did not distribute its money evenly among candidates, but "estimates of electability dominated the party choice," and a committee spokesman said "neither ideology nor issues entered into decisions." F. Christopher Arterton, "Political Money and Party Strength," in Joel L. Fleishman, ed., *The Future of American Political Parties: The Challenge of Governance* (New York: American Assembly, 1982), p. 129.

35. Paul C. Light, *The President's Agenda: Domestic Policy Choice from Kennedy to Carter* (Johns Hopkins University Press, 1983), p. xii, reports that promises of financial support—or threats to withhold it—were effective in holding congressional Republicans in line in 1981. But President Reagan disavowed the use of presidential power to discipline members of Congress at his news conference of March 21, 1985. Asked about whether he was satisfied with the loyalty of some Republican members of Congress, he responded: "Well, I suppose this comes from the suggestion that I am supposed to penalize some members in the coming campaign. No, I've never done that. . . . I'm dedicated to doing my best to see if we can't maintain the majority we have in the Senate and someday get ourselves a majority in the House. . . . So, no, I'm not going to hold a grudge on anyone." *Weekly Compilation of Presidential Documents,* vol. 21, p. 347.

infuses the organs of government with a sense of common purpose. But, as in the case of so many other of the reform ideas canvassed in this book, the end is easier stated than the means designed— assuming that one takes into account the problem of political acceptability of proposals for change.

The state of the party organizations is not essentially an independent variable, subject to manipulation, but a dependent one, the product of tradition and deep-seated public attitudes. The American people have been, in a real sense, antiparty since the framers in the 1787 convention and George Washington in his farewell address inveighed against "the spirit of faction." Distrust and hostility crested in the heyday of the corrupt political machines, but as patronage diminished and graft was rooted out, the public attitude changed but slowly. Moreover, the trend toward democratization within parties, epitomized by the direct primary as the means of choosing candidates for every office up to the presidency itself, has contributed to the decline of party organizations.

At the margin, party organizations can be strengthened through the judicious use of money for systematic institution-building, as the Republican party in particular is now demonstrating. Yet ultimately, the organizations can exercise no more authority than the people are willing to confer on them. And from every indication, the public is not prepared yet to accept and trust political party organizations to exercise any real degree of discipline over elected officeholders. They expect their senators and representatives to be independent spirits, not cravens who allow party leaders or party majorities—or even the president as party leader—to tell them how to vote. Nor will the voters accept party discipline themselves. They will continue to prize their right to split their tickets and to put in place, if that is the outcome, divided government.

Even if party organizations become gradually stronger, then, that strength will not be translated directly or immediately into greater party unity within the Congress. That will come only slowly and gropingly, as attitudes change among voters and within the political elites—if, indeed, they do change. And party organizations can do little to bring about united party control of the presidency, the Senate, and the House as the normal state of affairs; that in turn must await the completion of the realignment of the party system that will convert ticket-splitters, notably in the South, into straight-ticket voters.

Since 1981, it has not been party weakness as such but divided government and the pressures of electoral politics that have rendered the government impotent to cope with such problems as the mounting deficit. To equip the governmental system to discharge its responsibilities effectively in this period, one must look to the constitutional remedies suggested in the preceding chapters. Strengthening political party organizations, even if that could readily be done, would have only a tardy, indirect, and limited effect.

The various proposals for formal institutional linkages between the branches likewise hold little promise. Joint executive-legislative councils or cabinets, suggested over the years in many variations, are, like political parties, dependent variables—only as effective as the participants would want them to be. When executives and legislators are disposed to cooperate, ample means for cooperation exist and additional formal mechanisms are scarcely needed. But when they are not so disposed—and those are the times when the creation of councils is advocated—the mechanisms would fail and fall into disuse. Dual officeholding is a remedy worth experimenting with, if the Constitution can be altered to permit it, but even its strongest advocates would hardly expect the resistance and the practical difficulties that would stand in the way of its widespread use to be quickly overcome.

CHAPTER EIGHT

Altering the Checks and Balances

The shield against despotism, thought the framers, was the system of checks and balances they had artfully constructed for their new experiment in government. The executive and legislative branches would restrain each other through an interlocking mechanism of mutual vetoes, and an independent judicial branch would keep its watch on both.

The checks and balances have assuredly served their purpose. None of the three branches has been able to overreach itself and dominate the others—for any sustained period of time, at least. Ambition has indeed countered ambition, as Madison hoped and foresaw. Legislative excesses have been thwarted by the power of the presidential veto and by the authority successfully claimed by the judiciary to strike down acts of Congress that exceeded constitutional limitations. Imperial presidencies have been curbed by congressional assertion of the power of the purse, by legislative investigations and oversight with their appeals to public opinion, by judicial enforcement of constitutional restraints, and in extremity by impeachment of the president or the threat to impeach. Judicial ambition and assertiveness have been controlled through the power of the Congress and the president to reconstitute the court system, including the Supreme Court, by statutory law, and through the authority vested in the president and the Senate to decide who shall wear the judicial robes.

It is a truism, however, that the power to prevent bad acts can also be employed to prevent good ones, however those two adjectives may be defined by any individual. The system of checks and balances that has been so secure a safeguard against tyranny has also given rise to the problem with which this book deals. For government to function effectively, the legislative and executive branches that are so well endowed with veto powers to thwart each other must somehow be induced to rise above their conflicting political ambitions and move in concert on essential matters.[1]

Other chapters consider how greater harmony between the two branches may be brought about without altering the basic structure of reciprocal vetoes. But to make it easier for the government to reach decisions and take forceful action, the weakening of one or more of the veto powers can be a direct and effective means. The disharmony that now so often saps the effectiveness of government is not overcome through this type of measure; it is simply circumvented, by making it more readily possible for one side of the controversy to override the other and impose its will. The risks of such a consequence must be weighed, obviously, against the advantages. A presidency can be too weak in relation to the Congress but it can also be too domineering; a Congress can be too subservient to the president but also too overbearing. The executive-legislative balance of power that has evolved over two centuries may not strike the happiest possible medium between the extremes, but each proposal to alter the constitutional structure of vetoes must be analyzed in terms of whether it keeps the balance close to that which the people have come to accept and expect, or whether it might lead to an unacceptable dominance of either branch over the other.

The most important of all the checks and balances is, of course, the presidential veto—the right of the president to reject legislation passed by the Congress, subject to override by a two-thirds vote of

1. Fifty years ago, the judicial checks on the executive and legislative branches would also have to have been discussed as a central constitutional problem. A series of Supreme Court decisions during President Franklin D. Roosevelt's first term invalidated major acts of Congress designed to cope with the crisis of the Great Depression, and the president's response was his famed court-packing plan. The proposal was rejected by the Congress, but whether partly because of the threat or wholly for other reasons the Court has ceased to be an obstacle to the policy aspirations of the other branches. Since the 1930s, no major legislative act has been declared unconstitutional. The decision in *Immigration and Naturalization Service* v. *Chadha*, 103 U.S. 2764 (1983), that outlawed the legislative veto may have invalidated a large number of statutory provisions, but the same policy objectives can presumably be achieved by other, constitutionally acceptable means.

both houses. It is the possession of the veto that makes the executive branch a full partner in the legislative process. The president's views must be taken into account on every single measure, for the advocates of a policy know that if they flout the president's wishes, they are hardly likely to be able to prevail. In the four decades 1945–84, only 36 of 353 presidential vetoes of public bills were overridden, or barely 10 percent.[2] To lower the override requirement from two-thirds to, say, 60 percent would certainly facilitate the enactment of legislation, but it would do so by reducing the bargaining power of the president and hence altering the executive-legislative balance in favor of the Congress. Conversely, to raise the two-thirds standard would shift the balance toward the president. While there would appear to be no theoretical reason that two-thirds should be the perfect standard for overriding the presidential veto, the undisputed acceptance of that figure by everyone concerned throughout the two centuries of national history suggests that it must come close to the ideal. No suggestion to alter the two-thirds requirement has ever been seriously advanced.

Five other issues relating to the checks and balances have, however, attracted attention in recent decades. One proposal would authorize the president to exercise his constitutional veto power not just over entire bills but, in the case of one or more types of spending bills, over individual items. A second would restore, in one form or another, the legislative veto that had come into widespread use but was declared unconstitutional by the Supreme Court in 1983. A third would seek to settle the constitutional division of responsibility between the branches in committing the United States to military action, which the Congress sought vainly to resolve in the War Powers Resolution of 1973. A fourth would lower the two-thirds requirement for approval by the Senate of treaties negotiated by the executive branch. The fifth would introduce a national referendum as a way of breaking legislative deadlocks. Constitutional amendments dealing with these questions would not necessarily have the effect in every case of aggrandizing one branch at the expense of another; some may have the potential of encouraging harmonious collaboration between the branches.

2. Congressional Quarterly, *Guide to Congress*, 3d ed. (Washington: CQ, 1982), p. 763; *Congressional Quarterly Weekly Report*, vol. 42 (November 17, 1984), p. 2957.

The Item Veto

Facing his record budget deficits, President Reagan in 1985 was campaigning vigorously for the Congress to grant him "the power forty-three governors now have to veto individual items of wasteful overspending in appropriations bills."[3] In his State of the Union Message, he specifically endorsed a bill by Senator Mack Mattingly, Republican of Georgia, that had the cosponsorship of forty-six other senators—nearly half the membership of that body. The Mattingly bill would grant the president the item veto (now usually called the line-item veto, through the ingestion of bureaucratic jargon) on a two-year trial basis, simply providing that each appropriation bill be divided after passage into as many separate bills as the measure contained items, each then to be presented to the president for approval or veto.

Prodigious claims have been advanced as to the volume of "wasteful overspending" that the item veto would eliminate. Proclaimed the *Wall Street Journal* in 1983, for instance: "Resolution of the budget crisis clearly lies with the president, and we know of one proven mechanism for getting the job done. . . . Mr. Reagan should make the line-item veto the centerpiece of his reelection campaign, and he shouldn't flinch from claiming it as the Republican answer to the deficit issue."[4] Senator Mattingly was more modest. He termed the item veto "just one small step to fiscal sanity," not "a quick, total solution to the budget deficits."[5]

Even a cursory look at the figures is enough to demonstrate that the item veto would indeed be a "small step." President Reagan's proposed budget for fiscal 1986, with all "wasteful overspending" presumably eliminated, still forecast a deficit of $180 billion, by his own estimate ($186 billion by the estimate of the Congressional Budget Office).[6] That figure took account of all changes he proposed

3. "Radio Address to the Nation, February 2, 1985," *Weekly Compilation of Presidential Documents*, vol. 21, p. 118.
4. September 14, 1983.
5. Letter to editor, *Washington Post*, October 2, 1984.
6. Congressional Budget Office, *An Analysis of the President's Budgetary Proposals for Fiscal Year 1986* (Government Printing Office, 1985), p. xviii. The Reagan administration in the summer of 1985 revised the economic forecasts on which these figures were based, adding another $20 billion to the estimated deficit.

in legislation that mandated expenditures. Even if, by employing the item veto, the president eliminated every dollar added by the Congress, that shortfall would remain.

Moreover, the item veto, in all of the versions being discussed, applies only to "controllable" items in appropriations bills, and these amount to less than 20 percent of the government's total expenditures. Of the $1,001 billion in outlays proposed in the president's 1986 budget, $746 billion are classified by the Office of Management and Budget as "relatively uncontrollable." This includes $143 billion for interest payments on the public debt; $187 billion to liquidate prior-year contracts and other obligations, mostly for the Department of Defense; and $403 billion for entitlement programs, including $203 billion for social security payments.[7] Only $255 billion of the appropriations are classified as "relatively controllable," and of these $176 billion are for defense, only $79 billion for all of the other programs of the government.[8] Finally, the item veto would not apply to tax expenditures—that is, subsidies of various kinds granted in the form of tax credits or deductions rather than through direct appropriations—which add to $383 billion in the president's 1986 budget.[9]

Congressional "overspending" through the appropriations process has been, at most, only a minor contributor to the massive deficits of the Reagan era. In the four budgets enacted during the president's first term, the Congress added a net of only $3.4 billion to the executive's appropriations request, according to the calculations of the Senate Appropriations Committee.[10] This net is compounded, however, of increases in the totals of individual bills of $56 billion, almost entirely for domestic programs, and reductions of $53 billion in other bills, almost wholly for defense. If the entire $56 billion had

7. The president has his opportunity to control the levels of entitlement payments through the use of his regular veto power when the bills that establish the entitlements are presented to him. Once he signs an entitlement bill into law, however, the expenditures are beyond the reach of the president and hence classified as "uncontrollable." The Congress can make some or all entitlements "controllable" by delegating authority to the president to reduce the payments at his discretion. But since these payments, once they are established by law, do not again appear as items in any bill presented to the president for approval, any such grant of authority would have to be made by a specific statute rather than encompassed in a general item veto authority.

8. Office of Management and Budget, *The Budget of the United States Government, Fiscal Year 1986*, pp. 9-44, 9-45.

9. "Special Analyses," ibid., pp. G43–47.

10. *Congressional Record*, daily ed. (February 5, 1985), p. S1003.

been vetoed (and the president would undoubtedly accept some of the increases, either because circumstances had changed or for various political reasons), that would have reduced the deficits of $743 billion amassed in the four years by only 7.5 percent.[11] The essential problem, clearly, is not the congressional additions to the Reagan budgets but those fiscal plans in their original form. The maximum level of revenue the president has believed to be tolerable, or feasible, simply falls too far short of the minimum level of spending he has considered to be desirable. The Congress has transferred some spending from military to domestic purposes, within approximately the same aggregate spending totals. Which branch one holds responsible for "wasteful overspending" depends on whether one considers the military expansion that was retarded by the Congress to be a more worthy object of federal expenditure than the domestic programs that it preserved instead.

If an item veto had been available to the president, in other words, he could have used it to try to impose his preferred distribution of expenditures on the Congress, but that would not have significantly reduced total spending, or the resulting deficit. President Reagan could have eliminated some of the relatively low-cost programs he opposed but the Congress sustained, such as the Legal Services Corporation and economic development programs. But no president would use his veto power in a mechanical way, to ferret out and excise all of the expenditures that exceeded his original budget requests. If the president were to routinely reject every alteration in his budget, the Congress would, in all probability, attain bipartisan solidarity to just as routinely override his vetoes in order to protect its institutional authority. The item veto would be essentially, then, a bargaining chip in the hands of the president, to be used selectively and occasionally, and its importance would lie more in the threat of

11. The $56 billion reflects only the aggregates of the thirteen bills into which the Congress divides the budget. Some added amounts that are offset by reductions in other items in the same bills are not reflected in the aggregates. If, for instance, an increase of $5 billion over the president's request in a particular bill is compounded from increases of $6 billion and reductions of $1 billion, the higher figure would be the proper one to use in assessing the potential of the item veto. No such detailed item-by-item tabulation of congressional budget increases has been published, but Joel Ostrow, comparing all enacted bills with presidential requests for the years 1984 and 1985, found a total of $77.4 billion in additions, or 10.4 percent of the $743 billion deficit.

its use than its actual use. In the 1985 battles over the MX missile, aid to the Nicaraguan "contras," and increases in military spending in general, the president would have been given added leverage to win the votes of dissident legislators. And to the dismay of those who see the item veto as an expenditure-cutting device, the result would have been increases as well as decreases in spending—even an increase, conceivably, in total outlays.

The effect of the item veto on budget deficits, then, would be miniscule at best, given the magnitude of those deficits, and might even be adverse. It is surely illusory to suggest that the proposed procedure can be *the* answer to the deficit issue, that it can "get the job done," that it can "resolve the budget crisis." And to the extent that it diverts attention from other, realistic solutions to that crisis, the illusion can be a dangerous one.

In exchange for whatever inconsequential budgetary savings might eventuate, the advocates of the item veto would effect a considerable shift in power from the legislative to the executive branch, with ramifications felt in areas of executive-legislative relations far removed from budget policy. The president's bargaining power would be enhanced in putting through any policy resisted by the legislators or opposing any policy advanced by them. Looking at the whole range of matters over which presidents have quarreled with Congresses in the last two decades, one might ask whether one truly wishes the president's authority to be materially strengthened. Should presidents have greater power to undertake military adventures that the legislators have resisted? To impose domestic spending cuts the legislators have rejected, in order to support military expenditures they have thought excessive? To conduct foreign policy without congressional restraint and participation? Is the system now out of balance in favor of the legislature? Perhaps, on examination, one would conclude that it is, that the president needs a new accretion of power in his rivalry with the legislature. But in any case, those are the criteria by which the desirability of the item veto should be measured. The general enhancement of presidential influence at the expense of the Congress would be the significant consequence of this innovation.

In the 1985 Senate debate on the Mattingly bill, Senator Charles McC. Mathias, Jr., Republican of Maryland and chairman of the Senate Rules and Administration Committee, quoted the retiring director of the Office of Management and Budget, David A. Stockman, as saying that the item veto does not have to do with deficits but with power. Mathias agreed:

> For example, if President Reagan does not like my position on the issue of school prayer, and if he acquires the power to kill funds for the program that I have long supported to save the Chesapeake Bay without affecting his Pentagon program or any other administration request, then the President, whoever he may be, has a hostage. He can hold the Chesapeake for the ransom of my support for a major change, for my support for State-sponsored prayer in school, or any other subject that he might want my support on. And it would be a major change in the relationship between the executive and the legislative branches.[12]

Senator Mark O. Hatfield, Oregon Republican and chairman of the Appropriations Committee, concurred:

> I can visualize, with a line item veto in the hands of the President, reminding the President that there was a project in the energy water appropriation bill that was very important to those of us in the Northwest— the Bonneville lock on the Columbia River. I can imagine a President, whoever he might be, saying: "Well, I need your vote on nerve gas" or, "I want your vote on the MX missile" or, "I want your vote on Contra aid to overthrow the Government of Nicaragua"—all issues on which I have fought the President. . . . Members of Congress should not be in the position of casting or withholding their votes on major issues, be it AWACS sales to Saudi Arabia, troops in Lebanon, a Panama Canal treaty, or the confirmation of a controversial nominee just because that vote might affect the enactment of local but urgent priorities.[13]

The Mattingly bill died in a filibuster, when the proponents could muster only 59 of the 60 votes necessary to shut off debate on a motion to consider the measure. But this may have overstated the bill's strength, because senators knew that they could cast a popular vote and gain favor with the Reagan administration without having to worry that the bill would ever become law. The Democratic-controlled House was certain to reject such a shift in the balance of power in favor of a Republican president.

Two years earlier, the Senate had defeated a more restricted grant of authority, offered by Senator Alan J. Dixon, Democrat of Illinois, by a decisive 53-to-25 vote. Dixon sought to put the Senate on record in favor of a constitutional amendment patterned on a provision of the Illinois constitution, which would authorize the president to eliminate or reduce appropriations items but allow the Congress to

---

12. *Congressional Record,* daily ed. (July 17, 1985), p. S9601.
13. Ibid., p. S9610.

override his actions by majorities of the membership of both houses, rather than by the usual two-thirds of members present and voting. Senator Dixon made the argument, not repeated in the 1985 debate, that the item veto would unclog the machinery of government because, if the president and the Congress were disputing only a few items in an appropriations bill, the entire bill would not, as at present, have to be held up by a presidential veto or the threat of one. The controverted items could be vetoed and the rest of the bill enacted. Thus would be averted the annual October 1 crisis, when the government enters a new fiscal year without operating funds for some departments because major appropriation bills are held up by disputes over a few programs. In 1983, Dixon noted, "many programs not in dispute were either brought to a standstill or nearly so. Major parts of the government once again went to the brink. Social security checks were nearly not mailed, thousands of government employees were unnecessarily laid off, and many worthy and necessary government activities were curtailed."[14]

The reduced override requirement would appear to produce a less drastic shift of power to the president, because the Congress could easily prevail on the disputed items, after the president had scored his political and public relations points. But the Congress could override the veto only if it were still in session. More than 40 percent of presidential vetoes on public bills in the 1945–81 period were pocket vetoes—that is, disapproval of bills after the adjournment of the Congress, giving the legislators no opportunity to override.[15] In recent years, major appropriations bills have normally been among the last measures passed by the Congress before adjournment. Even the seemingly innocuous Dixon amendment, then, would give the president the equivalent of an absolute veto over items in those bills—unless the Congress changed its ways and passed its appropriations before the final days of the session. An amendment making the item veto constitutional could, of course, be written so as to exclude pocket vetoes, but that would enable the Congress to circumvent the provision altogether by simply delaying final action on controversial spending items until just before adjournment.

If a constitutional amendment were adopted to require a balanced budget (which at this writing does not appear entirely unlikely), the

14. Alan J. Dixon, "Restoring Veto Power," *Washington Post*, October 19, 1983.
15. Congressional Quarterly, *Guide to Congress*, p. 743.

item veto question would undoubtedly arise again, because the Congress would have to determine a method for assuring that the intent of the amendment was carried out. The same arguments for shifting power to the president that were offered during the item veto debates—and, indeed, the same ones that were presented during consideration of the Congressional Budget and Impoundment Control Act of 1974—would again be heard. On those occasions, however, the Congress ultimately reaffirmed its determination to exercise final decision over the nation's fiscal program, both in general outline and in detail, and in the 1974 act it created new congressional machinery for that purpose. One can anticipate that the Congress would strive again, through the reinvigoration of the congressional budget process possibly coupled with a mild version of the item veto such as the Dixon proposal, to maintain essentially the present balance of power between the branches and forestall the loss of its cherished power of the purse.

The Legislative Veto

From the viewpoint of the Congress, the constitutional system of checks and balances has suffered from a glaring omission. All of the constitutional checks by which the legislators control the executive branch must be applied either before the fact or after the fact—not *during* the exercise by the administrators of the power the Congress has granted to them. But, in many areas of governmental activity, control must be exercised at the time the administrator acts, or prepares to act, if it is to be effectively exercised at all.

Before the fact, the legislature can write detailed instructions and restraints into the authorizing statutes, and the Senate has the power to confirm or reject the president's nominees for administrative office. The Congress is often criticized for writing broad, ambiguous statutes that give insufficient guidance to the administrative agencies, and there is truth in the complaint. But there is clearly a limit to what the Congress can hope to anticipate and resolve in advance; the most obvious illustrations arise in the field of foreign affairs, where the executive branch must have authority to deal with crises that flare up without notice in the middle of the night, Washington time, but unanticipated events may require immediate response in domestic affairs as well. As for controlling the administrators through the confirmation process, the Senate must almost always act on faith, for it cannot know in advance which executive officials will exceed or misuse the powers placed in their hands.

After the fact, the Congress can investigate, write clarifying legislation if it concludes that the law has been misinterpreted, chastise misbehaving officials and even drive them to resign or, as a last resort, impeach them. But by that time the administrative action to which the legislators object may have been fully accomplished. The damage will have been done.

It was to resolve this dilemma that the legislative veto was invented. By the use of that device, the Congress could authorize actions by the executive branch but require that before those actions took effect they would be subject to review and rejection by both houses, by one house, or even by a single committee of the Congress. It would thus assert its control during the fact, which might be the only kind of control that could really count. The oldest and longest-running series of legislative veto provisions—those contained in acts authorizing reorganization of executive agencies—well illustrate both the nature and utility of the mechanism. For more than half a century, the Congress has recognized that the legislative branch lacks both the capability and the interest to plan the restructuring of the executive branch that is necessary from time to time to accommodate its changing responsibilities. Yet it has been unwilling to give the president a completely free hand to organize and disband bureaus and departments and transfer functions among them, for on many such decisions a legislator's constituents may have strong views. In 1932, the Congress found a way out. It authorized President Hoover to reorganize the government by executive order, but each order had to be submitted to the Congress and could be disapproved by either house within sixty days. That procedure was continued, with modifications from time to time, in a long series of reorganization acts spanning the subsequent decades. After World War II, the Congress began incorporating the legislative veto in occasional other acts, usually in the form of a requirement that an executive agency "come into agreement" with designated congressional committees on particular types of actions. But after the historic constitutional clash between the Congress and President Nixon in 1973–74, the legislators began applying the veto on a broad scale, for a time attaching it almost routinely to new grants of power to the executive. In the period 1973–79, it was incorporated in more than sixty laws, and sometimes in a dozen or more sections of a single law. By 1983, a total of 122 statutes containing 207 legislative veto provisions was on the books.[16]

Since all of these laws were subject to a presidential veto in the first place, the legislative veto provisions had somehow obtained the chief executive's acceptance. But presidents did not always accept them gladly. Shortly after the 1932 reorganization act was signed, the Justice Department took a stand that the legislative veto was unconstitutional, and it maintained that position with unbroken consistency afterward. On its recommendation, several presidents disapproved bills containing veto provisions and so forced the Congress to delete them. But often the legislative vetoes were added as incidental and minor elements of major bills in the president's own program, or they were incorporated in the authorization bills required to continue essential governmental activities. The presidents might protest—Eisenhower, Nixon, and Carter all went so far as to announce that their administrations would not comply with certain of the vetoes, on the grounds the Congress was acting unconstitutionally—but they had to sign the bills. One statute containing a legislative veto—the War Powers Resolution of 1973—was passed over President Nixon's veto. But frequently the executive branch acquiesced happily in a veto provision, because it preferred a delegation of power under that limitation to the alternative, which would have been no delegation at all. Such was the case with the series of reorganization acts. In at least some instances, the executive branch initiated the suggestion for a legislative veto in order to win a grant of authority that the legislators were reluctant to approve. Even as he was denouncing legislative veto provisions as wholly unconstitutional, for example, President Carter publicly advocated inclusion of a veto procedure in a standby gasoline rationing bill; that provision broke the resistance, and the bill was passed. Inclusion of a similar provision was an essential compromise in enactment of the Congressional Budget and Impoundment Control Act of 1974, a statute that Nixon welcomed.

In its zeal to control the executive in the 1970s, however, the

16. Department of Justice, Office of Legal Counsel, "Compilation of Currently Effective Statutes that Contain Legislative Veto Provisions" (July 15, 1983). The evolution of the legislative veto from 1932 to 1980 is sketched in James L. Sundquist, *The Decline and Resurgence of Congress* (Brookings Institution, 1981), pp. 344–54.

Congress overreached itself. Instead of acting selectively in cases where the administration might find the legislative veto grudgingly acceptable, legislators began enacting blanket veto provisions covering the entire range of regulations issued by particular agencies, such as the Federal Trade Commission and the new Department of Education. In 1976, almost two-thirds of the members of the House voted for a bill that would have subjected all rules and regulations issued by all agencies to a legislative veto, and the Senate passed a similar measure in 1982. Legal scholars began to condemn the legislative veto of agency regulations as a corruption of the rule-making processes that had been carefully designed and prescribed by law to protect the rights of affected parties; as permitting irresponsible, secretive, and inexpert meddling by congressional staff in what should be open and expert proceedings; and as conducive to delay and deadlock.[17] The Justice Department decided that the time had come for a judicial showdown on their long-argued contention that the legislative veto violated the Constitution.

In June 1983 it won its case, in a sweeping Supreme Court decision that Associate Justice Byron R. White, in a dissent, said "strikes down in one fell swoop provisions in more laws enacted by Congress than the Court has cumulatively invalidated in its history."[18] The six-justice majority, through Chief Justice Warren E. Burger, took a simple, strict-constructionist approach. "Every order, resolution, or vote to which the concurrence of the Senate and the House of Representatives may be necessary (except on a question of adjournment) shall be presented to the President of the United States," says the Constitution in Article I, Section 7; "and before the same shall take effect, shall be approved by him, or being disapproved by him, shall be repassed by two-thirds of the Senate and House of Representatives." Similarly, every bill must be presented to the president. Legislative vetoes, being legislative acts, fall within the requirements of these "presentment clauses." True, adhering to the strict language of the Constitution may "impose burdens on governmental processes that often seem clumsy, inefficient, even unworkable," Burger ac-

17. The most influential study, conducted for the Administrative Conference of the United States by Harold H. Bruff and Ernest Gellhorn, is summarized by them in "Congressional Control of Administrative Regulation: A Study of Legislative Vetoes," *Harvard Law Review*, vol. 90 (May 1977), pp. 1369–1440.

18. *Immigration and Naturalization Service* v. *Chadha*, 103 U.S. 2764 (1983).

knowledged, "but those hard choices were consciously made by men who had lived under a form of government that permitted arbitrary governmental acts to go unpunished." One may question the chief justice's reasoning: what prevents arbitrary governmental action is not the independence of the legislative and executive branches that Burger was upholding but their interdependence through checks and balances. The legislative veto was an additional check and balance that the framers did not think of. While it has no express sanction in the Constitution, it did in fact serve the very constitutional principle the chief justice chose to cite in striking it down.

A month after *Chadha*, Senator Dennis DeConcini, Democrat of Arizona, and twenty-two cosponsors introduced a constitutional amendment to authorize one-house or two-house legislative vetoes as an exception to the presentment clauses. DeConcini foresaw a "tumultuous period of readjustment" as the Congress confronted its old dilemma: to rewrite the 120-odd statutes with the specificity necessary to control administrative agencies was impossible, but to transfer wholesale the lawmaking function was unacceptable.[19] Similar proposals were introduced in the House. But the constitutional amendment process is time-consuming, the Congress had to move immediately to decide what to do about all its invalidated laws, and as Representative Elliott H. Levitas, Democrat of Georgia, put it, "there are other ways to skin the cat." Levitas, who had established himself as the House's leading advocate of the legislative veto, expressed certainty that the Congress would "in some way, or more likely in various ways, reassert the type of control of requirement for accountability" that the legislative veto had given it and "the end result will be a much lesser delegation of power and much more tightly drawn laws constraining the discretion and delegation that had previously been given by Congress."[20] Since then the Congress has been proceeding slowly to reassert control, on a case by case basis, procrastinating where possible in the absence of pressing issues and, where delay was not possible, experimenting with various approaches.

At one extreme, the Congress has simply withheld delegations of power that in the pre-*Chadha* years it had granted contingent on the right of veto. Thus, predictably, the 1984 version of reorganization

19. *Congressional Record*, daily ed. (July 27, 1983), pp. 11015–16.
20. Address to the American Bar Association, Atlanta, August 21, 1983.

legislation simply authorized the president to recommend plans that the Congress would then consider approving by joint resolution. (A joint resolution is subject to approval by the president and, when so approved, becomes a statute.) The only innovation was a "fast-track" provision, which promised to be widely used in instances where the former veto procedure was converted to a requirement for affirmative action by both houses; to prevent defeat of a presidential proposal through congressional inertia or neglect, each house is required to bring a resolution of approval to the floor within ninety days.

Similarly, the House chose a joint resolution of approval as the procedure to be followed in the sale of the Conrail system to a private operator. In 1981, the Congress had authorized the Department of Transportation to sell Conrail unless both houses, in a concurrent resolution, objected to the negotiated terms. (A concurrent resolution is approved by both houses but not submitted to the president. It was the means by which two-house legislative vetoes were imposed and hence was outlawed, for that purpose, by *Chadha*.) In the debate three years later, Representative James T. Broyhill, Republican of North Carolina, protested that substituting a requirement for affirmative congressional action would force the buyer to negotiate not only with the executive department but with 535 members of Congress, who could amend "any or every detail of a proposed plan," but the House overwhelmingly approved the reservation of final approval for the legislative branch.[21] As it happened, the Senate did not have to decide whether to concur in the House decision, because new legislation turned out to be required in any case to make the sale financially feasible, but the House action was enough to bear out the Levitas prediction that the result of *Chadha* would be less delegation of executive power. Under the 1981 act, the support of one house would have been sufficient to sustain the sale as negotiated, but under the 1984 House bill the approval of both would have been required.

At the other extreme, the Congress could decide to let an executive action stand unless a statute in the form of a joint resolution of disapproval was enacted. Since such a resolution would be subject to a presidential veto, two-thirds of both houses would be required to overrule the executive if he insisted on his course. This was the

21. *Congressional Record*, daily ed. (March 6, 1984), p. H1305.

procedure adopted by the Congress in the case of the War Powers Resolution of 1973, which provided that if the president engaged the military forces in hostilities the Congress by a vote of both houses could force him to withdraw them. Robert C. Byrd of West Virginia, the Senate Democratic leader, who sponsored the new legislation after *Chadha*, admitted that two-thirds of both houses were hardly likely to oppose the president in a crisis but contended that a mechanism should be in place in the event of such "a very extreme difference in judgment between the President and the Congress."[22] The law incorporated a fast-track procedure, including a twenty-hour limitation on Senate debate to forestall a filibuster on a motion to override a presidential veto.

Intermediate between these extremes was the ever-popular appropriations rider, a means by which a majority of both houses could write the equivalent of a resolution of disapproval with normally no risk of presidential veto. By simply adding to an appropriation bill a sentence beginning "No part of any appropriation under this Act shall be available for . . . ," the Congress can effectively prevent an administrative agency from developing or enforcing a particular rule, or taking a specific action. Such limitations on executive discretion have been upheld by the courts as legitimate exercises of the legislature's power of the purse. When Secretary of the Interior James G. Watt in 1983 announced he would ignore a formal instruction from the House Interior Committee to postpone granting leases for coal mining on certain public lands, on the ground that the committee veto was unconstitutional, the committee simply got the moratorium included as a rider on the department's appropriation bill. Other riders prohibited the export of timber from the Western states and halted oil leasing on designated sections of the continental shelf off both the Atlantic and Pacific coasts.

Finally, the Congress can continue to enact legislative vetoes, in the full knowledge that they are unconstitutional but in the equally full expectation they they will be adhered to anyway. Louis Fisher of the Congressional Research Service counted thirty new legislative veto provisions in laws enacted in the first year after *Chadha*. Nineteen of them required advance approval by the two appropriations committees of various administrative actions, and one called for consent

22. Ibid. (October 19, 1983), p. S14164.

by both the appropriations and the authorizing committees. Two
others authorized committees to delay certain types of actions. Six
required administrators to report proposed actions to the Congress
and allow thirty days for comment, unless designated committees
waived the waiting period.[23] One was a two-house veto the Congress
chose not to remove from a bill that was reported to the House before
Chadha. The last was a provision allowing either house to prevent
the extension of a program.[24]

Particularly in the case of the committee vetoes, administrative
agencies may well prefer to follow what they hold to be an unconstitutional procedure than to risk the displeasure of the congressional
authorizing and appropriating committees that can reduce the agencies' budgets or take reprisal in countless other formal or informal
ways. Indeed, even after *Chadha*, one continuing form of de facto
legislative veto is the formal resolution by a committee, or a house,
or both houses, expressing disapproval of something the executive
branch has done or proposes to do. Such a resolution lacks the force
of law, but it is bound to exert a powerful influence on responsible
administrators. Committees have often controlled administration by
incorporating directives and instruction in committee reports and
other communications, which the administrative agencies have voluntarily accepted as binding. Realism suggested that they might as
well do so—witness the appropriations rider that overrode Secretary
Watt's rejection of such an order.

While the committees responsible for individual statutes have been
striving to perfect their individual solutions, those legislators who
before *Chadha* were seeking to extend the legislative veto to all agency
rules and regulations have transformed their efforts into a search for
a uniform method of control that will now be constitutionally
permissible. Various bills introduced in 1983 would have required
waiting periods before proposed rules could take effect and established uniform fast-track procedures for considering joint resolutions
of disapproval or, in some cases, joint resolutions of approval.

23. A statutory requirement for a waiting period is not, strictly speaking, a legislative
veto provision, since the proposed action cannot be prohibited by the Congress *alone*
during that period, but the language authorizing committees to shorten the period
presumably falls afoul of *Chadha* because it amounts to an official action of the legislative
branch in a form that circumvents the presentment clauses.
24. Louis Fisher, "One Year after *INS* v. *Chadha*: Congressional and Judicial
Development" (Congressional Research Service, Library of Congress, June 23, 1984).

Following hearings by the House Rules Committee on these general approaches, Representative John Joseph Moakley, Democrat of Massachusetts and chairman of the Subcommittee on Rules of the House, offered his solution early in 1985. A joint committee on regulatory affairs would be established to review all agency rules, including rules in effect and those proposed. The committee could request any agency to suspend a rule during the committee's investigation and it would be the "the sense of Congress, that any such request should be accommodated." The committee could report a resolution of disapproval and, if the resolution were adopted by both houses, consideration of any appropriation that could be used to issue or enforce the disapproved rule would be out of order. Thus the two-house veto would be extended to all rules and regulations and would be enforced, like an appropriation rider, through the power of the purse.

The question is whether a simple constitutional amendment that would restore the legitimacy of the legislative veto as it was employed before *Chadha* would be preferable to this panoply of statutory approaches. Events since that decision appear to be confirming Representative Levitas's prediction: whenever the Congress is intent on controlling administrative action, it can find a constitutional way to do so. That fact accounts, no doubt, for the lack of support on Capitol Hill for trying to resolve the problem by constitutional amendment. In the end, too, Levitas is likely to be proved right in predicting that the executive branch will be the loser, because some powers previously delegated to administrators on a contingent basis— such as reorganization—will be withheld. But the legislature will be a loser, too, for the alternative ways of "skinning the cat" are less convenient, and more burdensome and time-consuming, adding to the volume and complexity of matters that must be handled on the floors of the two houses. And efforts to streamline the process through fast-track procedures have even aroused apprehension among members of the House Rules Committee that that body's ability to maintain an orderly flow of business through the House will be impaired.

If the executive branch is conceived, however, to be the winner in the *Chadha* decision—and Justice Department officials have boasted of their victory on behalf of the entire branch—then the opportunity exists for a tactical trade. Former Representative Melvin R. Laird,

Wisconsin Republican who subsequently served as secretary of defense, has suggested that a single constitutional amendment might combine some form of item veto for the president with restoration of the legislative veto to the Congress. Legislators who now believe they are doing quite well in finding substitutes for their former vetoes might not consider that an even trade, but if they conclude at some point that public pressure is going to force them to accede to the item veto eventually anyway, they might find it expedient to combine a relatively mild form of the item veto, such as one providing for an override by constitutional majorities, with a legalization of the legislative veto.

The War Power

On the war power, the Constitution is direct and clear: "The Congress shall have Power . . . To declare War . . . To raise and support Armies . . . To provide and maintain a Navy . . . To make Rules for the Government and Regulation of the land and naval Forces." And "The President shall be Commander in Chief of the Army and Navy of the United States." Waging war, then, was intended to fall into the same set of relationships that governed any other undertaking. Policy decisions and the power of the purse would be the legislature's responsibility; carrying out the policy would be the president's.

But that simple language was written in an age of sailing ships and horse-drawn cannons, at a time when the United States was a minor power with no global interests to defend. The same deliberative process that was suitable for regulating commerce or organizing the postal system might have been appropriate enough, in that day, for deciding questions of war and peace as well. Now, however, the United States has grown to the rank of superpower, with a vast structure of alliances supported by bases and military forces across the seas, and weapons move at supersonic speeds. The national interest may be threatened almost anywhere on the globe, at any time, and the decision to defend an interest, or repulse a threat, must be instantaneous—made in minutes and hours, not weeks and months—and the Congress may be out of session. Moreover, the Constitution did not define war. Is every use of military force a war requiring formal declaration, or are there "police actions," "punitive expeditions," defenses of U.S. lives and property that are less than war? And can they be carried out by the president as commander in chief wholly on his own authority, relying perhaps on his own interpretation of treaty obligations? As early as 1798, the country fought an undeclared naval war with France, and since that time it has entered into hostilities far more often without a formal declaration of war than with one. On many of those occasions, the legislative body had no part in the policy decision. The lawmakers were told about it after it was made.

In the twentieth century, the United States entered both world wars through congressional declarations. But it carried out other military operations, in Asia, in Mexico, in Central America and the Caribbean—as lately in Grenada—without any such formality. Some of these interventions, even when the United States overthrew a foreign government and occupied its territory, have been called by other names than war. But two, at least, were wars in everybody's lexicon. Those were the Korean War, which was initiated by the president without explicit and prior sanction by the Congress, and the Vietnam War, authorized not by a declaration of war but by a congressional resolution that pledged support to the president if he chose to engage in military action.

It was the latter experience that precipitated the War Powers Resolution of 1973. The congressional resolution of support had been whipped through the Congress in 1964 in an atmosphere of crisis, after President Lyndon Johnson had told the legislators that two American destroyers had been fired on by North Vietnamese torpedo boats, without provocation, in the Gulf of Tonkin. The resolution was broad enough to authorize a full-scale war in alliance with South Vietnam, but Johnson had assured leading legislators that he had no such intention.[25] When, within three years, Johnson had cited the resolution as authority for plunging half a million American troops into Southeast Asia, many of those who had voted for the resolution felt betrayed, particularly J. William Fulbright, who as chairman of the Foreign Relations Committee had pushed the resolution through the Senate. And they felt doubly so when Fulbright's committee developed evidence that Johnson had misrepresented the facts about

25. Remarks of Senator Fulbright, during floor debate on the resolution, *Congressional Record* (August 6, 1964), pp. 18403–04, 18409–10.

the Gulf of Tonkin incident, that perhaps the United States had actually provoked the encounter to provide grounds for seeking the congressional action.[26]

Yet whether President Johnson could have thrust the United States into the Vietnam War without the Tonkin Gulf resolution, on the ground that he was executing treaty obligations, was never settled. In ordering troops into Korea fifteen years before, President Truman had found legal justification in the country's duty under the United Nations Charter to oppose aggression, but the validity of that claim was never established either. Truman's Republican opponents challenged the president's right to unilaterally take the country into war, but Truman insisted that the Korean engagement was not a war but a "police action," and Democrats defended the president on various grounds. Senate Majority Leader Scott W. Lucas, of Illinois, contended that the president could dispatch military forces whenever he believed "that the safety, the security, and the honor of this country are involved." Paul H. Douglas, Lucas's Illinois colleague, invoked technology and hoary Senate rules: "The speed of modern war requires quick executive action . . . even the slightest delay may prove fatal," but the Senate did not even have a way to shut off filibusters. The ultimate defense came from Lucas: "Well, it [the commitment of troops] has been done."[27] The debate on the Tonkin Gulf resolution found senators divided over whether the Congress was delegating power to take military action to the president or whether he already possessed the power, and the wording of the measure carefully evaded the question.[28] In any event, those who believed they were delegating power did so willingly, under the pressure of the assumed crisis, and the president got what he wanted. Some years later, Fulbright could say that "The Congress has lost the power to declare war as it was written into the Constitution. It has not been so much usurped as given away."[29] And Under Secretary of State Nicholas deB. Katzenbach, speaking for the Johnson administration, could tell Fulbright's committee that "the expression of declaring a war is one that has become outmoded."[30]

26. Comments of Fulbright and other senators, ibid. (March 7, 1968), p. 5645; *Congressional Quarterly Almanac, 1968*, p. 714.

27. Senate debate, June 28, 1950, summarized in Sundquist, *Decline and Resurgence*, pp. 108–09.

28. Ibid., pp. 120–23.

29. *Congressional Record* (July 31, 1967), pp. 20702–06.

30. Sundquist, *Decline and Resurgence*, pp. 245–46.

As senators in the late 1960s discovered that undeclared warfare had spread to Cambodia and Laos, supported by forty-five thousand troops in Thailand, the movement to bring presidential warmaking under control became irresistible. Senator Jacob K. Javits, Republican of New York, who emerged as the leader of the movement, introduced a resolution that would delegate precise and limited powers to the president, specifying the circumstances under which he could order the armed forces into hostilities without prior approval by the Congress. The Senate approved the Javits measure by a big majority, but the House Foreign Affairs Committee would not accept the idea that all possible contingencies could be anticipated and the president's powers therefore "codified" in advance, and the House passed a resolution differing in that respect. The conference committee of the two houses found their compromise in that convenient—and then legal—device, the legislative veto. The Senate's proposed restrictions were made advisory. The president was required to consult with Congress before ordering the military into action and to report immediately thereafter, but otherwise was left free to act. If, however, both houses of Congress objected, they could by concurrent resolution compel the president to terminate hostilities. And in any case, if the Congress did not within sixty days give its affirmative approval to the president's course, he must abandon it.

The Congress thus conceded Senator Douglas's argument about the speed of modern war and Katzenbach's point that the constitutional provision for declaring war was indeed outmoded, but salvaged what it could. Presidential freedom and flexibility were assured and legitimated, but only for sixty days, and even within that time the Congress could step in to reverse the executive. The legislators felt they had once more brought the executive-legislative balance of power as close to the constitutional intent as today's technology permits. The trouble is, the executive did not agree then or later. President Nixon vetoed the resolution as an encroachment on his constitutional responsibilities, and the measure became law only when the Congress overrode his veto.

Every subsequent president has upheld Nixon's constitutional position. Presidents Ford, Carter, and Reagan have complied with the reporting provisions of the resolution, but without acknowledging any legal obligation to do so. Their reports were submitted not "pursuant to" the terms of the statute but "consistent with" or "taking note of" it. When Reagan sent marines to join a multinational force in Lebanon in 1983, the Congress hastened to authorize their presence there for eighteen months (they were withdrawn well before that time expired). The few other actions reported, including the invasion of Grenada, have all been terminated after a few days, so the power of the Congress to impose the resolution's sixty-day time limit on the president's authority has not been tested.[31] Its power to exercise a legislative veto during the sixty days was, of course, stricken by the Supreme Court in the *Chadha* decision, but the rest of the statute is presumably unaffected. So the basic constitutional question remains as unsettled as it was at the time of the Vietnam War or the Korean War or, for that matter, the Mexican War more than a century ago. The executive branch has carefully preserved its contention that it is not bound by the War Powers Resolution and any compliance with its terms is strictly voluntary. If a future president chooses to act as unilaterally as Truman did in Korea or Nixon in Cambodia and Laos, defying the Congress and taking it upon himself to declare the legislature's constitutional responsibility "outmoded," the Congress can fall back only on relatively ineffective checks—the power of the purse, which can be exercised only clumsily and late, and the impeachment power, which in addition to all its other difficulties would come into operation so late as to be almost surely useless.

If the constitutional design is indeed outmoded, as even the War Powers Resolution seems to concede, should a new design be written for the modern age? Is unrestrained presidential warmaking authority still a menace, as the Congress found it to be in Southeast Asia? If so, and if effective control is to be restored to the legislative branch, some variant of the War Powers Resolution would have to be added to the Constitution. The notion that presidents know best and should be trusted has been severely undercut by the experience in Southeast Asia. One may argue that that debacle will forever chasten presidents, and no future leader, even one holding as expansive a view of presidential power as Truman, Johnson, or Nixon, will risk initiating a war without full popular support. If that argument seems dubious, perhaps a sounder one is that a new constitutional provision would not matter; in a crisis, the Congress would give the president whatever

31. In the Grenada case, a resolution limiting to ninety days the president's authority to use military forces, in the absence of further action of the Congress, passed the House but was not acted on in the Senate.

support and authority he asked for.[32] But not all constitutional checks are designed for everyday use. A new war powers provision in the Constitution would be intended only as a safeguard in the event of another feud between the branches as rancorous and unrelenting as that of Richard Nixon's era, or Andrew Johnson's. Such constitutional collisions have occurred often enough in the nation's history, and have involved the war power frequently enough, that the question of whether the constitutional ambiguity needs to be resolved should not be lightly dismissed.

Approval of Treaties

In the long struggle for control of U.S. foreign policy that marked the two decades between the First and Second World Wars, the internationalists had cause to complain that the Constitution was stacked against them. At the end of the first global conflict, the then-minority isolationists had succeeded in blocking the will of the internationalist majority that wanted to take the United States into a fully participatory role in world affairs. The thirty-five senators who voted against approval of the Treaty of Versailles had overridden the forty-nine who voted for it, backed by the president and, from all of the evidence, most of the country; and in doing so, the minority had blocked U.S. entry into the League of Nations. When that body proved ineffective as a guarantor of peace, its weakness could be blamed to some degree on the fateful minority decision that kept the world's strongest country from asserting the leadership that was its clear responsibility. It is hard to argue that any League of Nations, however strong, would have been potent enough to check the ambitions of the dictators who brought on World War II, but it remains on the national conscience that the United States did not do everything it could.

No treaty of equal significance has been rejected by a minority since the Versailles vote. Learning from that experience, the country achieved a rare and overwhelming national consensus after World War II to approve full participation in the United Nations that

32. See comments of Senator Frank Church, Democrat of Idaho, a future chairman of the Foreign Relations Committee, quoted in Sundquist, *Decline and Resurgence*, p. 267.

superseded the defunct League and to sustain American leadership in erecting a series of regional alliances to check the spread of communism around the globe. As long as the consensus existed, the country's foreign policy could be truly bipartisan, and the two-thirds requirement for treaty approval was no barrier to any major foreign policy objective. But popular agreement and bipartisan harmony dissolved in the Vietnam War, and that fact has given the provision renewed importance.

The effect of the two-thirds requirement is not to be measured by the number of treaties rejected; by that standard its effect has been negligible for nearly half a century and may well continue to be. The provision has to be judged, instead, by its pervasive influence on the development and conduct of foreign policy at every stage. Every president and secretary of state know that they may go no further in any negotiation than the minority of the day will finally accept. In a very real sense, then, basic foreign policy decisions are controlled not by the governmental majority that is elected by the popular majority but by the governmental minority whose policies may have been soundly rejected in a whole series of elections—just as the minority determined the national position on the Treaty of Versailles. Today, as an example, an equally irreconcilable minority could prevent any arms control agreement, however promising, from taking effect. The nation's leaders and negotiators must therefore pay as much, or more, attention to the views and position of the diehard opponents of arms control as to those of its supporters. The opponents gain a bargaining power that they can use in various ways, depending on the political climate at any given time. They can discourage negotiation altogether. They can discourage U.S. negotiators from proposing, or accepting, what the administration may conscientiously believe to be fair and reasonable concessions. In effect, the opponents rather than the responsible administration can define the treaty's ultimate terms. No one can be sure what would have happened to the Strategic Arms Limitation Treaty (SALT II) that President Carter submitted to the Senate if he had not withdrawn it, but it seems likely that it would have been defeated by a minority of senators. Yet the Reagan administration found it worthy of voluntary adherence.

It is sometimes difficult to distinguish, when treaties become controversial, how much of the opposition represents genuine policy objections and how much reflects the constant struggle in any democratic system for partisan advantage (or individual advantage, for a senator may use his bargaining power to obtain a concession, perhaps one wholly unrelated to the treaty, from the president). That "politics stops at the water's edge" is a myth; except in the rare periods of national consensus like the one that prevailed after World War II, politicians dispute foreign policy with the same intensity that they debate domestic policy, both within each party and between the parties. Politicians of the opposing party respond to public opinion, of course, and do not risk appearing to oppose a popular treaty just for the sake of opposition. But if a significant segment of public opinion has doubts about the agreement, the opposition's opportunity—and, many will say, its duty—lies in responding to the doubts, giving them a hearing, and exploiting them. The opposition view, after all, is entitled to an advocate. If it can be made to prevail, politicians reason, it probably deserves to. And if those who negotiated the treaty sink with it, that—in the inevitable perception of the partisan opposition—will be for the long-run greater good of the country anyway.

This being the necessary nature of democratic politics, the de facto requirement imposed by the two-thirds rule that every treaty have bipartisan support—since the president's party rarely commands two-thirds of both houses—sets a standard of extreme severity. Defenders of the requirement contend that the standard should properly be severe; a treaty is binding not just on the administration and the party that negotiated it but on successor administrations of the other party too, and agreement by the opposition in advance of its responsibility is therefore not an unreasonable rule. The opposing argument is that the necessity for bipartisan agreement can render the country incapable of acting on any issue that is to any significant degree divisive and susceptible to partisan exploitation.

Even the most vigorous opponents of the two-thirds requirement would probably concede some merit to the view that a treaty, because of its binding character, should rest on a broader base than a simple majority in popular opinion reflected in a bare majority, made up entirely of one party, in the Congress. If supporters of the extraordinary majority would concede that the two-thirds requirement calls for a base so broad as to be in many reasonable circumstances unattainable, a solution might be found in the substitution of a lower percentage figure—60 percent, say (though that figure would not have saved the Treaty of Versailles, which garnered only 58.3 percent of those voting, unless the proponents somehow mustered additional support).

All this leaves out of account the House of Representatives. The constitutional amendment overwhelmingly approved by that body in 1945 would have authorized approval of treaties by a majority of the membership in both houses. There is good reason to involve the House as well as the Senate on treaty matters, for the implementing legislation and appropriations that most agreements require must win the approval of both bodies. The framers' concept of the Senate as a kind of privy council to the president, which was the origin of its special role in treaty approval, has long since given way. But if a constitutional amendment must win the approval of the Senate in order to be submitted to the states for ratification, any proposal to admit the House to equal responsibility stands little chance of passage. Perhaps a reduction of the Senate approval requirement to 55 or 60 percent could be combined with a provision for approval also by a simple majority of the House to form an acceptable, though awkward, solution.

What is difficult to justify, or even comprehend, is the view often encountered in the Senate that to reduce the two-thirds requirement would in itself denigrate that body and diminish its status and responsibility. True, the power of individual senators to defeat a treaty would be diminished, but their power to approve agreements would be enhanced. In the case of those treaties that would be affected by lowering the two-thirds standard—those with majority but not two-thirds support—more senators would always gain influence than would lose it; in the Versailles treaty instance, a requirement of 58 percent or less would have stripped thirty-five senators of their power to block the agreement but conferred on forty-nine the power to approve it. As is shown in other instances as well—notably in the case of the filibuster rule—senators appear to place greater value on their power to obstruct than on their power to concur. A senator willingly accepts minority rule in order that he or she may rule, as part of a minority, on some future occasion and inflict defeat on some president—even though the mathematical certainty is that, with minority rule, most members of the Senate will rule less often.

One way to escape the stringent two-thirds requirement for treaty approval while leaving the Constitution unchanged would be to expand the use, and the concept, of the executive agreement, which presidents have extensively employed in carrying out the terms of treaties and of statutes such as the Trade Agreements Act.[33] As in the case of trade, the Congress could authorize the president to negotiate international agreements covering particular subjects—arms control, for example—that would take effect if ratified by act of Congress, or, as was provided in the original trade statute, on the president's own authority. If that became the practice, the purpose of modifying the treaty clause of the Constitution might be largely achieved without altering the clause itself. But to legitimately remove any questions as to the legality and the propriety of using this approach on a broad scale, some constitutional language might be necessary and would certainly be useful. One approach would be to encompass international agreements in any amendment restoring the legislative veto. The Congress could then authorize the president to enter into agreements that would not require affirmative action but would be binding unless they were rejected by the legislators.

Breaking Deadlocks by Referenda

If the branches of government reach an impasse on a single crucial issue at a time when their relations are otherwise reasonably effective, a means of overcoming the checks and balances that produced the deadlock could be made available through constitutional amendment. That is the device of the referendum, by which the people themselves vote yes or no on a legislative or constitutional proposition.

A comprehensive study of national referenda, published in 1978, counted more than five hundred such votes. A third of the countries belonging to the United Nations, including a majority of the European states, had employed the device at least once. Of the countries with an uninterrupted democratic history going back to the nineteenth century, only the United States and the Netherlands have never submitted a question to a direct popular vote. Most have used the device sparingly, but at the other extreme stands Switzerland, which has "accepted the principle that almost every major national decision

33. As of January 1, 1983, the State Department reported that 966 treaties and 6,571 executive agreements were in force. The two types have the same status under international law; they differ only in the approval process.

could become the subject of a popular vote." Of the five hundred referenda, Switzerland accounted for 297, Australia 39, France 20, and Denmark 13.[34] The measures may be submitted for decision by the voters or simply for advice, as when the British parliament in 1975 asked the electorate's view on withdrawal from the European Community. (It voted to retain membership, and the government followed its advice.) The questions are normally presented to referendum by the government, but in some countries a question can be placed on the ballot by petition, as when in Italy a national divorce law was appealed to referendum in 1974 and a law modifying cost-of-living wage increases was similarly taken to the people by the Communist party in 1985. (Both laws were upheld.)

The American states have used the referendum device extensively. In every state but Delaware, constitutional amendments must be approved by referendum. Changes in city charters usually require similar popular approval, and so do bond issues in many states and cities. In many states, constitutional amendments as well as statutory proposals may be placed on the ballot by petition—as, perhaps most notably, California's tax limitation amendment (Proposition 13) adopted by referendum in 1978. A Gallup poll of 1977 found that a decisive majority of the nation's voters would approve establishing a similar right of the people to legislate by popular initiative at the national level.[35] But the Congress has never seriously considered establishing a referendum procedure.

Without amending the Constitution, the Congress could by statute submit measures for advisory votes, and the submission could be acompanied by a moral commitment on the part of the legislators and the president to accept the verdict of the voters. But such an approach would require agreement between the president and both houses of Congress, and therefore would be of least utility when it was most needed—that is, when the president and one or both houses were in hopeless disagreement, immobilizing the government on some urgent matter. To make the referendum serviceable to break

34. David Butler and Austin Ranney, *Referendums: A Comparative Study of Practice and Theory* (Washington: American Enterprise Institute, 1978), pp. 5–7.

35. Austin Ranney, "What Constitutional Changes Do Americans Want?" *This Constitution: A Bicentennial Chronicle* (Winter 1984), reprinted in Donald L. Robinson, ed., *Reforming American Government: The Bicentennial Papers of the Committee on the Constitutional System* (Westview Press, 1985), p. 283.

such a deadlock, it would be necessary to amend the Constitution to let the people finally decide the issue; popular approval would enact the law. Moreover, one side of a controversy would have to be able to initiate the referendum over the opposition of the other. The logical approach would be to authorize any two elements of the policymaking triad—president, Senate, and House—to ask the public by referendum to overrule the third. The Senate and House now have the power to impose their will on the president, of course, but it requires a two-thirds vote by both houses.

The question arises as to whether an extraordinary majority should be required for the Senate or the House to act in concert with the president in a new referendum procedure. As with a limitation on the power of the Congress to call a special election, if the purpose is to make it possible to break deadlocks, demanding an extraordinary majority can defeat that purpose, allowing the debilitating impasse to continue. Any requirement more stringent than a constitutional majority encounters that difficulty. But if the president and a constitutional majority of one house were authorized to submit a measure to referendum, the same right should apply to the two houses acting in opposition to the president. If they failed to override a presidential veto, they should be empowered also to take their case to the people by a constitutional majority of both houses.

The principal objection to use of the referendum device in national legislative matters concerns the capacity of the people to exercise soundly the responsibility that would be entrusted to them. Executive-legislative conflict in recent years has centered on fiscal policy, but the budget is made up of thousands of expenditure items on which the public could not hope to become educated. On any complex measure, enormous expenditures would be required to educate the electorate, and that would tilt the scales toward the side with the greatest financial resources. The contest between the president and the legislators would also be unbalanced in favor of the executive, given his superior access to the media and his other advantages in gaining the attention of the people. The president and either house, particularly if they were allied with wealthy interests with a financial stake in the outcome, would be in a strong position to flood the country with advertising and overwhelm the other house.

The experience of the states with referenda has been mixed. Some measures submitted to the people have been poorly drafted and some have been complex and technical, forcing the voters to rely for their understanding on oversimplified and even misleading advertising campaigns. But this is partly because the referendum in the states is associated with the popular initiative; the measures are placed on the ballot by the people themselves. National referenda on measures selected for submission by the president and congressmen would involve issues that had been the subject of mature consideration in both houses. Presumably, those submitting the measures would exercise a responsible judgment that the issues involved could be readily grasped by the voters and were of sufficient interest to stimulate voters to inform themselves. Perhaps useful legislation submitted to a national referendum would be beaten by confused voters who, in doubt, would choose to play safe by voting no. Since a defeat in referendum would weaken a measure in future Congresses, presidents and legislators would be inhibited from overusing the device. But as an additional safeguard, the number of measures eligible for referendum could be limited, perhaps to two at the conclusion of each Congress—one initiated by the president and one or the other House, the other by the two houses acting together.

The most significant effect of such a referendum provision would probably not be the actual resolution of deadlocked issues by the people but rather the incentive that would be created for presidents and legislators to avoid the risks of the referendum process by working things out themselves. A Democratic House, for instance, might find itself pressed to compromise on a controverted piece of legislation lest a Republican president and Senate take their case to the people; and the pressure would apply to the Republicans as well, for the chance would always exist that they might lose. In any case, the purpose of resolving a debilitating stalemate would have been served, and it would be more difficult for timid politicians to evade critical issues by blocking action altogether.

Preserving the Executive-Legislative Balance

Although they do not deal in any fundamental way with the central problem of executive-legislative stalemate to which this book is mainly addressed, all five of the proposed constitutional amendments discussed in this chapter are worth consideration on their merits as part of any broad effort to adapt the country's charter to the needs of modern government.

The item veto would give the president an additional means, although a relatively minor one, to bring the alarming national budget deficit under control. Restoring the legislative veto would give both the president and the Congress a device that both branches have found useful in the past. Writing the essence of the War Powers Resolution into the Constitution would do as much as probably can be done to limit and control what some presidents have contended is their unilateral power to make war. Modifying the two-thirds requirement for treaty approval would give the president and the congressional majority, when they are in agreement, the right to determine the nation's foreign policy free of minority domination. And providing for a national referendum on disputed measures would make it possible to resolve some legislative impasses that now persist.

To make any of these changes, however, runs the risk of upsetting the present balance of power between the executive and legislative branches—a balance that has evolved over two centuries and that appears, on the whole, to satisfy both the country's political leadership and the public. If some modification of the existing system of checks and balances appears desirable, then, the objective should be to construct a combination of amendments that would grant roughly equal accretions of power to both branches. Quite apart from the intrinsic desirability of maintaining the present balance, if any set of proposals were seen as tilting the scales decisively in one direction or the other, the proposals would be doomed politically.

The most powerful of the proposals, in terms of potential subversal of the executive-legislative balance, would be the item veto in any form that required a two-thirds majority of both houses to override the president. That would so enhance the president's bargaining power that no combination of other measures could offset it. But a milder form of the item veto, such as the Illinois variant that permits an override by an absolute majority of both houses, would pose nowhere near so great a threat—provided that the Congress remained in session long enough to consider the presidential vetoes. In that case, the president would have the opportunity to bring the offensive items to the attention of the country, but the legislators could still work their will if they were determined to do so.

In return for gaining a limited item veto, the president might be willing to support a restoration of the legislative veto. Again, a limitation might be in order, restricting the legislature's authority to two-house vetoes, and thus excluding the one-house and committee vetoes that were often enacted in the days before the *Chadha* decision. And international agreements could be encompassed in the legislative veto language, to encourage the Congress to authorize wider use of agreements as a substitute for treaties. A reduction of the two-thirds requirement for treaty ratification would still be desirable. Either, or both, of these would presumably be interpreted as a concession to the executive—although they should not be, for in fact either would enhance the power of the congressional majorities. But a war powers amendment could easily be added to the package as a step favoring the Congress. The referendum amendment might come close to being neutral in its impact, for any two of the policymaking triad—president, Senate, and House—could initiate its use to break a deadlock with the third. But in all of these measures, the opportunity to assemble a combination of amendments that would be both constructive and politically appealing seems clearly to exist.

CHAPTER NINE

The Prospects for
Constitutional Reform

That there has been no powerful popular, or even elitist, movement on behalf of fundamental alteration in the governmental structure at any time in two hundred years testifies that the government has, most of the time, lived up to the expectations of the people. When failures have occurred, they have proven to be temporary and correctible. Yet some of the experienced leaders who are advocating constitutional revision today are profoundly convinced that the United States has been lucky in the past and that, in the future, the deadlock and indecision built into the governmental structure will place the nation in continued peril. Perhaps the country's luck, if that is what it has been, will continue. But there have been enough periods of governmental failure in the nation's past to suggest the imprudence of continuing to rely on providence if the weaknesses in the governmental system can be identified and timely remedies adopted.

In today's world, two dangers seem paramount. One is that the division of power among the president, the Senate, and the House—coupled with a split in partisan control—will render it impossible to achieve what Budget Director David Stockman called "fiscal sanity," and budgetary deficits will grow until they produce a sudden, or a gradual, economic calamity. The other is that division of power will produce a paralysis in foreign policy, with no president of either party able to conduct foreign relations in a coherent and effective manner with the harmonious assured participation and support of congressional majorities. And the consequences of foreign policy failure are magnified with every new generation of more deadly, destructive weapons.

If one accepts the proposition that indecisive, stalemated government can place the nation in peril—and that those risks outweigh the danger that decisive government will make unwise decisions— the preceding chapters suggest a range of remedies. Without regard to the question of what may or may not be politically feasible, an ideal series of amendments to the American Constitution would include these, roughly in order of importance (and in the order discussed in the earlier chapters).

1. *The team ticket.* The separation of powers is far more likely to lead to debilitating governmental deadlock when the organs of government are divided between the parties. Several measures give promise of discouraging the ticket-splitting that produces divided government, but only one would prevent it altogether. That is the team ticket, which would combine each party's candidates for president, vice president, Senate, and House into a slate that would be voted for as a unit.

2. *Four-year House terms and eight-year Senate terms.* Even a united government is constantly distracted by the imminence of the next election, which normally limits an incoming president to barely a year as his "window of opportunity" to lead his party in enacting the program for which it sought its victory. The midterm election now gives the electorate an opportunity to express its objections if an administration performs poorly but it gives them no chance to remedy the situation, for the president remains in office. To eliminate that election and thereby lengthen the period of relative freedom from election pressure would require four-year House terms and either four-year or eight-year Senate terms, with the latter more in accord with the staggered-term tradition of the Senate. Presidents and Congresses alike would be better able to undertake short-term measures that might be unpopular, in order to achieve a greater long-run good, and the legislative process would profit from a more deliberate tempo.

3. *A method for special elections to reconstitute a failed government.* Chapter 6 explores the almost infinite variations in form that a procedure for calling special elections might take. If the mechanism is to be suitable for use in all of the kinds of emergency circumstances

that can produce governmental failure, the special election should be callable at any time, by the president or a majority of either house of Congress. All seats in both houses, as well as the presidency and vice presidency, should be filled at the election. Those elected should serve full terms (except half the senators would serve for only four years), and the terms could be adjusted by a few months so that the next regular election would fall on the customary November date.

4. *Removal of the prohibition against dual officeholding.* Permitting members of Congress to serve in the executive branch might turn out not to be practical, but removing the prohibition would permit constructive experimentation with that means of linking the executive and legislative branches.

5. *A limited item veto.* An item veto that could be overridden by absolute majorities of the two houses would give the president an important new power with which to combat the rising deficit, yet not upset the executive-legislative balance of power.

6. *Restoration of the legislative veto.* This, too, might be limited, permitting only two-house vetoes.

7. *A war powers amendment.* Writing the essential terms of the War Powers Resolution of 1973 into the Constitution would clear up the unsettled question as to whether that resolution is valid and presidents are required to conform to its provisions.

8. *Approval of treaties by a majority of the membership of both houses.* This would remove the power to dominate critical foreign policy decisions from a minority of the Senate and restore it, like other governmental powers, to the majority.

9. *A national referendum to break deadlocks.* Measures that are in deadlock could be submitted to referendum by both houses of Congress, or by the president and one house. The number to be submitted in any year could be limited to one or two.

These constitutional amendments could be supplemented by statutes and changes in party rules that would serve the same objectives, such as increasing the proportion of members of Congress, candidates for Congress, and other party leaders in presidential nominating conventions and providing for partial financing of congressional campaigns with public funds administered by party committees.

As observed in chapter 8, items 5 through 8 on this list of amendments all affect the balance of power between the executive and legislative branches and hence could best be combined in a single package that would come as close as possible to preserving the present balance.

The Difficulty of Doing Anything

Even those most profoundly convinced that the United States government has serious structural weaknesses come to ask themselves and one another: Why even try to change the Constitution? Why not take for granted that it cannot be altered, and settle for whatever improvements can be made by lesser means—by passing laws, or changing party rules and structures, or concentrating on electing better officials to high office? The process of amending the country's two-hundred-year-old charter is so formidable that reformers can be excused for being daunted at the outset, and theorists forgiven for devoting their analytical energies to other subjects. Not only may an amendment be blocked by 34 percent of the voting members of one house of Congress but, if it passes that hurdle, it can still be defeated by the adverse vote, or simple inaction, of as few as thirteen of the ninety-nine state legislative houses, or fewer than 14 percent.[1]

No other country has a mechanism for constitutional amendment that requires so high a degree of national consensus. Nor does any state of the United States. Of the fifty states, twenty-one permit legislatures to submit amendments to the people by simple majorities (in three of these, the legislature must act twice in separate sessions), one by a two-thirds vote in its senate but only a majority in its house of representatives, nine by a three-fifths vote in each house, eighteen by a two-thirds vote in each house, and one by a two-thirds majority of the membership of each house. But while eighteen states make the initiation process as difficult as in the federal government (and one makes it even higher), in forty-two of the states a simple majority approval by a popular referendum completes the process. One state

1. To make matters still more difficult, 7 states require extraordinary state legislative majorities for ratification of federal constitutional amendments. Arkansas, Colorado, Georgia, Idaho, and Kansas require a two-thirds vote of both houses, Illinois three-fifths of both houses, and Alabama three-fifths of the lower chamber of the legislature. For an attack on these requirements as "unnecessary, undesirable, and unfair," see comments of Representative John J. LaFalce, Democrat of New York, *Congressional Record*, August 9, 1978, p. 25255.

does not require approval; five require approval by a majority of the votes cast in the election (as distinct from votes cast on the amendment itself), one requires that the majority be equivalent to the majority of votes cast for governor, and only one requires a two-thirds vote of the electorate. Moreover, seventeen states permit constitutional amendments to be placed on the ballot by initiative, and thirteen of these provide for their approval by simple majorities of those voting. Finally, the states make it relatively easy to convene constitutional conventions; in all, two hundred and thirty such conclaves had been held through 1981, or more than four per state.

As the consequence of these comparatively workable amendment procedures, the states had approved 4,988 amendments to their constitutions as of the end of 1981, or nearly 100 per state as compared to 26 for the federal government. Given that the states were then, on the average, only 139 years old, that represents a frequency of constitutional change more than five times that of the national government.[2] Among the changes were many that altered the basic structures of state governments, including lengthening the terms of governors and other officials, strengthening the governor's power, shortening the ballot, eliminating executive councils, and so on. The circumstances are not strictly comparable, of course, because state constitutions have been more in need of amendment; in contrast to the federal charter, they have been widely criticized for incorporating too much detail that should be left to statutory law, and many of the amendments accomplished purposes that in the federal system can be, and have been, achieved by statute. Nevertheless, whenever the people of the various states have become aware of deficiencies in their governmental structures, the ease with which their constitutions can be modernized is impressive.

The question arises, then: Should the advocates of constitutional change in the interest of more effective government turn their attention first to modifying the amendment process itself? Probably not. A simplified amendment procedure would never be considered in the abstract, simply as a theoretical proposition in the interest of

2. Council of State Governments, *The Book of the States, 1982–83*, pp. 136, 137, 121, 117. These figures include amendments proposed by constitutional conventions. Of the 21 states listed as permitting submission of amendments by simple legislative majorities and the 42 allowing approval by electoral majorities, 1 requires a three-fourths approval in each case for certain specified matters.

good government. To win any significant backing, it would have to be seen as making the course easier for one or more specific, popular amendments whose supporters could then be mobilized behind it. But arrayed against the change would be the opponents of not only those amendments but all the many other changes in the Constitution that might be under public discussion at the time, including those that would modify the Bill of Rights. The proposal would be seen as a devious attempt to slip into the Constitution bad ideas that could not win approval otherwise, on their merits. It would simply carry too much baggage.

Variations in the Amendment Process

Reformers might find some slight promise, however, in two elements of the existing amendment process that have been little used. One is the option of state ratification by unicameral conventions rather than by bicameral legislatures, which would—in theory, at least—somewhat reduce the mathematical odds against approval of any proposition by three-fourths of the states. On the one occasion that method was used—the Twenty-first Amendment repealing Prohibition—it was resoundingly successful. Ratification was completed in the course of barely nine months, between February 20 and December 5, 1933. As to why that expeditious procedure was not chosen by the Congress in any other instance, the historical record is a blank; presumably the sponsors of the various amendments were confident that they could win approval by the legislatures readily enough, obviating the need for the expense and trouble of organizing state conventions. Or perhaps they feared that taking their case to the people, who would elect the convention delegates, would involve more risk than relying on the more experienced politicians who constitute the legislatures. If a proposed amendment is unpopular, as the Senate debate of 1924 (described in chapter 3) brought out, the powerful lobbying organizations that support it are sometimes able to prevail on the legislators to approve it anyway.

The second optional procedure is the initiation of amendments by constitutional convention rather than by the Congress. A convention must be called, under the Constitution, on petition of the legislatures of two-thirds of the states. No such gathering has ever been held, but for any amendment that would be seen by a substantial bloc of legislators as restricting in any way their own powers, the convention process would appear to be essential as the only way of bypassing the opponents in the Congress. Such was the case early in this century, when advocates of the direct election of senators began a drive for a convention in order to circumvent the Senate, which was stubbornly refusing to reform itself. When one legislature after another passed the necessary resolution and the move appeared headed for success, the Senate reluctantly yielded and joined the House in proposing the amendment to the states. Since then, the only significant attempt to call a convention has been the one that as of 1985 was still proceeding, organized by advocates of an amendment to require a balanced federal budget except in certain specified circumstances.

Constitutional lawyers dispute whether, if the Congress attempted to limit a convention to a single subject—such as a balanced budget amendment—the limitation would be binding. In the total absence of precedent, no one can be sure. It is unlikely that the delegates would choose to disregard any congressional limitation, because they would have been chosen to deal with only one subject and would not be prepared to cope with others. But if they did elect to broaden their agenda, it is clear that no one outside their body would have authority to prevent their doing so. The delegates of 1787, after all, had been assigned only to propose amendments to the Articles of Confederation but, once they met, they set their own agenda. Another such "runaway convention" is not beyond the realm of possibility, then. The question would be what happened afterward. To the extent that the convention exceeded its mandate from the Congress, it would plunge itself into a public controversy that would create a negative presumption against all of its actions, and the accusation of illegality could be exploited in the state ratification process. But if, nevertheless, three-fourths of the states took cognizance of the challenged proposals and gave their approval, the amendments would no doubt ultimately become part of the Constitution—either because the Supreme Court validated the disputed amendments or the Congress took the initiative to resubmit them. Should the balanced budget movement succeed in compelling a convention, then, and that body decide to consider additional matters, critics of the governmental structure would have an opportunity to advance any proposals that, because of their effect on the Congress itself, would not be likely to be initiated by the legislators in the normal manner.

The Problem of Gainers and Losers

Still, ratification by three-fourths of the states would remain as formidable a barrier as ever. Institutional structure is not an issue likely to arouse popular fervor, in the absence of a patent breakdown in the functioning of government, and even then—as at the time of Watergate—most people are inclined to place the blame on the failure of individual leaders rather than of institutions. Proposals for structural change may not arouse fervent opposition either, but in the absence of popular support any organized institutional opposition is likely to be sufficient to prevail. If either of the major parties sees its interests jeopardized by a proposal, or incumbent legislators discern a loss of power for their branch, or the president and defenders of presidential power foresee a weakening of the executive, the proposal is doomed. Any significant ideological bloc, also, would surely have enough strength in enough states to block an amendment; so no proposal has much chance of success if it arouses conservative concern that it hides a bias toward big government, or liberal concern that it favors weak government, or elitist worry that it embodies an excess of democracy, or antiestablishment fear that it upsets the balance the other way.

But institutional changes are seldom neutral, and even if one could be conceived that is truly neutral—and would be perceived that way—neutrality is not enough. Each of the elements of the institutional system, and each major ideological group as well, must see some benefit. Unless something is to be gained, why risk change at all? But gains for everyone is a logical impossibility. True, the government as a whole can accrue power, as it has been doing for most of two centuries, but the division among institutions and officeholders of the right to exercise any given aggregate of power becomes a zero-sum game. If one institution or one political party or one ideological group gains, another loses. That, at bottom, is why there has not been a single amendment in two hundred years that redistributed governmental power. The two amendments that can be classed as even affecting the institutional structure at all—the Seventeenth and the Twenty-second—concerned only the selection of the individuals who would wield institutional power, not the scope of the institutional authority itself.

But the distribution of power among the elements of the governmental system is what all of the constitutional changes discussed in this book would, in one or another degree, affect. The scale of the benefit to governmental effectiveness to be derived from any measure or set of measures would depend on the magnitude of that effect. But so would the vigor of the opposition each measure would incite. It becomes an axiom of constitutional reform, then, that any structural amendment that would bring major benefits cannot be adopted—again, barring a governmental collapse that can be clearly attributed to the constitutional design—while any measure that stands a chance of passage is likely to be innocuous.

The strategy of reformers, in such a circumstance, must be to search for trade-offs, based on the possibility that institutions and groups affected may weigh gains and losses on different scales. If party A to a negotiation considers proposition X to be far more important than proposition Y, while party B perceives them in the opposite relation, then party A will gladly trade Y for X and party B will accept the trade. Constitutional amendments are, unfortunately, not easily combined in logical packages for trade-off purposes, nor can the parties involved be brought to a table for direct negotiations.

If one concludes, for instance, that much of the problem of governmental incapacity arises from divided government, as discussed in chapter 4, there appears to be no practicable remedy. The axiom applies: the only modifications that would come close to forestalling divided government—bonus seats and the team ticket—would encounter insurmountable opposition. Bonus seats would dilute the power and influence of every legislator elected through the normal process, thus solidifying the entire Congress as an opposition bloc. As for the team ticket idea, only one of the two parties, at any given time, would see a possible gain, while the other would anticipate a certain loss. In 1984, the team ticket would have helped the Republicans. Ronald Reagan's strength would surely have won for the GOP control of the House as well as the Senate. Even so, Republicans might fear the idea, anticipating that at some future date the situation might be reversed. Meanwhile, the Democrats would look at 1984 and reflect on how many House and Senate seats they would have lost if their congressional candidates had been tied to Walter Mondale. They would provide opposition enough but, meanwhile, ideological opponents would also appear. The right to split tickets would be touted as one of the inalienable rights of citizenship, not to be abridged for the politicians' gain. The other two proposals discussed in chapter 4 would arouse less opposition simply because they would be potentially less effective, but at least one of the parties, at any given time, would find any measure that tended to promote united government against its short-run electoral interest. In the current period, when Republicans succeed in presidential elections while Democrats win more congressional contests, why would any Democrat wish to increase the chance that every time the Republicans won the White House they would sweep the House and Senate also?

Of all the proposals considered in this book, lengthening of congressional terms would seem to come closest to making everyone concerned a gainer, and none a loser—at least at first glance. House members should be expected to prefer terms of four years instead of two, Senate members ought to like eight-year terms better than six, and presidents should see benefit in electing congressmen only in presidential years. But the rejection of Lyndon Johnson's 1966 proposal for four-year House terms coincident with the president's is instructive. Republican representatives saw their party placed at a disadvantage vis-à-vis the Democrats, and Democrats came to fear a loss of congressional independence vis-à-vis the president. Perhaps the latter worry could be shown to be ill founded—representatives would not have to run on a presidential ticket any oftener than they do at present—but the former concern is surely real, for one party or the other. In recent midterm elections, one of the parties would have been the gainer, and that party would be loath to see its opportunity for future gains eliminated. Only if recent midterm elections had been close to a dead heat would it appear possible to persuade members of both parties to assess the personal convenience of a longer term as outweighing any potential partisan loss.

As for the public reaction, the Johnson proposal met with some approbation, much indifference, but no mass cry of outrage. Perhaps that was because the amendment made so little progress on Capitol Hill. If a new proposal were to win serious consideration, a principled opposition would undoubtedly arise to contend that popular control over elected officials was being lessened. The public, it would be argued, should have the right to "throw the rascals out" at less than four-year intervals. The argument would be persuasive, and rightly so. As suggested in chapter 6, the country has always needed a mechanism for reconstituting failed governments, and lengthened terms would make the need more evident.

The prospect for winning longer terms might be enhanced, then, if that proposal were accompanied by a companion scheme to retain for the people the opportunity, in times of need, to redirect the course of government between presidential elections. The midterm election is now seen as accomplishing that purpose. In fact, it offers only a partial and unsatisfactory control; only the Congress can be remade, and if the fault for ineffective government lies with the president, reconstituting the Congress may do no more than strengthen the opposition, rigidify the deadlock between the branches, and compound the public dissatisfaction. The exploration in chapter 6 of the range of remedies that would permit reconstitution of the government between presidential elections to extend to the presidency as well confirms that no conceivable remedy is apt to be perceived as making all gainers and no losers. Presidents and congressmen alike are sure to suspect that any proposed scheme for special intra-term elections would remove whatever advantages might be conferred by the lengthened terms. If the public gains control, the politicians lose it; that, too, is a zero-sum game. Perhaps it is not out of reason that a combination of longer terms and special elections could be so designed that presidents, senators, and representatives would all see more benefit than loss. But the task for institutional architects is a forbidding one.

The proposal in chapter 7 for removing the prohibition against dual officeholding might encounter minimal opposition, for both branches might be seen to be the gainers. The president would gain the right to appoint legislators to executive office, yet without compulsion to do so; and legislators would gain at least a chance for broader responsibilities. Moreover, the amendment would require each specific use of the new authority to be approved by the Senate, and perhaps by the House too, as provided by law. The issue of gainers and losers would simply be deferred, and each particular appointment would have to worked out in such a way that both branches at that time were perceived to gain. The difficulty of achieving that objective would probably be great enough that, when the practical obstacles to combining executive and legislative work-loads were also considered, the amendment would turn out to be inconsequential.

The proposals for strengthening political parties discussed in chapter 7, which are the only ones not requiring constitutional amendment, are clearly more feasible for that reason, but they nevertheless encounter the same problem of winners and losers. Passing laws requires, usually, some degree of bipartisan support, and any fundamental redesign of party institutions would have to be backed by all of the major factions within a party. But changes in election laws, including controls over campaign finance, inevitably favor one party against another, some factions against others, incum-bents against challengers or vice versa. Modifications in the presi-dential selection process may also run afoul of state laws and of popular sentiment in favor of the broadest possible public participation and control. Changes in party and electoral institutions have occurred in the past, however, and reforms that enjoy broad though not overwhelming popular support can—unlike constitutional amend-ments with the same degree of public approval—eventually win adoption.

The possibility that the item veto and the legislative veto might be combined in a trade-off is noted in chapter 8. The president might find the item veto so appealing that he would concede the legislative veto in exchange, in the knowledge that the Congress will find ways of imposing its veto anyway and that the executive branch has often gained because of a veto provision a delegation of power it would not otherwise have received. The trade might not be seen by the legislators as an even one, unless the item veto it granted the president could be overridden by a majority of the membership of both houses, as in Illinois. In that case, of course, the president might lose his interest. But the issue does appear to be one that lends itself to more or less formal interbranch negotiation. The war power and the requirements for treaty approval might be included in the bargaining as well.

All of the seemingly insurmountable obstacles to constitutional change could be overcome, of course, if the government were indeed to fail, palpably and for a sustained period. But the necessity to experience governmental failure, in order to prepare for it, is not a happy prospect. This book must end, then, on a pessimistic note. Nothing is likely to happen short of crisis—which is, of course, the case with all fundamental constitutional reform, in every country of the world and throughout history.

Nevertheless, nothing can be lost if, during the bicentennial period, the public can be brought to look hard at the weaknesses of the American governmental system and consider what, if the worst comes to pass, the remedies might be. Even among those who believe no constitutional crisis lies ahead, few argue that the workings of governmental institutions are beyond improvement. Whatever the future may hold, much is to be gained if politicians, statesmen, and scholars carry forward the kind of analysis this book has attempted to begin, trying to separate the workable modifications in the constitutional structure from the unworkable, the effective from the ineffective, the possibly feasible from the wholly infeasible, exploring an uncharted area of institutional design where there are few precedents to be evaluated and no one can be sure.

Index

system, 69; on presidential tenure, 46: reelection, 129

Women: caucus system and, 187; in House, 61n; party representation, 184; suffrage, 56–57, 94

Works, John D., 44

World Court, 58, 166

World War I, 5; League of Nations and, 58; Versailles treaty, 11, 53, 58, 229–32

World War II, 14, 58

Wright, Jim, 193

Yates, Robert, 23n

Zablocki, Clement J., 67